TERROR, LOVE AND BRAINWASHING

Written by a cult survivor and renowned expert on cults and totalitarianism, *Terror, Love and Brainwashing* draws on the author's 25 years of study and research to explain how almost anyone, given the right set of circumstances, can be radically manipulated to engage in otherwise incomprehensible and often dangerous acts.

Illustrated with compelling stories from a range of cults and totalitarian systems, from religious to political to commercial, the book defines and analyzes the common and identifiable traits that underlie almost all these groups. It focuses on how charismatic, authoritarian leaders control their followers' attachment relationships via manipulative social structures and ideologies so that, emotionally and cognitively isolated, they become unable to act in their own survival interests. Using the evolutionary theory of attachment to demonstrate the psychological impact of these environments, and incorporating the latest neuroscientific findings, Stein illustrates how the combined dynamic of terror and 'love' works to break down people's ability to think and behave rationally. From small local cults to global players like ISIS and North Korea, the impact of these movements is widespread and growing.

This important book offers clarity and a unique perspective on the dynamics of these systems of control, and concludes with guidance to foster greater awareness and prevention. It will be essential reading for mental health professionals in the field, as well as policy makers, legal professionals, cult survivors and their families, as well as anyone with an interest in these disturbing groups. Students of social and developmental psychology will also find it fascinating.

Alexandra Stein is a social psychologist who lectures and writes on cults and totalitarianism. She is an associate lecturer at Birkbeck, University of London, UK and has also taught at the University of Minnesota, US and the University of Westminster, UK. As a young woman she was a member of a political cult, an experience she described in her first book, *Inside Out*.

TERROR, LOVE AND BRAINWASHING

Attachment in Cults and Totalitarian Systems

Alexandra Stein

Routledge
Taylor & Francis Group

LONDON AND NEW YORK

First published 2017
by Routledge
2 Park Square, Milton Park, Abingdon, Oxon OX14 4RN

and by Routledge
711 Third Avenue, New York, NY 10017

Routledge is an imprint of the Taylor & Francis Group, an informa business

© 2017 Alexandra Stein

British Library Cataloguing in Publication Data
A catalogue record for this book is available from the British Library

Library of Congress Cataloging in Publication Data
Names: Stein, Alexandra, author.
Title: Terror, love and brainwashing : attachment in cults and totalitarian
    systems / Alexandra Stein.
Description: New York : Routledge, [2017] | Includes bibliographical
    references and index.
Identifiers: LCCN 2016027933 | ISBN 9781138677951
    (hardback : alk. paper) | ISBN 9781138677975 (pbk. : alk. paper) |
    ISBN 9781315559223 (e-book)
Subjects: LCSH: Brainwashing. | Ideology—Psychological aspects. |
    Totalitarianism—Psychological aspects.
Classification: LCC BF633 .S84 2017 | DDC 153.8/53—dc23
LC record available at https://lccn.loc.gov/2016027933

ISBN: 978-1-138-67795-1 (hbk)
ISBN: 978-1-138-67797-5 (pbk)
ISBN: 978-1-315-55922-3 (ebk)

Typeset in Bembo
by Apex CoVantage, LLC

To Rosa and Carlos

CONTENTS

ACKNOWLEDGMENTS

My thanks go to Spencer Ward, Mary Russell, Paul Beckford, Sally Harding, Malcolm Rund, Madeleine Chapman, Helen Young, Roger Bailey, Bea Cabrera and Cilla Walford. They read all or some of this book as it developed. Their comments, critiques and encouragement have been invaluable.

I also thank those who encouraged and helped in other important ways: my sister Lyndall Stein, my children Carlos Rybeck and Rosa Rybeck, and Ida Susser, Mark Krivchenia, Paula Westmoreland, Grace Connoy, Mike Dunford and Masoud Banisadr. Rebecca Stott provided invaluable advice at a critical stage in the publication process.

The participants in my original doctoral research generously and sometimes bravely shared their stories with me. I would like to thank them again for their contributions. I am grateful to Alan Sroufe who has supported my attachment-based work for many years. Joachim Savelsberg was a wise advisor as I developed the basis for this work. Finally, I would like to thank Mary Main for her permission to develop the Group Attachment Interview modeled on the groundbreaking Adult Attachment Interview.

INTRODUCTION

My colleagues are an interesting bunch. They are professors, artists, managers, writers, activists, psychologists, teachers, medical professionals, therapists, directors of charities, social workers. Even a record-breaking around-the-world cyclist. But what brings us together – our common interest – is that we all share a particular past. This group with their varied careers have had even more varied previous lives. They were Jehovah's Witnesses, Islamist extremists, neo-Nazi skinheads, a Jew who spent years in the allegedly anti-Semitic LaRouche cult, a former Moonie, extreme fundamentalist Christians, guru-worshippers, and adults who grew up in, variously, a Trotskyist cult, a sexually abusive Christian cult and an ultra Orthodox Jewish sect. As for myself, I existed for ten years in a state of suspended animation in a supposedly "leftwing" political cult. Since I escaped (and it did feel like an escape) I have spent the last 25 years studying, writing and teaching about the cultic experience and it is through this that I have met and worked with this interesting group of people.

What we have in common is that we all suffered for years within a specific type of social structure – a social structure that I, and many others, call a cult. This same social structure forms the basis of totalitarian movements and states.

The groups we belonged to clearly did not all share the same ideology. They were not the same size, did not share goals. But when we are together, my colleagues and I know that we have lived through almost eerily similar experiences. We all experienced the chronic terror and powerlessness of living in closed environments where the leader's control was absolute and where the group dictated often the most mundane details of daily life. Wrenching ourselves out of these systems we count as among the most difficult and bravest acts we have each had to do.

After getting out, we have all tried to contribute in some way to helping others, either by helping people get out and recover from cults, or by trying to educate the public to prevent others from recruitment into such groups. We do this because we know that these groups – these cults and totalitarian systems – take control over people's lives to such an extreme extent that life itself ceases to belong to followers. In the worst cases – such as the violent terrorist cults – this annihilation of life is directed not only at followers but at outsiders, with acts of terrorism and war taking thousands of lives. Other groups focus the terror only internally (so it is not visible to the outside world), seeking to maintain their grip on followers in this way.

My colleagues and I share the experience of having been indoctrinated, having been put through the fear-driven process of brainwashing where we have been – at least for some period of time – trapped by a psychopathic leader, locked in by a psychological trauma bond. Something that we all understand – and certainly wish we didn't – is how an ordinary person can end up donning a suicide vest and killing themselves along with their unknown victims.

As a group we were not crazy, especially needy, or subservient. We have gone on to useful careers and generally typical personal lives (though sadly this is not an outcome that is in any way guaranteed for many former members). I say this because I want to emphasize that the people who find themselves in cults, extremist groups or even totalitarian nations are ordinary people who did not choose that situation. Rather, the situation – or the group – chose them.

As you read this book, perhaps you will reflect back on some experiences that you yourself have been through that may fit this picture: a political group, a church or other religious group, a meditation or wellness center, a workplace or a personal growth training program? As this is a topic that is still largely hidden and stigmatized, if you have come across cultic or totalitarian organizations you may not have identified them as such. But in my experience most of us have run into these groups at one time or another or have known friends or family who have. None of us are immune given the right come-on and the right situation, yet those who do become victims are demonized. This demonization prevents us from recognizing our own potential vulnerability.

Cults and totalitarianism are a continuing and ever-present danger – from political and religious terrorism on the world stage to the intimate terror of controlling one-on-one personal relationships. I have written this book with the hope that I can make a contribution to the development of a public health approach to prevention of these social ills. It is my belief that societies can best protect themselves through a widespread understanding of how ordinary people can be recruited and controlled, and by teaching people the warning signs and the mechanisms of this coercive control and the variety of contexts in which it can occur. Far better, I think, for people to learn this in the classroom or community than through the school of hard knocks that brought me to writing this book.

★ ★ ★ ★ ★

Most of us don't see the small beginnings, relationship zero as I call it. The first wielding of power by a psychopath over another person. The first gaining of control and finding that it works, that it has staying power. We see the middle, the second act, a little more often – and from these scenes we make our judgments. Sad souls with fixed smiles give out flowers at airports, or knock on doors on a weekend. An excited friend tells us they have found the answer to personal success at some seminar or other. On a busy street a stranger offers a free personality test, while another pushes leaflets at us announcing a political or religious apocalypse. Crowds – sometimes whole nations – chant, waving the Little Red Book, the Bible or the Qur'an.

It is the third act that makes the headlines with a numbing regularity. It is here we see the explosive endings, the final results. Endings of outsiders, of enemies, of followers, of children. We see the genocides of totalitarianism from Hitler to Stalin to Pol Pot. Or the smaller tragedies such as Aum Shinrikyo's 1995 gassing of commuters in the Tokyo subway. Propaganda films show a young Londoner turned ISIS/Daesh executioner beheading hostages in Syria. Perhaps saddest of all are the children, from child soldiers to the children who die in cults, sacrificed to the leader's will.

Along with the deaths of children, the most difficult endings to understand are the suicides. Sometimes the whole group self-destructs – always at the orders of the leader – as in the group suicides of Jonestown in 1979, Heaven's Gate in 1997 and the Solar Temple in 1994. In the 21st century, suicide bombings continue on an almost daily basis, ending the lives of followers and outsiders at one and the same moment. Then there are the suicides of the survivors; the ongoing fallout of trauma that may finally catch up to the Holocaust survivor or, more recently, to the children brought up in sexually and physically abusive cultic environments such as the Children of God cult.

There are also many more smaller suicides of the self that occur in the range of groups and relationships about which I will be talking in this book – the rejection of one's inner self, of one's family, friends, beliefs, morals. An essential ingredient in this process of inner coercion is the attempt by the psychopathic leader to control the very *self*, the interior as well as the exterior world of the follower. It is in this way that group suicides, or suicide bombings, can perhaps indeed be termed suicide rather than murder engineered by the leader – the follower takes his or her own life, in a sense intentionally.[i] But what is the meaning of "intentional" when the self has been hijacked, the core of the follower's cognitive and emotional self has been pulled into pieces that no longer form a coherent whole?

It is this question that forms the heart of this book. What is the process that allows a leader to gain such control over his or her followers that they will obey his or her orders even to the point of killing themselves, and sometimes even sacrific-ing their own children? This defeats in such an extreme way our understanding of ourselves as humans. It defeats the view that we are hard-wired to protect our-selves and those we love. Yet an evolutionary-based analysis can help us to under-stand how this happens. Behaviors and ways of feeling and thinking evolved over

---

i Although in Jonestown the victims were prevented from escaping by armed guards, so in this sense the deaths at Jonestown must more accurately be termed murder.

millennia, can, in particular environments, be turned against our own survival. The very behavior that protects us within the environment to which we are adapted becomes a dangerous vulnerability outside of this environment.

I will try to describe why and how this happens. It is possible to understand this, yet so often the wrong question is asked: What was wrong with *those* people that they chose to join such a group? We know that, in fact, most of these followers were ordinary people, people who got caught up in situations beyond their control. As a social psychologist I am trained to ask different questions: What was the situation that these people found themselves in when these things happened? What processes unfolded in that situation to cause such a tragic and seemingly incomprehensible result? What is this dangerous environment to which we are not well adapted? Why, in fact, are most of us vulnerable to these influence processes, given the right circumstances at the right time?

It is not all grim. There is much evidence that knowing how these processes work is protective. That is the main goal of this book: to add to the literature that exists to educate the public, to increase people's resilience to these types of dangerous human relationships, and to offer evidence-based suggestions for strengthening social resilience overall.

The stories that contribute to this book come from interviews, memoirs, newspapers and history books. They are the stories of real people caught up in situations that few of them chose. Certainly none of them chose these situations with informed consent of either the motives of the leadership or where the situation would ultimately lead. Here I introduce just some of the people we will meet in the course of this account.

I interviewed Marina Ortiz in 2002, in New York City where she lived.[ii] We sat in a cozy Puerto Rican restaurant with Salsa music stirring up the atmosphere in a particularly pleasant way. This was her neighborhood, her choice of restaurant, the music of her Nuyorican people who she now served by editing a website on the local politics and culture. I turned on my tape recorder and sat with pen in hand. She began her story. For two hours I listened as she told how, some 18 years prior she had responded to an ad in a free newspaper offering "non-racist, non-sexist therapy." She was then a single mother of a small child, pregnant with her second and suffering from depression. The story rolled on. Within two years this "therapy" had transformed her into a full-time cadre of an underground political organization headed by Fred Newman. Fred is a charismatic white man who had set up shop as a Marxist therapist (without, however, the benefit of any training or qualifications in psychotherapy) in the early 1970s. By 1990, after five years as a full-timer, working "24/7," supposedly for social justice and equality, the group was pressuring Marina to put her daughter into foster care so that she would not be distracted from her organizational commitments. At that point she was finally able to break away.

---

ii All names and identifying details of individuals have been changed unless real names have been used in quoted published material, or in cases where individuals prefer to have their real names used.

What was her journey? How did she get there? What allowed her to break free? Marina and her comrades' stories form a central element of this book. Though not as dramatic, or as violent as many such groups, nonetheless they demonstrate clearly the methods and dynamics central to this form of social psychological control and serve as an in-depth case study.

Masoud Banisadr wrote an extraordinary memoir of his years with the extremist and cultic Iranian Mojahedin to which he was recruited while a student in New-castle in the UK.[1] I met him in Middlesbrough, an industrial town in the north of England, where he cooked me an exquisite Persian meal of beef stew enfolded with sheaves of green herbs. This he served with a dome of crusted rice scattered with sunbursts of saffron. The appreciation of food, he told me, was allowed in this group, though love was abolished. He and all his comrades were forced to leave their marriages by submitting to "ideological divorce." At the very same time, the leader, Rajavi, took a new wife, fortuitously now freed from her marriage through the enforced ideological divorce of one of his lieutenants.

I first heard of Anne Singleton in 2008, when I discovered she had posted some of my own story on her aptly named website, *Cultsandterror.org*. It turns out that she, like Masoud, had been a member of the Iranian Mojahedin. She had been recruited through meetings at Manchester University, which she and her Iranian boyfriend attended together. She went from an ordinary Yorkshire background to training with a Kalashnikov in full military uniform in the Iraqi desert. The group showed her, over and over again, videos of female suicide bombers. Anne was able to step back from the brink. Now she is back in Yorkshire, raising a son and working to raise awareness of the problem of cults, terrorism and brainwashing. How did she end up in such a group and how did she find a way to leave?

And there is my story, which I have already written about in my book *Inside Out*.[2] In that book I describe how I was unwittingly used to cover up a murder committed by the leader of the small and damaging group to which I belonged for ten long and dreary years in the 1980s. Masoud and I had found each other's stories, and though he had been in a terrorist group and I had been in a political cult, we recognized that these were the same type of organization with the same methods of control.

Then there are the religious cults. Peter Frouman is a young man born into the Children of God cult (now renamed The Family). His story of violence, sexual abuse and enforced separation from his parents is just one of hundreds of stories from the children raised in this group. As a teenager Peter was able to escape although his siblings were kidnapped and hidden within the cult for many more years.[3] Peter is now an activist working to support others who grew up in similar environments, and to educate the public about these secret and isolated worlds. He is joined in this work by, among others, three young women who wrote the moving book *Not Without My Sister*,[4] which tells of their equally difficult experiences in this group.

We will learn more about these and other stories as this book unfolds.

I wanted to write this book because I believe there needs to be an accessible, read-able book that pulls together the various strands of research, of experiences and of theoretical advances that can help us understand this phenomenon of extreme control, and so help us to protect our citizenry, ourselves, our children and others we love. I also wanted to add my voice to the developing chorus that is trying to make itself heard over the dull and unhelpful clamor currently dominant in academia on this topic. This view states that coercive persuasion or brainwashing doesn't exist, doesn't occur. There is no such thing, says this group of scholars, as cults, just deviant "new religions," which should be left alone to practice their rituals. The fact that many of us were not in religious groups is steadfastly ignored by such critics. These scholars say that persons such as myself and those I mention above are simply disgruntled followers (some use a mangled sociologese to call us "angry apostates" who are "carriers of atrocity tales").[5] According to these scholars we are simply trying to avoid responsibility for our own mistakes by blaming the groups we were in. In fact, they say, we exerted free will and now are trying to cover our ill-judged tracks.

But on the contrary, myself, Marina and Masoud, among many, many others, have attempted to shoulder responsibility by learning the lessons presented to us through the difficult experiences we have lived through. We are all involved in working to prevent others from going through the killing of self that we encountered. And in that process to also prevent actual suicides, including the suicide bombings that kill not only followers but also countless innocent bystanders.

Perhaps more to the point, the scholars who deny these very real forms of extreme social influence are unable to help us prevent the very real loss of life that results. Their analysis does not help us understand or prevent the ongoing problem of more or less average young people continuing to be recruited into terroristic or cultic organizations. As of this writing, 20 Somali-American youths brought up in Minnesota have disappeared from their family homes, turning up months later as new recruits to the Jihad. One of them became the first-known American suicide bomber and at least five others have died in Somalia.[6] Similarly, four high school girls from London's East End are only a few of hundreds of young women who have recently disappeared from their homes in Western countries to become "jihadi brides" in Syria.[7] Their story also is one of recruitment, indoctrination and, finally, brainwashing until they sacrificed potentially promising futures. My intent in this book is to help make plain the mechanisms and the structures of such groups, and the sadly general vulnerability of most of us to these situations.

Brainwashing[iii] takes place within a wide variety of social situations. It occurs in cults, like the one Peter grew up in, in cultic terrorist organizations where political violence is an organizing principle, in totalitarian movements and in totalitarian states where, as Hannah Arendt[8] put it, terror has achieved state power. On the other end of the spectrum brainwashing can occur in very small or even one-on-one cults: relationships of one leader and only one or two followers.[9] Similar mechanisms and structures of control can also be found in certain cases of highly controlling domestic violence or abuse, such as the Fritzl case in Austria.

---

iii In the next chapter I discuss the difficulties of vocabulary in this field.

It is due to this wide reach of brainwashing and extreme social control that it is of concern to all of us in the contemporary world. Terrorism continues to be a threat throughout the world. Cults, though they are secretive and often hidden, are far from abating, and in fact, though we may not always be aware of it, rub up against us in our daily lives more often than we know. While controlling domestic violence may sometimes erupt as in the horrors of the Fritzl case, more often it is silent and hidden, yet sadly commonplace: over one hundred women in the UK are killed every year by their male partners,[10] and in the US in 2000, 1,247 women were killed by an intimate partner,[11] usually the outcome of highly controlling relationships. Reaching to another point in this unhappy constellation of social control, we find totalitarian movements, such as the Lord's Resistance Army in Northern Uganda and the Sudan, which terrorize whole segments of the population. And totalitarian states like North Korea live on as others, such as Pol Pot's Cambodia, fall.

This may seem an overly ambitious agenda. However, it is not my goal to explain all the evils of the world. Rather, the central aim of this book is to show the common social psychological and structural elements that link these varied situations and that result in charismatic, authoritarian leaders shaping the minds of followers so that they are not able to act in their own survival interests. This mind-shaping activity can be usefully termed brainwashing or coercive persuasion. The structures in which this takes place I refer to as totalist systems.

This book will argue that the belief systems or ideologies we see in these systems mirror and shore them up; indeed, total or absolutist ideologies reflect the totalist and all-encompassing nature of the social structures they represent. Understanding the structure of these all-or-nothing ideologies is a helpful and critical element in being able to determine if the underlying relationships that they represent are indeed totalist in nature.

The social structures of totalism and the belief systems they exhibit enter deep into the lives of those targeted. They penetrate the most personal and tender parts of us: our hearts, the places in us that seek attachment and intimacy with others. And they penetrate our brains, the places in us that usually work to help us solve the problems of survival. They detach our higher-order cognitive thinking from our sensory perceptions and emotions and leave us, thus, helpless to understand which way to turn to avoid danger. It is these processes that I hope to clarify through the course of this book.

Notes

1   Banisadr, Masoud. 2004. *Masoud: Memoirs of an Iranian Rebel*. London: Saqi.
2   Stein, Alexandra. 2002. *Inside Out: A Memoir of Entering and Breaking Out of a Minneapolis Political Cult*. St. Cloud: North Star Press of St. Cloud.
3   Frouman, Peter. *Family Values*. Retrieved January 12, 2009 (http://www.frouman.net/kidnapping/).
4   Jones, Celeste, Kristina Jones and Juliana Buhring. 2007. *Not without My Sister*. London: Harper Element.

5 Bromley, David. 1998. "The Social Construction of Contested Exit Roles: Defectors, Whistleblowers, and Apostates," in *The Politics of Religious Apostasy:The Role of Apostates in the Transformation of Religious Movements*, edited by D. Bromley. Westport: Praeger Publishers, pp. 19–48.

6 Elliott, Andrea. 2009. "Charges Detail Road to Terror for 20 in U.S.," in *New York Times*, November 23. New York.

7 Sherwood, Harriet, Sandra Laville, Kim Wilson, Ben Knight, Maddy French and Lauren Gambino. 2014. "Schoolgirl Jihadis: The Female Islamists Leaving Home to Join Isis Fighters," in *Guardian*, Vol. 29 September. London: Guardian.

8 Arendt, Hannah. 1948/1979. *The Origins of Totalitarianism*. Orlando: Harcourt Brace.

9 Lalich, Janja and Madeleine Tobias. 2006. *Take Back Your Life: Recovering from Cults and Abusive Relationships*. Berkeley: Bay Tree Publishing.

10 McVeigh, Tracy and Clare Colley. 2015. "'We Record All the Killing of Women by Men. You See a Pattern'," in *The Observer*, Vol. 8 February. London: Guardian News and Media.

11 Rennison, C. 2003. "Crime Data Brief: Intimate Partner Violence, 1993–2001." *NCJ no. 197838*.

1

THE OVERTHROW OF THE RULERS OF THE MIND

In 1985 Marina Ortiz, a young woman with a pretty, round face, was in her third year of university at Hunter College in New York City, studying media and communications and editing the college magazine. She was pregnant with her second child and had just broken up with the father of her children. Understandably, perhaps, she was depressed. She found a therapist advertised in a free newspaper distributed at Hunter. After two months the therapist shunted her into group therapy, despite Marina's misgivings. This was "social therapy," the invention of Fred Newman. In 1974 he described it thus: "Proletarian or revolutionary psychotherapy is a journey which begins with the rejection of our inadequacy and ends in the acceptance of our smallness; it is the overthrow of the rulers of the mind."[1]

The therapist and others in the therapy group began to deluge her with invitations to various events: a workshop on sexism, productions at their Castillo Theatre, alcohol-fueled social functions held on riverboat cruises down the Hudson. At a meeting in Harlem on women's empowerment another therapist said she was impressed by Marina's comments and invited her to write for the *National Alliance*, a political newspaper produced by the New Alliance Party. From the first therapist to the *National Alliance* newspaper, all these involvements were the products of the Newman Tendency,[i] an organization run by therapist-in-chief Fred Newman.

---

i Since the organization changes its name frequently, morphing as needed, cutting elements and adding others, I refer to it here as the Newman Tendency. This uses one of its own names – The Tendency – while acknowledging the formative and central role of its charismatic and authoritarian leader, Fred Newman.

About a year into the process of engulfment by the Newman Tendency, two of its leading women therapists sat Marina down over drinks in a Manhattan bar, announced that the group was actually part of an underground political organization fighting for social justice, and invited her to become a full-time cadre of the International Workers Party. As Marina was, by this time, living with a man she had met in one of the therapy groups and her life already revolved around the various group activities, and, not least, she believed in the group's stated goal of organizing to create a non-racist, non-sexist, non-exploitative society, she joined. Her personal life was already attached to the Newman Tendency through therapy, her lover and her social connections developed through the group. Her political and professional life, which previously had expressed itself in a variety of ways, including the college newspaper and other activities, had also fallen under the domain of the organization. So it was not really such a big step when Marina said "Yes." Thus began a secret, closed life where she was under the organization's discipline "24/7." This outcome was not accidental or random. It was the result of a systematic, orchestrated and deceptive process of grooming and recruitment.

Marina's initial action had been to seek therapy for depression. She was trying to help herself, to improve her life and that of her children. She was certainly not looking for a life-consuming commitment to a secretive political group. The result, however, of that initial action was that she fell under the control of Fred Newman. Newman was a former itinerant university teacher who, during the last of the six academic posts he held during the sixties, started an encounter group under the aegis of the City College of New York philosophy department. At the time of Marina's involvement the group had grown to around 500 members.

Marina became a loyal follower with Fred now her therapist as well as her leader. Her children attended the group's rather shoddy school (Marina described it as a "rat-hole"). Unusually for most group members, she kept her day job, although she did as much group work as possible there. She laughed as she told me: "I did as much of their work at my job as I could, so that was typing, xeroxing – anything you can get away with time-wise – stealing supplies." Then straight after work she went off to her second, unpaid and full-time shift for the Newman Tendency working on the *National Alliance* newspaper or other projects. Often, additional meetings or "socials" with other group members were scheduled late into the night, usually rotating through different bars in Manhattan. Twice-weekly therapy was yet another demand on her time. And she could be summoned to attend rallies and demonstrations whenever additional bodies were needed.

She regularly slept overnight in the newspaper's office as "security" and now put her two young children to bed only two nights a week, childcare being shared with the other families with whom she lived. She lost contact with her own family: "You were discouraged from seeing your family. The family was holding you down, the family unit was not encouraged." She became utterly committed to the group, convinced of their mission, which in her understanding was to create a "peaceful socialist revolution."

But what was the group actually doing? During her tenure, Marina found not social justice, not anti-racism or anti-sexism. Rather, she saw families pulled apart, women ordered to have abortions, money laundering and fraud, including the bilking of both Medicaid and the Federal Elections Commission.[2] As Newman so eloquently put it, highlighting one of the goals of his bizarre revolution:

> There's big money right now in Marxist Leninist organizing if we set up the structure. . . . I don't know how big the money is but, there is in fact real money to be made in the model we developed – real money, serious money. The damn New York Institute for Social Therapy and Research is a bloody goldmine. . . . There's big money out there. In all of its versions – Marxist version, cleaned-up version – all the different versions. There's heavy money.[3]

During this time, cadres were being trained in armed self-defense and an arms cache was set up. According to Bill Pleasant, a group member in whose house the arms were stored:

> Well there were this group of people who were known as gunmen. Everyone went through that class, but there was a clique who had not only enjoyed that stuff but they went around armed . . . But the theory was, it wasn't so much that we would go gunning for the police, it was that we had so much money hanging around that it was necessary to defend our offices.

Ruiz, another former member, put it this way:

> We did do weapons training. You know, there was a group of us that went into the woods once in a while. . . . The reality of the situation at that point for us was that we were trying to create a revolution in the belly of the beast. At a certain point in time it would become a physical struggle, so weapons training was important. You had to learn how to deal with weapons so that you could teach how to deal with weapons, you know. In the early days there were discussions about where to put the bombs, when it came to that. Later on it didn't. It was more about fundraising, more about the emotional underpinnings and psychological underpinnings and how to move that to the Left through culture, through propaganda. It was a different look and feel, so it became protectionist when we moved down to Castillo, when we moved to the office on Greenwich Street, it was more protecting what we had.

Along with this weapons training, former members have also alleged that the group funneled money for weapons to a variety of guerrilla groups in Africa and South America.

Newman, meanwhile, was engaging in numerous sexual relationships, some of which involved breaking up other couples in the group in order for him to take over the female partner. All of his (known) relationships involved women who had first been his therapy patients, and several of these women became part of what was to become known as his "harem." Such was the nature of the much-touted women's leadership of the Newman Tendency.

Far from creating a peaceful socialist revolution, this was an organization where Newman exerted almost total power and control over followers. Loyalty, labor, money and sex flowed up to Newman. Marina found herself trapped in a totalist organization, and was now fully indoctrinated. In fact, and as promised by Newman, she had indeed accepted her smallness and overthrown herself as the ruler of her own mind. Now it was Newman who ruled her mind.

Fred Newman's "Tendency" is just one example among thousands. No matter the ideology – left, right, religious, commercial, for "personal growth" or to get rich quick – the leadership, structures and processes are remarkably similar. What constitutes this type of group? In later chapters I'll detail the steps in recruitment and – more importantly – retention and indoctrination processes along with each element of the structure of these groups, but for now I'll focus first on vocabulary and definitions, and then give an overview to provide some context.

A note then on vocabulary. There are difficult word choices a writer on this topic must make. Some words – like "totalist" – convey important meaning and have solid roots in the field (Lifton introduced the concept in his study of brainwashing or thought reform in China and North Korea[4]). I like this word. It conveys the all-encompassing nature of the beast. The way a total eclipse utterly covers the light, so do totalist organizations attempt to block out any alternate relationships or beliefs, locking daylight out of the picture. The word "totalist" gives an appropriately oppressive sense, the suffix "-ist" conveying the active role required in creating this total environment, thus flagging the actions of the leader and the organization as the agent of their wishes. The suffix "-ism" denotes "a belief in or practice of," and so "totalism" is the practice of a total worldview or a total ideology (I discuss this in depth in Chapter 7). As Hannah Arendt said of totalitarian ideologies, they are "isms that pretend to have found the key explanation for all the mysteries of life and world":[5] the ideologies of totalism claim to supply the answers to all possible questions for all time.

Two other words in this field are tricky. First is the word "cult," about which much has been written. I will use it here in its simplest sense, believing that most people share a visceral understanding of the word: that is, a cult is a group of people led and generally exploited by a charismatic and authoritarian leader, who hold an extreme (totalist) set of views. A cult employs brainwashing in its efforts to keep members under its control. I use this word "cult" interchangeably with the terms "totalist group" or "totalist system."

Finally, the word "brainwashing" demands some attention. It originated in the study of the prisoner of war and reeducation camps of the early days of Communist China and North Korea.[6] The term was translated literally from its usage in Maoist China where it meant to wash or cleanse the brain. It described the process whereby these regimes used methods of indoctrination to neutralize opponents of the regime and, in many cases, to convert them to sometimes enthusiastic support. This process involved the alternation of assault and leniency,[7] of threat and apparent safety, within an isolating environment. The downside of the term is that it became popularized through such movies as *The Manchurian Candidate*, which portrayed a sleeper agent flipping hypnotically into a murderous robot-like state in response to a preprogrammed stimulus. This is a simplistic caricature of the actual, sometimes complex and subtle, process that occurred in China and North Korea, and that continues to take place with great frequency today in totalist groups. I will make use of the word and concept "brainwashing," but I also use terms such as coercive persuasion,[8] which originated during this same period of research. Other terms – thought reform,[9] mind control,[10] resocialization[11] – similarly refer to the same process of control.

We need a clear definition of what a cult or totalist group is. I refer to a very specific set of groups or relationships. A clear definition is especially critical as academic wars ongoing since the early 1970s[12] have muddied the field until any conversation about this very damaging and pervasive social phenomenon has become unnecessarily confused. The discussion has become stalled within the constraints of a dead-end debate about religion.

A recent example of this confusion is in the best-selling book *The God Delusion* by Richard Dawkins,[13] a scholar with whom I share an evolutionary and multidisciplinary approach to understanding human behavior. Dawkins has, unfortunately, been dragged into this mire – perhaps coinciding with his embracing of "militant" atheism (itself a kind of fundamentalism). The heart of the problem is the lumping together of religions and totalist groups into one category. At the very start of his book he asks us to imagine "a world with no religion. Imagine no suicide bombers, no 9/11, no 7/7 . . ." His list goes on, from the troubles in Northern Ireland to "bouffant-haired televangelists fleecing gullible people of their money," to the Taliban blowing up ancient statues.[14] The difficulty with this way of looking at things is that sadly this would still leave the world with plenty of other horrors. Pol Pot's regime was hardly religious, yet it resulted in the death of one-quarter of the Cambodian population, picking out for particularly murderous attention musicians, artists or those who wore spectacles. The Symbionese Liberation Movement or the Baader Meinhoff gang were politically, not religiously, motivated terrorist groups. In the decade from 1995 to 2005, one monitoring group recorded about 60 right-wing terrorist plots in the United States, by groups ranging from the KKK to militia groups to racist skinhead organizations.[15] In the US it is not just evangelists who fleece the gullible by way of television, but get-rich-quick con artists with no religious claims at all but remarkably similar methods. Imagining the world without religion certainly does not bring to my mind a world without terror or con-men.

Though I share Dawkins's antipathy to magical thinking and other elements common to most religions, I do not share this view that all religions are harmful *per se* nor that all are liable to engage in the acts of terror that he lists. In this way he casts the net too widely. On the other hand, the net is cast too narrowly: looking at the problem of terror or cults as being only religious problems leads to missing out on an entire spectrum of non-religious groups[ii] that engage in terrorizing and cultic behaviors.

No, the issue is not religion as such. What is at the heart of the problem is not whether the ideologies of these groups are religious, political or otherwise, but how tightly they are structured and the levels of control they exert over followers. To fully understand this, our analysis must go beyond a distaste for religious or supernatural beliefs. Focusing solely on religion, as Dawkins does, results in a misrepresentation of causes. I will try to show that it is a particular form of leadership and the social and belief structures that flow from it that set up the conditions in which followers can be manipulated into certain types of terroristic or cultic behaviors. Focusing only on the beliefs, while they are an important component of these systems, gives us only a partial view of how these systems operate. In fact, the belief system can be seen as the outer layer of a whole system: it is the expression of the social structure, and the social structure is the expression of the leader. To understand these systems we must enter in and look at these other two aspects.

Without getting too much further tangled in this debate, the point is: cults and totalist groups are not all religious, and religions are not all cultic or totalist. To confuse the two in this way prevents understanding the particular set of characteristics that make up the totalist environment in which – importantly – traumatic brainwashing processes take place to create extraordinarily high levels of control over followers. There is a particular set of groups and relationships that are best understood as varieties of totalist systems that are highly controlling of followers and can be predicted to have psychologically or physically violent outcomes.

Dawkins and the sociologists of religion dominant in this field leave us analytically bereft when it comes to understanding the precise components and mechanisms of this set of groups that are able to exert such extreme control over their members. Some types of groups may have particular beliefs in certain areas of life, yet allow autonomy in other areas. These are not totalistic. For example, someone may be a regular, even a devout, churchgoer. Another person may believe in aliens, astrology or a past life as an armadillo. Yet such people may still belong to a football club, be married to someone of a different faith or beliefs, choose their own career, have a variety of friends who hold a variety of beliefs. Their belief system only forms a part of their life and their views.[iii] Their adherence to their perhaps odd belief or their faith and place of worship has an entirely different impact on their life than that experience by someone – like Marina Ortiz – whose whole existence becomes bound up within one organization.

ii   It is not only groups that are in question, but also cultic one-on-one relationships, such as that between serial killer John Allen Muhammad and Lee Boyd Malvo. Malvo met Muhammed at the age of 15, learned to call him "Dad," and after an indoctrination process eventually became his accomplice in a series of sniper killings in the Washington DC area. Bender, E. 2004. "Expert Witness Describes Making of a Serial Killer." *Psychiatric News* 39(23):13–44.

iii For a useful explanation of the difference between a *total* versus *particular*, or partial, ideology, see Mannheim, Karl. 1936. *Ideology and Utopia: An Introduction to the Sociology of Knowledge*. San Diego: Harcourt Brace Jovanovich.

The total ideology, the absolute belief system – whether religious, political, commercial or of any other type – is the reflection of the underlying totalist social structure. It is an important component, but not the driver of the system. The total ideology has a specific structure and function in supporting the totalist system, which I introduce in this chapter and discuss more fully in Chapter 7. However, totalist groups, cults, totalitarianism, even controlling forms of domestic violence, are set apart – not by the fact of religion or ideology – but by the nature of the *relationship* between leader and follower, the *relationship* between the group and the follower.

This is a relationship that is rooted in the creation of, and experience of, trauma. A helpful way to understand this relationship is by using attachment theory and trauma theory. Attachment researchers who study both child and adult relationships call this type of relationship one of "disorganized attachment." This concept lies at the heart of the ideas presented in this book and is introduced in the next chapter. Both attachment and trauma theory look at the impact of trauma on the brain and these ideas are key to understanding the response of followers to the totalist situation.

Totalist groups represent a very particular social form. They are defined by five dimensions of the group: leadership, structure, ideology, process and outcomes.[16] Let's take an initial look at each of these elements that unite these apparently disparate groups and relationships.

The leader

Most importantly, no totalist structure can exist without the engine, as Hannah Arendt calls it, of *the leader*. The leader drives the whole system. The system – the group's structure, beliefs and processes – reflects the personality, the preferences and the whims of the leader. The leader needs to have two core, and key, qualities: charisma and authoritarianism. In Chapter 6 we will see the importance of these specific attributes.

This leader generally builds an organization up from an initial exploitative relationship, which I refer to as relationship zero. In 1968, 18-year-old Hazel Daren was Newman's first recruit, the Tendency's relationship zero. Newman, a burly, mustachioed man with long, disheveled hair and a broad pale face, was then 33 and was Daren's teacher at the City College of New York. She stayed with the group, as Newman's number one "wife," until her death at the age of 54. That relationship became the core of Newman's first organized group – a therapy/encounter-group collective named *IF . . . Then*, which later grew into the full-fledged Newman Tendency.

The two aspects of the leader's personality – charisma and authoritarianism – set up the fundamental dynamic in the group, starting with this first relationship. That is, the followers love, worship and idealize the leader, endowing the leader with charisma and with, as Weber says, "magical qualities."[17] At the same time, the leader's authoritarian nature leads to actions that generate a feeling of fear, terror or threat. Threat can be introduced in myriad ways, for example through threatening to end the relationship, or by inducing fear of the outside world through introducing or fanning apocalyptic fears, or it could simply be through creating conditions of physical threat such as extreme fatigue, hunger or the outright threat of violence.

In the case of Newman, these two features of his personality and leadership were documented in the Tendency's own 1972 history: though the group was supposedly "anarchic" it was, according to their own account, "ruled by a benevolent despot."[18] Benevolence and despotism, of course, are one way of describing the two elements of charisma and authoritarianism, of a leader who induces feelings of both love and fear. A former member, Sidney, put it this way:

> Yeah, somebody taught him how to abuse people. . . . He's charming too, he's charming. Even though . . . I liked him! I would have a problem disliking him now even after I already know about him. If he sat down right there next to me, I'd say, "Hey Fred, how are you doing? Are you still corrupting people?" (laughs) – "Are you still screwing 18 women at the same time?" or trying to. But you know, he was a likeable guy!

The leader's primary goal is to create a set of guaranteed attachments to others. This drive for relational control is an outcome of the leader's own disorganized attachment. Nothing a totalist leader likes less than to be left. Purging followers is another matter (and is sometimes needed in order to get rid of troublesome members) – but the *control* of the relationship must rest with the leader. Secondary benefits accrue from this primary goal of control: the ability to control others opens up the possibility of sexual, financial and political exploitation. However it is my belief that these are indeed secondary, rather than the core personality elements that drive the leader. As in relationships of controlling domestic violence this combination of charisma and authoritarianism, of love and fear, is a potent one. These two elements of the leader's personality are reflected in the structure, ideology, process and outcomes of the group. (In subsequent generations of larger groups a leadership body may evolve after the demise of the individual leader, but this too will display the two elements of charisma and authoritarianism.) We will see below in the discussion of coercive persuasion why this particular dynamic is so central to the totalist system.

The structure

The totalist group grows by replicating the dynamics of relationship zero as recruits are drawn in. The pattern of relating to the leader set in this initial relationship remains, modeled by the existing members and so transmitted to new recruits. Structurally, the totalist group is dominated by the leader in all regards. In order for the leader to maintain control of followers, the structure must facilitate several functions: it must maintain the single point of dominance of the leader, isolate group members and, in most cases, provide controlled access to and from the outside world.

The group structure must serve the process of coercive persuasion, which requires an isolating environment. Newman achieves this in the Tendency by drawing followers into full-time commitments where, as in Marina's case, they live together, work on Tendency assignments, attend social therapy, socialize with other members and generally have no available time remaining to engage in non-group activities. The emotional and physical energies of the group members must be fully engaged in order to keep them from external relationships and influences.

The structure must be one in which the alternation of love and threat can take place, while severely limiting the group member's access to "escape hatch" relationships with persons outside of the group or its sphere of influence. Newman's proscription of what he calls "doing family" means that followers are not only discouraged from seeing family members outside of the group, but they are also systematically discouraged from developing close emotionally trusting ties with other group members. Many group "friends" now replace select trusted others. In this way the structure is closed, what Lalich calls a self-sealing system:[19] there are many tight and dense (yet interchangeable) ties that exist between members within the group, but few to none with persons outside the group.

The structure must also allow the transmission downwards of the leader's orders and ideological pronouncements while simultaneously funneling resources from followers back upwards to the leader. Levels of hierarchy may exist for this purpose. In the Newman Tendency, Fred's "wives" ("the harem") and assorted others form a small core who organize and manage the communication of his plans and whims to the larger organization. They in turn manage a group of about 40 "lifers," who themselves lead cells of full-time cadres.

A rule-bound bureaucracy is not well-suited to the domination by one individual of a group and so a flexible, non-bureaucratic structure is needed that can easily adjust to the leader's whims, changes of plans and changes, even, of beliefs or ideologies. So although the group is closed and steeply hierarchical, usually this hierarchy is fluid and fluctuating. There is generally a lieutenant layer in such groups, but as the leader must prevent alternative power bases developing he or she ensures that life as a lieutenant is insecure with frequent promotions and demotions in these higher ranks.

In the Newman Tendency, for example, Newman, already living with three women with whom he had been sexually involved, decided to take a new wife, Gabrielle Kurlander, a low-ranking follower who was 28 years his junior and then married to another cadre. After a "communist wedding," Newman promoted her to his inner circle and to a key, well-paid job running one of the Tendency's front groups. But this rapid promotion of a former peer (who, though well-liked, was not necessarily well-respected) caused dissension in the ranks. Hearing the rumblings, Newman called a meeting that would go down in Tendency lore – the "Want Fred" meeting. This was the beginning of a campaign and purge that would once again consolidate Newman's power by removing dissatisfied elements and shaking up the leadership. Cadre were instructed that if they didn't want Newman and Kurlander and their "hot, sexy relationship"[20] then they should leave.

How to "Want Fred" was demonstrated in several self-abasing letters from his wives and other inner circle women published in various Newman-controlled publications.[21] A typical example from a high-ranking "wife" and lieutenant follows:

> I am haunted by the spectre of this BEAUTIFUL LOVE! I admire it, and want to be near it within sight and sound of it. It's like a beautiful aria! But I can never have the aria. Ah, the division of labor! . . .

You and Rie! [*the new wife – AS*] You're in another, better world, a world of your own making. You deserve it! Good for you, comrades! . . .

I didn't want you. I didn't want you to touch it. And that's my anti-Semitism [*Newman is Jewish – AS*] that I see only now in the light of this BEAUTIFUL LOVE, and for this crime of rejection, dear comrades I am heartily sorry, and beg your forgiveness.

And I tell you with all my heart that I will learn to want you, to want you. I want to be more than an asset to the revolution, more than cannon fodder, more than a sacrifice (Jesus, till now, that was truly enough for me!) I want to want you. And I will![22]

Those cadres who could not stomach this level of submission and thus were not completely loyal either dropped out or were expelled for failing to "want" Newman. Membership was consolidated to a loyal 300, the weaker links having been purged.

Finally, many – though not all – totalist groups create front groups as the outer layer of their onion-like structure. These are the public face of the group and exist for purposes of recruitment, fundraising and other functions. The Newman Tendency, for example, has had many front groups over its existence, some of which come and go overnight, while others have remained for decades. The secretive inner party controls this changing roster of front groups ranging from the political (i.e. Independence Party locals), to social therapy centers in several cities, to theater and performance-based projects, to children's "development" programs. These front groups exist, as Arendt described it, as "transmission belts" from the group to and from the outside world.[23]

The total ideology

Whether an ideology or belief system is totalist is not determined by its content as such but by its *structure* and *function*. The structure of such a belief system is *total*: closed and exclusive, allowing no other beliefs, no other truths, no other affiliations and no other interpretations, proposing to be true for all time and under all conditions.[iv] Newman stated that the Tendency espoused a "historical totality that has no beginning, middle or end, no starting point."[24] At the same time he claimed that social therapy would teach people to think as "creators and transformers of everything that there is and all there is."[25] The ideology is determined by the leader and can be changed at a moment's notice by the leader, and only by the leader. Dissension cannot be tolerated. In its all-encompassing nature and its single point of origin, the ideology therefore mirrors the closed, steeply hierarchical structure of the group.

---

iv Although, as Arendt also pointed out, the ideology changes at the leader's whim, and sometimes the group must go through extraordinary contortions to keep up with these changes.

The key element of the total ideology is its focus on a single truth. This single truth, the sacred word, is the word of the leader, or sometimes, that of a deity to whom the leader is the only one to have a direct line. All knowledge comes from the leader. While the leader may change their mind as new "insights" appear, followers may never do so, although they must ever be on the alert to jump to the leader's sudden ideological shifts.

The functions of the totalist belief system are to shore up the totalist structure, ensuring the leader's absolute control; to justify loyalty to the group; to establish a rigid boundary between the group and the outside world; and to prevent the formation of alternate escape hatch relationships. Not least amongst these functions is that of maintaining the dissociation of the followers created by the traumatic relationship, preventing them from being able to adequately reflect on the reality of the situation in which they find themselves. Thus Newman says of social therapy that it is "a way to help the group members to have their conversation be 'about nothing'"[26] and, rather more grandly: "to support conversationalists (the group members) to abandon the realist assumption of truth referentiality."[27] This encouragement to sacrifice the distinction between truth and lies allows the leader to foist upon the isolated and traumatized follower his own opportunistic interpretation of the follower's experience. Thus day is actually night, and black is clearly white. Boxer, the super-exploited horse in Orwell's *Animal Farm*,[28] demonstrated this internalizing of the leader's view as he bravely repeated, in response to his exhaustion and misery: "Napoleon is always right" and "I will work harder." This, however, is a powerful vulnerability of totalism: that is, the frequently extreme contradiction between its heavenly or freedom-touting pronouncements and the grimly oppressive reality of life within the system.

Process: Brainwashing

Brainwashing[29] refers to the overall process set in motion by the leader, operating within the closed structure supported by the total ideology. There are several alternative terms scholars have used to name this process: coercive persuasion (Schein),[30] thought reform (Lifton),[31] resocialization (Berger and Luckmann),[32] total conversion (Lofland),[33] mind control (Singer, Hassan),[34] or, most recently by Lalich,[35] bounded choice. All these thinkers describe variants of the same essential process: the alternation of love and fear within an isolating environment resulting in a dissociated, loyal and deployable follower who can now be instructed to act in the interests of the leader rather than in his or her own survival interests.

Replacing followers' prior trusted relationships with the rigid relationships within the group, combined with the extremely strong compound of terror plus "love," entraps the follower within the group. Three important behaviors result from this. First the follower is glued in anxious dependency to the group. Being in a state of constant fear arousal means they constantly seek proximity to the group in a failed attempt to attain comfort.

Second, this seeking of contact with the source of threat causes a cognitive collapse, or dissociation, in the mind of the follower. There is no way out, no useful way to think through the trap that has been set – the mind ceases to function adequately in regard to that relationship. In my own account of my consolidation as a member of a political cult, detailed in my book *Inside Out*, I describe how I was sworn to secrecy after my first six-week stay with the group, leaving me with no one but those in the group with whom to try to understand what had been an extremely difficult experience:

> I came back with an intense culture shock and could talk to no one of it. Even with Andy and Leah, I was not to share the details of my trip. It was incredibly confusing and disorienting. I became more and more detached from my friends.
>
> I crumbled into loss, chased into panic by one nightmare after another . . . I have the kind of dream from which science fiction films are made. As I watch, my face begins to crumble and melt: the flesh beneath my eyes falls downwards, drooping like dough into my cheeks, down to my jaw. My forehead falls into my blue eyes, changing the round shape I'm so familiar with and attached to. The crumbling continues . . . a face is reforming. My face has destroyed itself. I wake up screaming.

Later I wrote in my journal:

> It has felt like madness. I have been sinking into a world where I do not want to go. . . . In sleep someone is trying to kill me, my friends are dying. I wake up with a dead emptiness inside as if I've lost everything, even my ability to know.

This sense of chaos and loss is the prelude to the next step. In my own case I resolved the sense of cognitive collapse caused by the group's isolating and dissociating strategies by turning more completely to the group – my only remaining source of comfort. Again I documented this in my journal, unconsciously echoing the poignant words of *Animal Farm*'s loyal horse Boxer:

> I must take myself in hand. I must struggle and face my fears. This chaos in my head has got to stop or I'll drown. The noise is unbearable.
>
> Commitment and discipline will hold me up. This I can control: I will work harder for the struggle. It's the one thing I know I can do.
>
> No more nightmares. I am moving on. I feel as if I've found solid ground. . . . I've decided to join.[36]

Many other accounts have vividly described similar moments of collapse: in the face of extreme pressures the recruit gives up the attempt to maintain rational thought about the group and submits to the demand for commitment and obedience.

In the third step, the leadership can now take advantage of this cognitive collapse and introject their own agenda into the cognitive vacuum thus induced. The total ideology is further introduced as both the explanation for the recruit's cognitive collapse, as well as the explanation of all other phenomena. These three elements function together to create what has been termed a "deployable agent":[37] that is, a follower who is hypercredulous and hyperobedient.[38] The process causes a change in beliefs, attitudes and behaviors in the follower that are not congruent with the follower's preexisting traits, nor – should the follower get out of the group – with their beliefs, attitudes and behaviors after leaving.

Denise, a former Tendency member, talked regretfully about her role in enforcing the psychological assault element of the social therapy process, and in the process demonstrates this change in her own attitudes and behavior:

> I used to beat up on the people in the group there. I was the bulldog in there 'cos I knew all about therapy and the therapist N. used to push me on (laughs ruefully). I can't believe I did that . . .

This is a mild example, but it illustrates the sense of estrangement and disbelief that former members may feel about actions taken while under the group's influence.

Families, friends and teachers of suicide terrorists struggle to convey this same sense of disbelief about the son, daughter, friend or student they had known. For example, these are statements from friends and family of three young men who were recruited to jihadi terrorism, respectively Hammad Munshi, Jamal Lindsey and Ramy Zamzam: "He was a normal boy, a good boy";[39] "He was a friendly, calm guy";[40] "He is a very nice guy, very cordial, very friendly";[41] "'He's a good guy', the brother said, 'He's a normal Joe.'"[42] The question that is always asked reflects this fundamental change in the follower: How could such a good person end up doing such a terrible thing?

In this book I am attempting to add to the understanding of the process of coercive persuasion by bringing in evolutionary-based attachment theory as an explanatory factor in how this mechanism works. The dissociation caused by a relationship of disorganized attachment (a relationship embedded in trauma) can help to explain this, and can show why cultic and terrorist groups predictably share the five elements described here.

Outcomes: Exploitation and deployability of followers

Coercive persuasion within the closed domain controlled by the charismatic and authoritarian leader leads to a triple isolation for the follower. Contrary to public perception, the key experience of membership in a totalist group is one of isolation, not community or comradeship. The follower is isolated from the outside world; he or she is isolated from an authentic relationship to others within the group – allowed only to communicate within the narrow confines of the group-speak and rigid rules of behavior; and, due to the dissociation that is created, the follower is also isolated from his or her self, from his or her own ability to think clearly about the situation.[v]

The result of this system is a leader with extreme control over hypercredulous and hyperobedient followers: they'll believe anything and do anything. Followers can now be exploited and deployed. They may be exploited financially; through use of unpaid labor; sexually; through exploitation of their children; and, in the extreme case, through giving up their lives in the service of the leader's needs, as for example in group suicides, or suicide terrorism. As Marina told me, sitting in that East Harlem restaurant, she would have done anything for Newman. She felt so strongly, so committed to him, that had it been needed, she would have "taken a bullet for Fred."

Not everyone who encounters a totalist group ends up successfully indoctrinated and deployable. As Zablocki puts it: "many are called, but few are chosen."[43] Cults typically do not attempt to retain unproductive members, or those who will be a drain on resources,[44] and some potential members are able, in various ways, to resist. There is, therefore, an important difference between recruitment and retention – that is, the creation of a deployable group member. Recruitment processes, and the motivations (or lack thereof) of the recruit, can differ vastly across groups. Chapter 3 deals with the wide variety of recruitment pathways from self-selection – the stereotype of the New Age cult "seeker" – to the recruitment of child soldiers at the point of a gun by groups like the Lord's Resistance Army in Uganda. But once within the group's sphere of influence, retention processes with the goal of creating deployable followers look very similar across these different contexts.

Retention involves the follower going beyond a passing interest in the group. It means also that the follower must be useful enough to the group to warrant the efforts needed to brainwash or indoctrinate them.[45] The follower must find themselves in a situation where resistance is difficult (i.e. where the isolation process is largely successful). Later in the book we shall see what conditions may allow escape or strengthen resistance to these systems.

A recent MI5 report[46] confirmed what many scholars of terrorist and cultic groups have long known: there is no single, or simple, demographic or psychological profile of those likely to be indoctrinated. From the adherents of David Koresh and Jim Jones who followed (or were forced to follow) their leaders to their deaths, to contemporary suicide bombers such as the Somali-American youths from Minneapolis who – among thousands of others – have disappeared to join the *jihad*, to eager proselytizers for highly controlling religious and personal growth groups, a range of persons across nationalities, age, class and racial categories have been successfully brainwashed. The toll in lost and wasted lives, in shattered relationships and communities and in broken beliefs continues to grow.

What happened to Marina Ortiz? She rose in the organization, not to the upper echelon of the Tendency, but she had a certain amount of status in the group, and

v Thanks to Doug Agustin for his useful concept of this triple isolation.

was one of a select number who attended a therapy group run by Newman himself. But the end came for her when, after five years, she was confronted in a household meeting by two Newman Tendency social therapists. Her young teenaged daughter had been "acting out," cutting class and generally being troublesome. The therapists wanted Marina to give up her daughter and put her in foster care. Marina described what happened:

> They said: "You know, she's getting in the way of your work as a revo-lutionary" and that was just the thing that snapped me, like, just of all of the stupid – you know, things that I overlooked, that was just a big slap in the face that helped me just to get the fuck out cause I left a few weeks later, you know, like even then, at that moment, I said, "I'm doing this for our future and you're asking me to throw away our future" – just like that. And that was just the most outrageous like, inconceivable thing that I, you know . . . I could never, you know . . . as much as I neglected them [the children] and overlooked things, you know . . . that was just too much.

Her love for, and her bond with, her daughter was strong and intact enough to overcome the ties to the group. In Chapter 8 you will see how important this is, as well as looking at other ways in which followers are able to escape (and most do experience it as an escape) the totalist systems in which they have become trapped. Marina later wrote:

> When I finally left the cult in July of 1990 – after finally becoming disgusted with the totalitarian internal structure which, in my opinion, basically relies on slave labor for profit in the name of justice and empowerment – I had to literally rebuild my life. I had damaged my relationship to my children and the rest of my family. I was thousands of dollars in debt. And my self-esteem and judgment had been severely impaired.[47]

After leaving Marina gradually succeeded in mending her family relationships and in rebuilding a professional and personal life. She became committed to speaking out about the manipulation, corruption and exploitation of the Newman Tendency. When she left the Tendency, Newman announced in a Tendency meeting: "The Marina Ortiz you knew no longer exists. She's dead to us. She's in the dustbin of history."[48] As I've said, leaders don't like to be left. They want that guaranteed attachment, the loyalty and obedience that binds the follower unambiguously to them. Fred Newman is no different.

Here is my working definition of a totalist system:

> A totalist system is formed and controlled by a charismatic authoritarian leader. It is a rigidly bounded, dense, hierarchical and isolating social system supported and represented by a total, exclusive ideology. The leader sets in

motion processes of brainwashing or coercive persuasion designed to isolate and control followers. As a result followers are able to be exploited, and
potentially become deployable agents, demonstrating uncritical obedience to
the group, regardless of their own survival needs.

We must understand this process, and we must, as a society, learn to disarm it. In
order to do so we need to understand – really understand – the way that it works.
The next chapter introduces some ideas that can help us begin to untangle the
mechanisms at the core of these totalist systems.

Notes

1 Newman, Fred. 1974. *Power and Authority: The Inside View of Class Struggle*. New York
   City: Centers for Change, Inc.
2 Gasink, Kellie. 1993, *Da Letter*. Retrieved June 5, 2007 (http://www.ex-iwp.org/docs/
   Ortiz-Others/DA%20Letter.htm).
3 Office of Economic Development. 1983, *OED Meeting: International Workers Party*.
   Retrieved September, 2006 (http://www.ex-iwp.org/docs/1983/OED_3–3–83.htm).
4 Lifton, Robert Jay. 1961. *Thought Reform and the Psychology of Totalism*. New York: The
   Norton Library.
5 Arendt, Hannah. 1994. *Essays in Understanding: 1930–1954 Hannah Arendt*. New York:
   Harcourt, Brace & Co.
6 Hunter, Edward. 1956. *Brainwashing*. New York: Farrar, Straus and Cudahy.
7 This is a useful formulation from Zablocki, Benjamin D. 1998a. "Exit Cost Analysis:
   A New Approach to the Scientific Study of Brainwashing." *Nova Religio* 12:216–49.
8 Schein, Edgar H. 1961. *Coercive Persuasion: A Socio-Psychological Analysis of the "Brainwashing" of American Civilian Prisoners by the Chinese Communists*. New York: W.W. Norton.
9 Lifton, *Thought Reform and the Psychology of Totalism*.
10 Hassan, Steven. 1988. *Combatting Cult Mind Control*. Rochester, VT: Part Street Press.
11 Berger, Peter L. and Thomas Luckmann. 1966. *The Social Construction of Reality: A Treatise
   in the Sociology of Knowledge*. Garden City, NY: Doubleday.
12 Zablocki, Benjamin D. 1997. "The Blacklisting of a Concept: The Strange History of the
   Brainwashing Conjecture in the Sociology of Religion." *Nova Religio* 11:97–120.
13 Dawkins, Richard. 2006. *The God Delusion*. London: Bantam Press.
14 Ibid., p. 1.
15 Potock, Mark. 2009. *Terror from the Right: 75 Plots, Conspiracies and Racist Rampages since
   Oklahoma City*. Montgomery, AL: Southern Poverty Law Center.
16 This five-part definition owes much to Arendt, Hannah. 1948/1979a. *The Origins of
   Totalitarianism*. Orlando: Harcourt Brace and Lifton, *Thought Reform and the Psychology of
   Totalism*.
17 Weber, Max. 1968. *Max Weber on Charisma and Institution Building: Selected Papers*, edited
   by S.N. Eisenstadt. Chicago: University of Chicago Press.
18 Centers for Change. 1972. *Cfc-a Collection of Liberation Centers*. New York: CFC Press.
19 Lalich, Janja. 2004. *Bounded Choice: True Believers and Charismatic Cults*. Berkeley: University of California Press.
20 Sadell, Cathy. 1989. "The Anti-Women's Club Club." *National Alliance*, August 3, n.p.
21 Collected in: Daren, Hazel, Cathy Sadell, Freda Rosen, Deborah Green, Alvaader Frazier
   and M. Ortiz. 1990, "Tributes": ex-iwp.org. Retrieved October 21, 2006 (http://ex-iwp.
   org/docs/1990/female_tesitmonials.htm).
22 Newman, Fred. 1990. "The Women I Live with/Maudie and the Men's Club." *Practice*,
   Winter.
23 Arendt, Hannah. 1948/1979a. *The Origins of Totalitarianism*. Orlando: Harcourt Brace.

24 Newman, Fred and Phyllis Goldberg. 1994. *Let's Develop!* New York: Castillo International, Inc, p. 234.
25 Ibid., p. 236.
26 Newman, Fred and Lois Holzman. 1997. *The End of Knowing.* New York: Routledge, p. 125.
27 Ibid., p. 116.
28 Orwell, George. 1946. *Animal Farm.* New York: Signet Classic.
29 Hunter, *Brainwashing*; Zablocki, Benjamin D. 2001. "Toward a Demystified and Disinterested Scientific Concept of Brainwashing," in *Misunderstanding Cults: Searching for Objectivity in a Controversial Field*, edited by B.D. Zablocki and T. Robbins. Toronto: University of Toronto Press, pp. 159–214.
30 Schein, *Coercive Persuasion.*
31 Lifton, *Thought Reform and the Psychology of Totalism.*
32 Berger and Thomas, *The Social Construction of Reality.*
33 Lofland, John. 1977. *Doomsday Cult: A Study of Conversion, Proselytization, and Maintenance of Faith.* New York: Irvington Publishers; distributed by Halsted Press.
34 Singer, M.T., and J. Lalich. 1995. *Cults in Our Midst: The Hidden Menace in Our Everyday Lives.* San Francisco: Jossey Bass; Hassan, Steven. 1988. *Combatting Cult Mind Control.* Rochester, VT: Part Street Press.
35 Lalich, *Bounded Choice: True Believers and Charismatic Cults.*
36 All these quotes are from Stein, Alexandra. 2002. *Inside Out: A Memoir of Entering and Breaking out of a Minneapolis Political Cult.* St. Cloud: North Star Press of St. Cloud.
37 Lofland, *Doomsday Cult.*
38 Zablocki, "Toward a Demystified and Disinterested Scientific Concept of Brainwashing."
39 Taylor, Peter [Director] S. Bagnall [Producer]. 2010. *Generation Jihad.*
40 Ibid.
41 King, Colbert I. 2009. "A Terrorist Threat in Our Midst?" in *Washington Post.* Washington DC.
42 Barrett, Devlin and Pamela Hess. 2009. "Worried Parents at Heart of Terror Probe after 5 Missing Americans Caught in Pakistan," in *StarTribune.* Minneapolis: McClatchy.
43 Zablocki, "Toward a Demystified and Disinterested Scientific Concept of Brainwashing," p. 176.
44 Singer and Lalich. 1995. *Cults in Our Midst: The Hidden Menace in Our Everyday Lives.* San Francisco: Jossey Bass.
45 Zablocki, "Toward a Demystified and Disinterested Scientific Concept of Brainwashing."
46 Travis, Alan. 2008. "Mi5 Report Challenges Views on Terrorism in Britain Exclusive: Sophisticated Analysis Says There Is No Single Pathway to Violent Extremism," in *The Guardian.* London. This was confirmed more recently by terrorism scholar Martha Crenshaw at the 2011 conference in Bielefeld, Germany on Processes of Radicalization and Deradicalization, International Journal of Conflict and Violence.
47 Ortiz, Marina. 1993. *Statement Issued by Marina Ortiz.* New York: Cult Awareness Network Meeting, June 6.
48 Ibid.

2

FEAR

It's screamingly obvious

> The first method in reasoning is to give the patients a powerful stimulus, yell at them 'you're sick!', so the patients will have a fright and break out in an over-all sweat; then, they can be carefully treated.[1]

This is how Chairman Mao Zedong described the first step of coercion, brainwashing – or "re-education" as he called it – that took place in China's prisons and reeducation camps during his regime. As Mao understood so well, fear was the "powerful stimulus" required to gain – apparently voluntary – compliance from any resisters to his regime. The combination of fear and isolation is what puts the coercion into coercive persuasion.

In 1958, John Bowlby, the originator of attachment theory, wrote this to his wife:

> Most people think of fear as running away from something. But there is another side to it. We run TO someone, usually a person. ... It's screamingly obvious, but I believe it to be a new idea, and quite revolutionary.[2]

Bowlby's revolutionary idea helps to explain the relationship that exists both at the heart of these systems – between follower and leader – and *in* the heart and brain of each individual who is successfully coerced or brainwashed. The leader positions themselves (or the group, as an extension of the leader) as the benevolent safe haven to which each follower will turn when afraid. The principal means of achieving this involves two subsequent elements: isolate the follower from any other possible safe havens and then arouse fear in the follower. The result? Frightened, stressed followers who "run TO someone": to the leader or group.

But this "running TO" is not an adaptive, healthy seeking of protection when frightened – something all of us do as both children and adults, seeking the comfort of our close relationships in times of stress. In the case of totalist organizations, it's a particular and problematic form of this hardwired behavior, a form termed *disorganized attachment*. In this chapter I outline the basic principles of attachment theory to explain this type of relationship.

But first, let's return to one of the people I met during my research. I last saw Masoud Banisadr when we shared a meal with his daughter – now a surgeon – and her infant son. Masoud played with his baby grandson while telling me about his latest research on brainwashing, which, like mine, was inspired by his own need to understand his history – a history that included an enforced abandonment of his family, including this same daughter. After years of difficulty he reunited with his children and they are making up for lost time with a shared love for this new child.

In the 1970s Masoud and his wife had come from Iran to the UK for his post-graduate studies in chemical engineering at Newcastle University in the north of England. He was politically aware and active in Iranian politics with a loose group of other Iranian students. In the late 1970s, the Iranian Mojahedin (also known as the Mojahedin-e-Khalq or MEK) approached him to support their movement from the UK. According to the group's slogan they were fighting for "freedom, democracy, and human rights in Iran." For some years he and his wife supported the MEK movement and its claims to be against imperialism and, later, against the Khomeini regime in Iran. The small support group he was in operated somewhat independently from the MEK, and was run on democratic lines. This independence, however, did not sit well with the MEK leadership. At a meeting to bring this fringe group into line, Masoud was targeted by an MEK leader who pointedly said of him:

> When part of a body has rotted, it must be cut out and discarded. It is painful; once it was healthy and functioning perfectly. But its disease might infect and destroy the rest of the body. Removing it is the only remedy. This is what the Mojahedin have done with some of their members.[3]

Masoud realized in panic that he "was the rotten part that had to be excised." He had grown up in a supportive, educated and liberal family in Iran. Though he was far from them in Newcastle, they had brought him up with a sense of himself as a good person and he argued and fought back against this dark assessment of him as the "rotten part." But his colleague in the group angrily exhorted him to

> forget your idealism and face reality. You must accept things, including the Mojahedin, as they are, not as you wish they were or think they should be.[4]

Masoud states that this was his "moment" – these words:

> were like a hammer banging on my head – but instead of awakening me, they knocked me unconscious . . . Instead of forcing myself to think, I shut my mind to all doubts and questions.[5]

This was just one moment – but importantly, this was the first of years of such moments – moments where clear and systematic thinking became so difficult, so dangerous, that giving up the effort seemed to make the most sense of all. This is the process that is central to brainwashing – the pushing aside of doubts and questions and beginning to passively accept the dogma on offer. Thus began Masoud's journey of submission to become fully immersed in the MEK, an immersion that required this dissociation in which "all doubts and questions" were shut out. After years of working as a supporter of the MEK, and with this involvement having already seriously weakened his relationship with his wife, he gave in and ceased arguing. It would be almost two decades before he regained his ability to think independently.

In Masoud's case this submission did not happen overnight (though in some cases – most famously the Unification Church, known as the Moonies – it can happen much more quickly). In most instances getting a person to this point is an iterative process. That is, it may involve many cycles of the basic dynamic that includes a progressively more isolating environment, establishing the group as the main (and eventually only) reference point for the individual, and generating levels of fear or stress arousal that cause the person to keep turning towards the group for support. It is this, often cyclical, process that causes the dissociation that is induced in the brainwashed follower.

Using attachment theory to understand totalism

Attachment theory is a key to understanding this dissociative mechanism that lies at the heart of a totalist system. It can help make sense of why the five elements of leadership, structure, ideology, process and outcomes are seen together, and what holds them together – they do not appear randomly, and they do not act randomly. Totalist systems are made up of a predictable pattern of behaviors and, with the help of attachment theory, we can go some way to explaining why they appear in concert and the function each serves in maintaining the system.

When I talk about attachment theory in this context, people are often prone to jump to the conclusion that I mean the follower has some type of attachment disorder that led them to seeking out a cultic or extremist group. "Aha," says the listener, "As I suspected, such followers are needy seekers, looking for some authority figure to tell them what to do." Let me make clear, at the outset, that this is not at all the direction of this explanation. In fact, it is my belief that followers start out with a similar variety of attachment-related dispositions as we find in the general population: some are well adjusted (securely attached) while others may be more or less so, and some, perhaps not well adjusted at all. My contention is that the system itself acts upon followers and, *regardless of their original attachment status*, attempts to *change* that status, to what is known as disorganized attachment. Further, the system aims to remove the follower's prior attachment figures and replace them with the leader or group as the new – and disorganized – attachment relationship. The people you love are pushed out and replaced by the leader or group as the new and sole focus of your emotional commitment.

It is, in fact, the primary task of the totalist system to effect this change: to gain control of followers it must, in fact, *rewire attachment behavior* and utterly reconfigure followers' attachments. If we understand this, then the features of totalism begin to make sense and to be predictable. We can then make sense of why the system is deceptive, why it isolates people from their loved ones and controls close relationships, and why its ideology is often impenetrable, contradictory, fictitious (as Hannah Arendt puts it[6]) and, in most cases, fairly insane. But first we need to learn a bit about attachment theory, and in particular how our attachment status affects both our emotional and our thinking lives.

The origins of attachment theory

In 1935 Konrad Lorenz, a scholar of animal behavior, published his study on the imprinting behavior of geese – a gosling became imprinted with the mother goose, and followed her around, even when that "mother" was actually a pair of wellington boots, a balloon or a box. If the gosling was exposed to the object on hatching, then they sought out that object and followed it as if it were, indeed, their mother. Similarly Harry Harlow discovered that baby monkeys clung to a comforting cloth "mother" in preference to a cold wire "mother" that dispensed food. The baby monkeys went to the wire mother only for long enough to feed, but otherwise sought the comfort of the cloth mother, even though no food was available there. These experiments began to open up thinking that a child's attachment to his or her caregiver went beyond the earlier belief that this was simply a conditioned response based on the mother being the source of food.[7]

John Bowlby was a child psychiatrist who, inspired by these and other studies, argued that the need for attachment was an independent instinct separate from the needs for food, shelter or sex. Building on Lorenz and Harlow's work, Bowlby saw that attachments to others served the independent function of *protection*. Further, he saw that attachment behavior was most in evidence under conditions of fear or signals indicating changes in the environment or in one's vulnerability to it (such as fatigue, the dark, illness) that required increased vigilance to potential threats.[8]

The core idea of attachment theory is that human attachment behavior has evolved as a survival mechanism. Attachment to others serves as a source of protection, and seeking attachments in order to gain such protection – a *safe haven*, in attachment theory terms – is as much an imperative for humans as seeking food, shelter or sex. Babies who stayed in close proximity to their caregivers survived to have their own children – and so attachment behaviors evolved with this function of maintaining proximity. Equally, Bowlby argued, successful caregivers evolved a reciprocal caregiving system with the function of protecting their young. He elaborated attachment theory from these roots, and created a field of research that continues fruitfully to this day. For the past 30 years, attachment theory has been the basis for research, not only of child development, but also of a wide-ranging set of topics spanning the life course and ranging from interpersonal violence to religious affiliation, and from altruism to prejudice and authoritarianism.[9]

Organized forms of attachment

How then does this attachment system operate? Like the fuzzy gosling, children turn to a familiar figure – usually their mothers (or other caregivers) – when they are stressed, frightened, hungry, tired or in pain. When all works well, and the parent is open, flexible and responsive to the child, *secure attachment* results. When the child experiences threat or stress their attachment system is activated and through an array of attachment behaviors (such as crying, smiling, reaching out to be held) they seek out their attachment figure, who, ideally, will provide appropriate comfort and protection. The child is then able to use the parent as a *safe haven* under these conditions of threat. The child's need for protection and their attachment behaviors trigger the parent's caregiving system. (Most of us have experience of how this caregiving system operates – think of how difficult it is to ignore the persistent cry of a baby.)

When the threat passes, and the child has been comforted and attains a state of "felt security," their attachment system is deactivated and the child is free to explore and move away from the attachment figure – but close enough to return in case of further threat. And the secure parent allows this exploration, letting the child return when needed. Imagine a young child running off to play, but turning from time to time to check that their parent is still there – with this reassurance they can relax and continue to play. The child now uses the parent or attachment figure as a *secure base* from which to explore their world. The link between parent and child is like an elastic band, contracting and expanding in response to the child's needs and to conditions in the environment. (See Figure 2.1.) About 58 percent of low-risk populations are securely attached.[10] Secure attachment is predictive of protective factors in life such as resilience,[11] protectiveness of others,[12] altruism,[13] and empathy.[14]

Bowlby saw this as a homeostatic control system with proximity-seeking behaviors (such as approaching, crying, seeking contact) alternating with exploratory behaviors. Attachment behaviors, according to Bowlby, need to be "terminated" effectively, through adequate and reliable comfort in order for the exploratory phase to take place. In other words, the child (or adult) must achieve a sufficient level of comfort to calm his or her fearful response (yet not so much comfort as to become smothering or oppressive).[i] But once the threat has passed and the fear response has been calmed, the need for the caregiver as safe haven also passes and the child is ready to explore his or her environment again. At this point the child's attachment behavior has been terminated effectively through the provision of adequate comfort, and his or her exploratory behavior resumes.

But caregivers may not always respond adequately, or situations may prevent a child (or adult) getting the care they need, and when such attachment is lacking or

---

i This can be detailed at a biochemical level, as a process of homeostasis between the arousal of adrenalin or cortisol and the comfort of opioids being stimulated by the processes of fear and comfort. See Smith, Thomas, 1992. *Strong Interaction.* Chicago: University of Chicago Press, for an interesting discussion of this process.

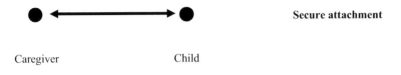

Secure attachment

Caregiver   Child

Attachment figure provides
protection: a **safe haven**
from situations of threat.

After threat has passed,
individual returns to
exploration. Attachment figure
is used as a **secure base.**

FIGURE 2.1   The attachment bond – secure attachment (organized)

impaired Bowlby and his colleagues uncovered predictable consequences on later development. Along with the secure attachment status, Bowlby then described two *insecure* forms of attachment: preoccupied and dismissing attachment.

For those who have unreliable, inconsistent attachment figures, where a safe haven is only intermittently available, attachment behavior is not effectively terminated through reliable comfort. As the child is never fully comforted they remain attempting to gain closeness with the attachment figure. The result is clinginess, separation anxiety and a failure to effectively use the attachment figure as a secure base from which to explore. This is termed *preoccupied attachment*[ii] and is characterized by a hyperactivation of the attachment system, ongoing attachment behaviors and impairments in being able to use the parent as a secure base – in other words, the child's exploratory behaviors are limited. Unsure of the parent's responsiveness, the preoccupied child remains on alert, demanding attention through attachment

---

ii The attachment categories have different names depending on whether one is discussing children or adults. For simplicity I use the adult categories as most of this book is concerned with adults in totalist groups.

behaviors and, from time to time, succeeding in getting that attention. The child takes on a disproportionate share of the task of maintaining connection with their caregiver.[15] This type of attachment has been correlated with, for example, later anxiety and hypervigilance, and being victimized by bullying.[16] About 19 percent of non-clinical populations have a preoccupied attachment status.[17]

The other form of insecure attachment occurs when the parent or attachment figure consistently rejects or neglects the child, and the child deactivates their attachment behaviors – resulting in *dismissing attachment*. Having not experienced positive, caring responses to early attempts to seek attachment, the child eventually gives up and avoids seeking it. This doesn't mean the child can regulate their fear responses on their own, but they do not go to the caregiver to try to get comfort or protection, and they avoid attachments and suppress attachment behaviors even while they are experiencing threat or fear internally. Those with dismissing attachment stay detached and unable to depend on others. They do experience physiological arousal when stressed but they are not able to seek comfort to attenuate the stressful feelings. This attachment status has been correlated with anger and aggressive behaviors such as bullying.[18] It is estimated that 23 percent of non-clinical populations have dismissing attachment.[19]

Although the preoccupied and dismissing attachment strategies may not be ideal in terms of securing attachment, they are useful responses, or adaptations, to particular attachment situations – the preoccupied may increase the chances of attachment through vigilance and availability, and the dismissing may prevent harm to the self by avoiding rejecting and possibly harmful behaviors on the part of the caregiver. Along with secure attachment these make up the three organized strategies that work as a homeostatic control system, ebbing and flowing within the limits of an environment of adaptedness. That is, these strategies work well enough within situations that, while not all are optimal, are at least predictable, and allow the child to develop a coherent – organized – way of responding to their environment.

So far, so good. But how does this relate to brainwashing and to Masoud's submission to his leader? The fourth form of attachment is the one that interests us. The effect of *disorganized attachment* on both emotions and thinking is dramatic and helps explain how someone as intelligent, curious and thoughtful as Masoud (or, for that matter, Marina, myself, of any of the many people described in this book) could shut his mind "to doubts and questions" about the group he had joined.

Disorganized attachment

The classification of disorganized attachment was developed by Mary Main and Judith Solomon[20] when they noticed unusual behaviors in a set of children who had been unpredictably frightened by their caregivers – whether directly as a result of frightening behavior by the caregivers, or indirectly resulting from the caregivers themselves being frightened. These children sometimes showed the typical secure and insecure (preoccupied, dismissing) strategies described above, but they also displayed brief but disorganized and disoriented behaviors including signs of confusion, fear, freezing and strange movements. This resulted in the addition of a new classification, *disorganized*.[iii]

These responses occur when a child has been in a situation of *fright without solution*. Their caregiver is at once the safe haven and *also* the source of threat or alarm. So, when the child feels threatened by the caregiver, he or she is caught in an impossible situation: both comfort and threat are represented by the same person – the caregiver. The child experiences the unresolvable paradox of seeking to simultaneously flee from and approach the caregiver.[21] This happens at a biological level, not thought out or conscious, but as evolved behavior to fear. The child attempts to run TO and flee FROM the caregiver at one and the same time.

In the face of this impossible situation the child's attachment strategies collapse, hence the term *disorganized*. He or she makes movements to approach the frightening or frightened parent at the same time as trying to avoid the fearful stimuli coming from the parent. Freezing, confusion and a variety of other behaviors are the result. These may be very brief episodes, and are usually combined with one or (often) more of the other types of attachment behaviors discussed above, sometimes, for example, rapidly switching between preoccupied approach and dismissing withdrawal. However, in most cases the need for proximity – for physical closeness – tends to override attempts to avoid the fear-arousing caregiver.[22] So usually the child stays close to the frightening parent while internally both their withdrawal and approach systems are simultaneously activated, and in conflict. (See Figure 2.2.)

While the three types of *organized* attachment responses – secure, preoccupied and dismissing – are more or less adaptive, *disorganized* attachment, on the other hand, is a breakdown of attachment and attentional strategies resulting from a frightening or frightened caregiver. The conditions in the environment – the situation of fright without solution – overwhelm attempts to adapt and the homeostatic system fails. To understand what happens when a homeostatic system fails, think of how the body regulates its temperature to keep at approximately 98.6 degrees Fahrenheit. Sweating or shivering, or cues to put on or remove clothes, or seek shelter, all serve, within the environment of adaptedness[iv] in which humans have evolved, to maintain this constant temperature. However, place a human in an extreme condition of excessive heat or cold that is outside our environment of adaptedness, and the regulatory system fails – it cannot cope with all situations, only those within which it evolved this regulation system. Similarly, the environment of fright without solution is no longer one that allows a coherent response: withdrawal to safety becomes paradoxically an approach to threat and results in dissociation and confusion.

Attachment disorganization in infancy predicts a variety of possible outcomes: future controlling behavior with caregivers, dissociative symptoms and/or increased

---

iii The full term for this in adults is *Unresolved/Disorganized*. For simplicity I will just refer to *disorganized* in this text.

iv The "environment of adaptedness" is a term coined by Bowlby and refers to the environment in which a given adaption is said to have evolved.

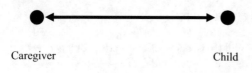

Individual has attachment to
perceived safe haven.

Caregiver   Child

Safe haven (source of comfort)
is **also the source of threat.**

Attachment strategy collapses.
Individual is disoriented,
confused, may dissociate.
Exploration phase is impaired due
to continued presence of threat.
Attachment bond may strengthen.

FIGURE 2.2   Disorganized attachment or the trauma bond

levels of psychopathology in adolescence and adulthood, and aggressive and fearful
relationships with peers.[23] People with disorganized attachment status are overrepresented in clinical and prison populations, suggesting that, indeed, this is not a
useful or adaptive strategy.[24]

This explanation has started with children, but the need for attachments and
attachment behaviors persists into adulthood, becoming the basis for close relationships with spouses, partners and very close friends, and for caregiving behaviors
towards children and other loved ones. As adults we seek comfort, help or reassurance from our close others when we are stressed or fearful, but otherwise we may
operate more independently, checking in once in a while. Similarly, disorganized
attachment does not occur only with children and their caregivers. It can also happen later in life in abusive, frightening or dangerous relationships, such as in situations of controlling domestic violence.

Disorganized attachment and dissociation

Disorganized attachment results in dissociation and it is this that makes it a
powerful and dangerous control mechanism. We can say that dissociation in a

situation of trauma with no escape means we can no longer *think* about what we are *feeling* regarding the frightening relationship. What happens in dissociation is that cognitive processing in the more recently evolved areas of the brain, including the frontal cortex and language areas, ceases to function while at the same time the older areas of the brain – the brain stem and central nervous system – continue to record the sensory information of that situation.[25] The sensory, emotional system becomes dissociated from the cognitive system. Or, to put it another way, the right, emotional, feeling side of the brain, cannot communicate effectively with the left, thinking, speaking side of the brain. In a dissociated state, thought and feeling become disconnected. But this does not necessarily happen globally – rather, it is dissociation in regard to the traumatic, disorganizing relationship.

There is a two-fold effect that results from this. On the one hand, the person cannot think clearly about the frightening relationship. The thinking part of the brain is not operating well. It is not able to think: "This is a dangerous situation, get out of here!" There *is* no escape, so no solution, no "get out" is available. On the other hand, the person – feeling frightened – tends to stay in proximity to their only remaining attachment, even when it is that attachment causing the threat. Panic is followed by giving up: giving up both independent thinking and emotional independence. The combination of isolation and fear is therefore, in many cases, able to create a dissociated follower with an anxiously dependent attachment bond to the group.

Why is all this important? Because totalist groups rely on disorganizing followers as the fundamental means of control. Given the dramatic effect on interpersonal relationships that we see in cults and totalitarian systems it is perhaps surprising that attachment theory is only now beginning to be applied to understanding the dynamics of these extreme social systems.[26]

The concept of what perhaps we can call *coerced* disorganized attachment can help us to explain why Masoud left the family he loved so much. Or why parents in the Children of God cult allowed the sexual abuse of their children. It can help to untangle the emotional and cognitive processes that led Marina to a state where she became ready to "take a bullet" for Fred Newman. And it can help us understand how so many ordinary young people can be turned into executioners at the service of terrorist organizations. The answer to these seemingly incomprehensible behaviors lies in understanding this powerful combination of terror and love. Remember, though, that followers do not have to *start* with disorganized attachment, but that this is created through the different elements of the totalist system.

Attachment status is malleable, not fixed

Patterns set in childhood are important, they provide a kind of template for future attachment relationships – Bowlby called this template the "internal working model." But Bowlby and other researchers noted that attachment statuses are not set in stone and can change later in life.[27] For example, someone with a dismissing attachment status from a rejecting childhood background can become secure later in life by means of a later secure relationship. And generally people tend to become more secure as they get older.[28] Even those with early disorganized attachment, with the help of a later secure attachment − perhaps in a close relationship, or with a reliable and skilled therapist − can become what is termed "earned secure." Through understanding their prior disorganized or insecure relationships, and developing new, secure relationships, security of attachment can be "earned" along with a new secure internal working model of attachment relationships. Thus, a childhood attachment status is not a life sentence.

In the same way, given that attachment experiences continue to adapt and change through the lifespan, it is also possible for a person's attachment status to adapt and change in a negative direction − for example: from organized to disorganized. In other words, if a person is immersed in a strong enough situation their secure or organized attachment can be shifted as a result of the new situation.

What is key here is that one's attachment status can change − either in a secure or insecure or disorganized direction − depending on attachment experiences and changes in one's environment over the life course. The early internal working models from childhood do have influence over these changes, but they are able to, and do, change. Although security of childhood attachment does increase − and predict − resiliency later in life, it does not offer blanket protection against all situations, and especially not situations that are outside the "environment of adaptedness" − that is, situations of fright without solution.[29]

Using the principles that Bowlby and later, Main, set out as evolutionary-based cornerstones of human development, we can trace how totalist systems set up this disorganized attachment between followers and the leader or group. So let's look at how this might play out in a cultic or totalist group.

A person of any preexisting attachment status − from secure to good-enough attachment, or even to disorganized − runs into a charismatic and authoritarian figure, or a group led by such a figure. The totalist leader sets in place an isolating structure, a fictitious and deceptive ideology, and processes of coercive persuasion. They can then isolate followers from any prior attachments, control attachments that exist within the group, set up the group as the new − and only − "safe haven," and generate stress, threat or fear in some form to create the disorganized attachment bond.

In Masoud's case, he was concerned about his home country suffering under the dictatorship of the Shah, and later that of Khomeini, and was attracted, and then recruited, to the MEK, who claimed to be fighting for freedom and democracy. The MEK later demanded that he dissolve the semi-independent group he had formed and this increased his isolation from the outside world. His wife belonged to the MEK as well and so did not represent a link to life outside the group. Their marital relationship was becoming more and more distant as he became busier and they spent less time together. Structurally, then, Masoud's attachments had become restricted to those within the group, and these attachments had to operate within the narrow limits set by the group's rules.

Meanwhile the MEK leader, Rajavi, and his wife, Maryam, were set up as the benevolent leadership:

> every moment a person spends for the leader, whether in thought or in deed, is spent for good, and every other moment, even when you are asleep or believe you are doing good, is spent in favour of evil.[30]

Rajavi was portrayed as "a kind of stern, but avuncular, almost mythical charismatic character."[31] They, and the group, represented the new safe haven for Masoud, the people who were right and good. Finally, the group became the source of fear, stress and threat for Masoud. Among the many other cumulative sources of stress, threatening Masoud with expulsion (and implicitly with violence) with their statement that the rotten part of the group must be "cut out and discarded" would certainly have aroused his fear response.

As is typical of such groups, the MEK subjected Masoud to harsh criticism, and put him on the "hot-seat" for confrontation by the group. The MEK attacked Masoud's sense of himself as a good person (forming a part of his previously secure internal working model). And as he became more isolated from his wife, his friends and others who might have been able to support him to stand up to these attacks, he took on, more and more, this new view of himself. This dynamic repeated itself throughout his tenure until he was finally able to break away after nearly two decades.

In this way, the MEK created a situation of "fright without solution." In this situation the follower is stressed by the group yet has no access to resources outside the control of the group. A state of chronic trauma in relation to the group is created. The first response to this is likely to be a state of hyperarousal or "frantic distress."[32] However, as a general rule, the soon-to-be follower does not attribute this distress to the group, but instead may attribute it to any number of other causes, causes that will be handily suggested by the group. In fact, as is typical of totalist groups, in Masoud's case his distress was attributed to his own faults. The group, if he would just accept it, would show him the way forward.

As another example, many "personal growth" groups encourage sharing of prior (and generally intimate) life traumas in front of a large audience. This escalates the narrator's remembered fear as well as arousing feelings of fear in the audience. Thus, feelings of fear, while aroused and manipulated by the group, will not be attributed to the group's actions, but to events in the narrator's past (and sometimes present). Rather the group will position itself as the comforter, the protector, the safe haven: the supposedly "safe" space in which those feelings can be felt and aired. Of course legitimate therapy groups *can* be safe spaces – the twist lies in the motivations of the group, and its control over the situation. Fear may, of course, also be aroused in many other ways, from fears of the apocalypse, to physical beatings, to fears of loss of the group itself.

In the first phase of a person's reaction to threat, their alarm response is activated, with increased heart rate, blood pressure and other signs of distress.[33] We can perhaps imagine Masoud's feelings of fear and panic at being threatened in that meeting – was he going to be expelled? imprisoned? executed? (The MEK already had a history of violence; many had been killed in the so-called struggle for democracy.) But if there is no useful action that can be taken using the physiological arousal that is now in play – if the struggle to escape the fear is unsuccessful – then eventually the body shuts down in order to conserve resources. Thus, if neither fight nor flight is effective, the only option is to freeze. Masoud's shutting down of thought and doubts was a result of this freezing process.

The second phase of a trauma response is dissociation: "detachment from an unbearable situation."[34] As previously described, in this state, both physiological states of hyperarousal and dissociation are activated: internal energy-consuming resources are simultaneously on full alert at the same time as the person is dissociating to try to shut down and conserve these resources. Imagine the toll on the body that this two-fold unresolvable process must take. Eventually, dissociation – freezing and giving up the failed effort to escape – comes to dominate. Along with giving up the struggle to fight against the group and the fear it has generated, the dissociated follower comes to accept the group as the safe haven and thus forms a trauma bond. This moment of submission, of giving up the struggle, can be experienced as a moment of great relief, and even happiness, or a spiritual awakening.

Roseanne Henry, who gave up her child to her cult leader, described this experience:

> After two months of hell I finally agreed to the plan. I remember the very moment when I flipped the switch. 'There is nothing greater that I could do for my child than give her to the divine mother,' I thought.[35]

In this quote we can see both the first hyperarousal phase (two months of hell) of struggling against the trauma of being ordered to give up her child, followed by the giving in, the dissociative phase where she stopped being able to think coherently about her and her child's survival ("I flipped the switch"), and at the same time confirming the "divinity" of the leader.

At this moment of giving up it appears that not only is the ability to think diminished, but also the effort to escape the source of the fear – the traumatic relationship – ceases. Like the disorganized child, the adult then also tends to seek proximity with the only remaining attachment – that is, the fear-inducing relationship – rather than continue to make efforts to avoid it. Recall that this disorganized attachment results with a double effect. In the emotional realm, the person ceases to struggle and the movement TO the source of fear dominates, creating a trauma bond. And in the cognitive realm the dissociated freezing impairs higher brain activity preventing normal complex processing of both the social world in which the dissociation is occurring, as well as the cognitive processing of the person's internal world. Clara, another mother whose bond with her child was under threat by a cult, said:

> I remember at one point saying, "I'll do it," and everything got quiet around me and the noise in my head stopped and I thought, "God, maybe that is right. . . ." And inside me I thought the quiet or sense of rightness means I'm doing the right thing.[36]

The "noise" in Clara's head is the hyperarousal of struggling against the leader's demand that she cease caring for her child as a mother. The quiet that follows is clearly the submission, the freezing – neither fight nor flight can work, and her ability to think about what is right is turned upside down.

Giving in – dissociating and ceasing to think – is experienced as relief. In my own experience I remember well this sensation: overwhelmed with confusion and exhaustion, the thoughts that were trying to enter the cognitive part of my brain just could not make it there and they fell back out of consciousness. Simultaneously I stopped struggling and decided to commit myself more fully to the group *even though I disagreed with it*. That too felt like relief – I didn't have to fight anymore. In fact, as we shall see later in more detail, key regions of the brain that connect emotional (largely right brain) and cognitive processing (largely left brain) are shut down in the disorganized and dissociated state.

Masoud continued to be isolated, threatened and prevented from forming safe relationships outside the MEK. In fact, the group actually condemned any outside relationships or activities by contemptuously labeling them as "attachments." These attachments were to be discarded and replaced by complete devotion to Rajavi and his wife, Maryam, which would result in "glorious joy and happiness" and the follower being "able to fulfill their true potential as a human being."[37] By 1989 Masoud had risen in the ranks of the MEK. Then another round of intense control was unleashed against followers: the Internal Revolution. Rajavi ordered all group members to "divorce your spouse, divest yourself of sexuality and devote your undivided self to me."[38] Despite his resistance, and following more confrontation, Masoud, too, acquiesced and divorced the wife he loved dearly. This was not just to be a legal divorce, but also an "emotional or ideological divorce." Masoud was ordered to divorce his wife in his heart and "learn to hate her as the buffer standing between our leader" and himself. At the same time the group restricted him from seeing his much beloved children. Love was now to be only for the leader and his wife, Maryam, and for the group.

Masoud did manage to break away after 18 years. After years of overwork, lack of sleep, and intense pressure, his body broke down and he returned from a long period overseas to get surgery in England. It was there that he managed to see his daughter again, along with old friends who would have nothing to do with the MEK. With these renewed attachments and with distance from the group and time to reintegrate his thoughts and emotions he was at last able break the stranglehold on his mind and feelings with which the group had trapped him. He finally resigned and "Suddenly" he said, "I had to think for myself."[39]

Totalist leaders – either directly or through their organizations – create a relationship of disorganized attachment by isolating people from their prior sources of support and replacing those with a new, and frightening, "safe haven." We know from attachment research that disorganized attachment, which involves seeking proximity with the frightening attachment figure when there is no other attachment figure or escape available, causes a dissociative response. Dissociation separates thinking from feeling. It dis-integrates the left, logical, verbal, thinking side of the brain from the right, emotional, non-verbal side of the brain. The dissociated person's ability to think clearly about the relationship is impaired and so they are now in a position to accept the group's views – its ideology. This ideology is in place to further bolster the elements of isolation, terror and "love" and to explain away the feelings of fear induced in the follower. Emotionally the dissociated person tends to draw closer to the group as it is now their only remaining "safe haven."

In understanding how this disorganized relationship works, the rest of the features of totalism start to make sense – in fact, they become predictable, because fundamentally these are systems that support the creation and maintenance of this central control mechanism that operates within the mind of each subjugated follower. In the following chapters we will explore how the core elements of the totalist system – leadership, isolating structures, totalist ideologies and brainwashing processes – work to create and maintain disorganized attachment and dissociation in followers.

But first we turn to recruitment and how followers find themselves within the sphere of influence of the totalist leader.

Notes

1　Mao Zedong in Opposing Party Formalism cited in Schein, Edgar H. 1961. *Coercive Persuasion: A Socio-Psychological Analysis of the "Brainwashing" of American Civilian Prisoners by the Chinese Communists*. New York: W.W. Norton, p. 37.

2　Hesse, E. and M. Main. 2006. "Frightened, Threatening, and Dissociative Parental Behavior in Low-Risk Samples: Description, Discussion, and Interpretations." *Development and Psychopathology* 18(2):309–43.

3　Banisadr, Masoud. 2004. *Masoud: Memoirs of an Iranian Rebel*. London: Saqi, p. 178.

4　Ibid., p. 178.

5　Ibid.

6　Arendt, Hannah. 1948/1979. *The Origins of Totalitarianism*. Orlando: Harcourt Brace.

7　Bowlby, John. 1982. *Attachment and Loss, Attachment*. Vol. 1. New York: Basic Books; Karen, Robert. 1998. *Becoming Attached: First Relationships and How They Shape Our Capacity to Love*. New York: Oxford University Press.

8　Bowlby, *Attachment and Loss, Attachment*.

9　Some examples include: Domestic violence and violent crime: Lyons-Ruth, K. and D. Jacobvitz. 1999. "Attachment Disorganization: Unresolved Loss, Relational Violence, and Lapses in Behavioral and Attentional Strategies," in *Handbook of Attachment: Theory, Research and Clinical Applications*, edited by J. Cassidy and P. Shaver. New York: Guilford Press; Political Extremism and "Authoritarianism": Hopf, Christel. 1993. "Authoritarians and Their Families: Qualitative Studies on the Origins of Authoritarian Dispositions," in

Strength and Weakness, edited by W.F. Stone, G. Lederer, and R. Christie, Springer Science & Business Media, 2012; Hopf, Christel. 1998. "Attachment Experiences and Aggression against Minorities." *Social Thought and Research* 211(2):133–49; Altruism and Prejudice: Mikulincer, M. and P.R. Shaver. 2001. "Attachment Theory and Intergroup Bias: Evidence That Priming the Secure Base Schema Attenuates Negative Reactions to Out-Groups." *Journal of Personality and Social Psychology* 81:97–115; and Religious Affiliation: Granqvist, Pehr. 1998. "Religiousness and Perceived Childhood Attachment: On the Question of Compensation or Correspondence." *Journal for the Scientific Study of Religion* 372:350–67. Granqvist, Pehr and Berit Hagekull. 2001. "Seeking Security in the New Age: On Attachment and Emotional Compensation." *Journal for the Scientific Study of Religion* 40(3):527–45. Kirkpatrick, L.A. 1998. "God as a Substitute Attachment Figure: A Longitudinal Study of Adult Attachment Style and Religious Change in College Students." *Personality & Social Psychology Bulletin* 24:961–74.

10 Bakermans-Kranenburg, Marian J., and Marinus H. van IJzendoorn. 2009. "The First 10,000 Adult Attachment Interviews: Distributions of Adult Attachment Representations in Clinical and Non-Clinical Groups." *Attachment & Human Development* 11(3):223–63.

11 Egeland, B., E. Carlson and L.A. Sroufe. 1993. "Resilience as Process." *Development and Psychopathology* 1993(5):517–28.

12 Troy, M. and Alan L. Sroufe. 1987. "Victimization among Preschoolers: Role of Attachment Relationship Theory." *Journal of American Academy of Child and Adolescent Psychiatry* 26:166–72.

13 Gillath, O., P.R. Shaver and M. Mikulincer. 2005. "An Attachment-Theoretical Approach to Compassion and Altruism," in *Compassion: Its Nature and Use in Psychotherapy*, edited by P. Gilbert. London: Brunner-Routledge, pp. 121–147.

14 Weinfield, Nancy S., L. Alan Sroufe, Byron Egeland and Elizabeth A. Carlson. 1999. "The Nature of Individual Differences in Infant-Caregiver Attachment," in *Handbook of Attachment: Theory, Research and Clinical Applications*, edited by J. Cassidy and P. Shaver. New York: Guilford Press, pp. 68–88.

15 Cassidy, J. 2001. "Truth, Lies, and Intimacy: An Attachment Perspective." *Attachment & Human Development* 3(2):121–55.

16 Troy and Sroufe, "Victimization among Preschoolers."

17 Bakermans-Kranenburg, Marian J. and Marinus H. van IJzendoorn. 2009. "The First 10,000 Adult Attachment Interviews: Distributions of Adult Attachment Representations in Clinical and Non-Clinical Groups." *Attachment & Human Development* 11(3):223–63.

18 Troy and Sroufe, "Victimization among Preschoolers."

19 Bakermans-Kranenburg and van Ijzendoorn, "The First 10,000 Adult Attachment Interviews."

20 Main, Mary and Judith Solomon. 1986. "Discovery of an Insecure-Disorganized/Disoriented Attachment Pattern," in *Affective Development in Infancy*, edited by T.B. Brazelton and M.W. Yogman. Nowrood, NJ: Ablex Publishing, pp. 95–124.

21 Lyons-Ruth, K. and D. Jacobvitz. 1999. "Attachment Disorganization: Unresolved Loss, Relational Violence, and Lapses in Behavioral and Attentional Strategies," in *Handbook of Attachment: Theory, Research and Clinical Applications*, edited by J. Cassidy and P. Shaver. New York: Guilford Press, pp. 520–554.

22 Schore, Allan N. 2002. "Dysregulation of the Right Brain: A Fundamental Mechanism of Traumatic Attachment and the Psychopathogenesis of Posttraumatic Stress Disorder." *Australian and New Zealand Journal of Psychiatry* 36:9–30.

23 Lyons-Ruth and Jacobvitz, "Attachment Disorganization"; Kobak, Roger. 1999. "The Emotional Dynamics of Disruptions in Attachment Relationships: Implications for Theory, Research, and Clinical Interventions," in *Handbook of Attachment: Theory, Research and Clinical Applications*, edited by J. Cassidy and P. Shaver. New York: Guilford Press, pp. 21–43.

24 Twemlow, Stuart W., Peter Fonagy and Frank Sacco. 2005. "A Developmental Approach to Mentalizing Communities: I. A Model for Social Change." *Bulletin of the Menninger Clinic* 69(4):265–81.

25 Siegel, Daniel J. 1999. *The Developing Mind: Toward a Neurobiology of Interpersonal Experience*. New York: Guilford Press.

26 To my knowledge, only myself, Mary Main, Ben Zablocki, and Judith Herman have so far begun such work, or suggested it be undertaken: Herman, Judith. 1992. *Trauma and Recovery*. New York: Basic Books; Main, Mary. 2000. "Attachment Theory: Eighteen Points with Suggestions for Future Studies," in *Handbook of Attachment: Theory, Research and Clinical Applications*, edited by J. Cassidy and P. Shaver. New York: Guilford Press, pp. 845–887; Stein, Alexandra. 2001. "Protea: Democratic Health and the Lessons of Authoritarianism." Masters, Liberal Studies, University of Minneapolis, Minneapolis; Stein, Alexandra. 2007. "Attachment, Networks and Discourse in Extremist Political Organizations: A Comparative Case Study." Doctoral Dissertation, Sociology, University of Minnesota, Minneapolis; Zablocki, Benjamin D. 2001. "Toward a Demystified and Disinterested Scientific Concept of Brainwashing," in *Misunderstanding Cults: Searching for Objectivity in a Controversial Field*, edited by B.D. Zablocki and T. Robbins. Toronto: University of Toronto Press, pp. 159–214.

27 Bowlby, John. 1980. *Attachment and Loss, Loss*, Vol. 3. New York: Basic Books; Bowlby, *Attachment and Loss, Attachment*.

28 Siegel, *The Developing Mind*.

29 Egeland, Carlson and Sroufe, "Resilience as Process."

30 Singleton, Anne. 2003. *Saddam's Private Army: How Rajavi Changed Iran's Mojahedin from Armed Revolutionaries to an Armed Cult*. Iran-Interlink. Retrieved June 22, 2013 (http://www.iranchamber.com/history/mojahedin_khalq/mojahedin_khalq_armed_cult01.php).

31 Ibid.

32 Schore, Allan N. 2002. "Dysregulation of the Right Brain: A Fundamental Mechanism of Traumatic Attachment and the Psychopathogenesis of Posttraumatic Stress Disorder." *Australian and New Zealand Journal of Psychiatry* 36:9–30.

33 Schore, Allan N. 2002. "Advances in Neuropsychoanalysis, Attachment Theory, and Trauma Research: Implications for Self Psychology." *Psychoanalytic Inquiry* 22:433–84.

34 Schore, Allan N. 2009. "Attachment Trauma and the Developing Right Brain: Origins of Pathological Dissociation," in *Dissociation and the Dissociative Disorders: DSM-V and Beyond*, edited by P.F. Dell and J.A. O'Neil. New York: Routledge, pp. 107–41.

35 Tobias, Madeleine and Janja Lalich. 1994. *Captive Hearts, Captive Minds*. Alameda: Hunter House, p. 235.

36 Deikman, Arthur J. 1990. *The Wrong Way Home: Uncovering the Patterns of Cult Behavior in American Society*. Boston: Beacon Press.

37 Singleton, *Saddam's Private Army*.

38 Ibid.

39 Banisadr, *Masoud: Memoirs of an Iranian Rebel*. London: Saqi Books, p. 464.

3

RECRUITMENT

The accidental extremist

If totalist groups are to attract recruits and set up the conditions for a later rearrangement of the recruit's close relationships they must first get the person within their sphere of influence. Then the organization can begin the isolation project, and start to position itself as the primary emotional and cognitive resource for the recruit – becoming the new, and eventually the only, safe haven. There is a three-fold process in setting the stage for the creation of a disorganized attachment bond to the group: the initial contact and gaining access to the recruit, positioning the group as a new perceived safe haven, and beginning to detach the recruit from prior attachments. Propaganda is the ideological tool wielded to accomplish this.

Pathways to followership

There are a variety of different pathways into totalist groups.[i] The stereotype is the path of the seeker, that is: a person seeking truth or enlightenment, or, more broadly, a cause to which they can commit themselves, sets out purposefully to find a group to join. Such people do exist – indeed, I was one of them. But there are other, possibly more common entry points to totalist groups: being "pulled in,"

---

i The 2008 MI5 report supports this view, stating that those who become terrorists:"are a diverse collection of individuals, fitting no single demographic profile, nor do they all follow a typical pathway to violent extremism"Travis, Alan. 2008. "MI5 Report Challenges Views on Terrorism in Britain Exclusive: Sophisticated Analysis Says There Is No Single Pathway to Violent Extremism," in *The Guardian*. Retrieved August 20, 2008 (https://www.theguardian.com/uk/2008/aug/20/uksecurity.terrorism1). A 2015 study of ISIS/Daesh recruits echoes this: Vidino, Lorenzo and Seamus Hughes. 2015. "Isis in America: From Retweets to Raqqa" (George Washington University: Program on Extremism, 2015).

usually by accident; being born or brought up from childhood in such a group; being press-ganged or kidnapped; or simply living in a totalitarian state.

Seekers are generally looking for some kind of spiritual or political commitment. But the stereotype gets an important fact wrong – these people are not seeking to submit to a malevolent authority figure, or to join a cult or a totalist group that will restrict their basic human rights. Most people who are seeking a spiritual or political commitment will find, and maybe join, a benign (or at least non-totalist) group. They may become active members of a mainstream political party, church or voluntary group, for example. But some will run into cultic groups and become recruited based on their interest in activism, charity work, spiritual commitment or personal development of some kind. In this type of recruitment there must be an initial fit between the recruit's interests and the stated program of the group. I say "stated" because, as I will explain in the sections on propaganda the stated, public program is often merely the fig leaf that obscures the inner workings and goals of the group.

The seeker, then, is looking for something the organization states they are offering. For example, Sidney was looking for a left-wing political involvement. He explained:

> I had become radicalized during the Vietnam War era in my college and I was quite specifically, specifically looking for a group to join. There were only a couple of groups in my home town, neither of which were very attractive to me for various reasons, and I didn't want to affiliate with them and there wasn't another alternative, so I went to New York City specifically to look for some folks to hang out with and to do some political organizing. . . . So I would go to bookstores that sold left-wing literature. I saw one of their papers and picked it up. . . . I responded to an ad in the paper that said "come to a meeting," and I just went to a meeting to check them out.

The fact that Sidney was seeking a political organization, however, does not imply that he was seeking what he found in the Newman Tendency, namely: a highly controlling organization that cut off his relationship with his family, mandated "therapy," arranged relationships and enforced long days of volunteer work often without enough money for food. As he said:

> Fred Newman cared as much about revolution as George Bush did, you know. He was basically in it for the women and the money and the power and, and this and that, and it was just another cult like the Moonies and LaRouche.

Sidney was seeking a revolutionary organization – whatever that may have meant to him. He was not seeking a cult.

My own recruitment was similar to Sidney's – I was looking for a political group to join to develop my organizing work with working women and to find like-minded people willing to try to maintain the anti-capitalist spirit of the 60s and 70s during the increasingly conservative Reagan era. The closed and exploitative organization I found in "The O." was not what I was looking for – but from the outside it looked promising: I was told of childcare centers, a women's health clinic and union organizing drives. These were exactly the kinds of projects I had already been involved with before I encountered the group. The grey and soulless reality of the O.'s programs, however, would not become apparent to me until much later.

Similar to the seeker in that they are looking for something when they get recruited are those who I refer to as "pulled in." But as terrorism expert Martha Crenshaw stated in regards to the recruitment pathway of most terrorists, they are pulled in "by accident" while on their way to other goals.[1]

This is what happened to Marina Ortiz, and, in fact, this was the pathway in for the majority of Newman Tendency members in my study. Marina wasn't looking to join any kind of group at all. What she wanted, and what she signed up for, was therapy to help her through a difficult patch in life. But the therapy became an entry point into something completely different: from individual therapy she was shunted into group therapy. And from there she was brought into a variety of political activities designed, supposedly, to "cure" her of her depression. Similarly, Gillian Trenton was looking for a supervisor for her training to become a therapist, not for any political or group involvement. But she became interested in the social activism that appeared to be tied to the social therapy practice she ran into and soon found herself targeted for recruitment, drawn into a round of activity and away from her husband and two young children. For both Marina and Gillian (and many others in the group), their interest in therapy became an entry point into a life more and more consumed by group tasks and relationships. Marina was finally successfully recruited as a full-time cadre of the underground political party whereas Gillian managed to get out before becoming consolidated but not before suffering what she described as devastation and intense, destabilizing confusion:

> Everything was confusing – everything, the texts were confusing, and they became more and more confusing. The social therapy sessions were confusing. My supervision was confusing. It, everything was confusing. It was – they wanted you to question things you took for granted, any sense of right or wrong, normal, was turned upside down – everything was questioned. Everything that you took for granted – everything. So it was just confusion, and, and then the relationship was confusing, with like, with, with my supervisor, because he became so intimate and I couldn't figure out any more if he was my friend? If he was my supervisor? If, I couldn't figure out if he was, if this was becoming like um, some sort of love relationship? It was incredibly intimate.

Some recruits to terrorist groups and cults are drawn in through their friendship networks. As Neumann states in regard to recruitment to ISIS: "[I]n many cases it's simply social obligation and feeling that one wants to be with one's friends."[2]

Many members of totalist groups were born into them, or came into them as children when their parents joined. While a good proportion of these rebel against their upbringing and leave these highly restricted environments as adults, not all do or can. However, those who do leave bring with them invaluable accounts of life within these groups. Juliana Buhring[3] was born and brought up in the emotionally, sexually and physically abusive Children of God/The Family cult – she and her two sisters have written an account of their experiences in *Not Without My Sister*. Their father entered the group as a young man and, since both monogamy and birth control were prohibited by the leader, he went on to father numerous children by different women giving Juliana siblings and half-siblings scattered around the world, most of whom, like Juliana herself, were separated from their parents at a young age. Peter Frouman was in the same group and, along with his siblings, he too was separated from his parents and was subjected to frequent sexual abuse.

Elissa Wall was born and brought up in the Fundamentalist Church of Latter Day Saints, a polygamous Mormon group. In a Nevada motel the leader, Warren Jeffs, forced 14-year-old Elissa to marry her cousin.[4] Jeffs is now serving a life sentence having been convicted for having sex with underage girls. Three other young women run a website – exscientologykids.org – that documents the experiences of some of those who grew up in the Church of Scientology. These stories make for compelling reading and are a reminder of all the young people still trapped inside such groups without the means to communicate to the outside world.

There are great numbers of young people who are press-ganged or kidnapped into totalist groups. This is particularly the case for children forcibly recruited into armies under the control of charismatic and authoritarian leaders. Among these are the estimated 20,000 girls and boys forced into Joseph Kony's Lord's Resistance Army – the girls used as sex slaves, the boys as child soldiers, and both serving as a slave labor force.[5] For years whole villages in northern Uganda were emptied of children every night as these "night commuters," as they became known, evacuated their homes to stay in the more secure towns to avoid kidnapping into the Lord's Resistance Army.

Other child soldiers were recruited in UN refugee camps, under the noses of the UN authorities. Emmanuel Jal documented this pathway into the world of the child soldier in his book *War Child*. At the age of 9, having escaped war in his village, and already separated from his family for two years, he became a child soldier in the Sudanese Peoples Liberation Army. He describes a scene from his recruitment:

> "This gun is my mother and father now," the officer screamed as he raised the Kalashnikov above his head. "How many of you are willing to say the same? All of you are alone here – you have left your families far behind, and now is your chance to have a new one with the SPLA."[6]

This quote grimly but accurately frames the children's futures: bereft of their own families they will become isolated within the closed world of the army – a brutal safe haven to which they must now turn.

In the last type of entry point – simply being part of a totalitarian state – we can include not just the populace of such states, but also those such as the prisoners of war in Chinese and North Korean POW camps so well-studied and documented in the 1950s by Lifton[7] and Schein[8] in their seminal works on brainwashing. These, too, are involuntary recruits. Most recently, the gripping book *Nothing to Envy* by Barbara Demick narrates the stories of six North Koreans who were able to escape the almost totally closed and repressive world in which they grew up.[9] As Mrs. Song, one of the six, told Demick: "I lived only for Marshal Kim Il-sung and for the fatherland. I never had a thought otherwise."[10]

The stereotype of the seeker, then, is incomplete when it comes to understanding how people enter totalist groups. In fact, in my own research, it was those who entered the non-totalist and non-coercive Green Party who were much more likely to be "seekers": that is, they were actively seeking political involvement. Newman Tendency members, on the other hand, were most often "pulled in" through front groups and cannot therefore be termed "seekers." They entered the group, as Crenshaw[11] says, by accident, and on their way to other goals. To understand how people find themselves in totalist groups we must take into account the multiple pathways that lead into these closed worlds.

Managing the first contact: Initiating a coordinated program of persuasion

Unless born into a group like Elissa Wall or Juliana Buhring, potential members must have some kind of initial contact with the group. Some scholars[12] state that the main way people encounter their groups is through their existing social networks – that is, through acquaintances, friends or family. While this is often the case, it is not true of those press-ganged or kidnapped. And in my study only half of the initial contacts of Newman Tendency members were through a person's social ties. The other 50 percent were "cold" contacts: through advertisements for therapists, fliers, recruitment in a public place or even the phone book. So while a person's existing social network can play a part in cult recruitment, it is only one pathway to the initial contact. What is more important to look at is how the initial contact is managed. A totalist group that is recruiting will follow up an initial contact in a concerted and orchestrated way whereas a non-totalist group is likely to leave much of the follow-up to the individual, or will have a very limited goal in developing the relationship.

The activities of the Newman Tendency present a clear picture of coordinated, planned recruitment. For instance, when Sidney attended the political meeting he saw advertised in the Tendency newspaper, he reported that a woman stationed at the door to the meeting obtained all his contact details as he entered:

> I had given my name and number – to a couple of the organizers at the beginning of the meeting – they were good with that, by the way, they knew some things. So they got me before the meeting, not the end! [laughs] And

one of them called me a couple days later ...They were ..."We are interested in doing organizing if you want to work with us."

Bernice's initial contact with a Newman Tendency therapist involved what she later remembered as a surprisingly rapid response to her phone message to his therapy practice:

> When I called them up for an appointment I was over at my girlfriend's house and then I got home and it was about ten o'clock at night [and he was] calling me back for an appointment. And that just struck me, that struck me as really weird. I mean what kind of psychologist or whatever is gonna – you know I just said I wanted, I was recommended by S. to set up an appointment – and he called me back at ten at night. And I mean, so that was kind of my first contact with him.

The Newman Tendency paid immediate attention to new contacts, which included gaining contact information, then efficient, responsive and quick follow-up. In fact, during my field research, I was subjected to this same process when I attended a play at their off-off-Broadway Castillo Theater. When I went to book my ticket the day before the show I was told to sit in the lobby and then interviewed by one of the managers – a long-time group member. She asked extensive questions about my interest in the play and took my contact details before I was granted a ticket (I am certain she was treating me as any member of the public as at that point the group was not yet aware of my research project). A few days later another Tendency member called, seeking support for the theater and the group. They finally ceased calling when I made it clear I did not live locally to any of their sites.

In contrast, none of the former Green Party members I interviewed reported being followed up by phone, or explicitly being asked for contact details. Sign-up sheets might be available at meetings, individuals might approach one, but there was no organized, concerted effort. Of course some organizations – particularly sales organizations – might follow up more rigorously, but generally with a limited agenda involving a particular sale of a particular product (although there are also sales organizations that are cultic in their methods, such as Quixtar).[13] Totalist groups, on the other hand, persist far beyond this, aiming for a total involvement of the targeted recruit.

Much has also recently been made of internet recruiting and certainly there are countless groups who use the internet to reach new recruits. Again, however, it is just one way in and although it may be the initial point of contact, a person-to-person interaction is still at the heart of the process. A 2009 Home Office report regarding Al Qaeda-influenced radicalization (Aqir) stated:

> That the internet does not appear to play a significant role in Aqir might be surprising, given that it is the social networking medium par excellence. However, the fact that the technology presents obstacles to the formation of intimate bonds could explain this counter-intuitive finding. Personal

attachments to radicalizing agents, be they peers, recruiters or moral authority figures, play a prominent role in Aqir.[14]

It is the face-to-face, personal dynamics that are consistent and key: a person may
have some contact via the internet but they are groomed and indoctrinated within
a charismatic authoritarian-led network. A case study of Hammaad Munshi, who at
16 years old became Britain's youngest convicted terrorist, illustrates this:

> Much of Munshi's extremist activism took place online, but his radicalisation
> had been initiated in the 'real world'. Through a common friend, Munshi had
> met Aabid Khan at Dewsbury central mosque. Khan had attended a terrorist
> training camp in Pakistan and served as a recruiter for the Islamist militant
> movement in the Dewsbury area. He also had a history of online jihadist
> activity and was closely connected to the 'superstar' of jihadism online, Younis
> Tsouli ('terrorist007'), as well as a number of foiled bomb plotters in Sarajevo,
> Washington DC, and Toronto. Khan spotted Munshi's knowledge of comput-
> ers, and carefully groomed him to become a leading part of his online network.
>   As with Khan, whose real world contacts informed his online activities,
> Munshi's radicalisation too was a combination of face-to-face interaction
> and virtual consolidation. His online communication with a closed network
> of like-minded and older individuals consumed much of his time and rep-
> resented the defining feature of his extremist existence. But it was the early
> meetings with Khan and some of his friends that helped turn a boy interested
> in religion into a young man dedicated to killing 'non-believers'.[15]

Larger totalist groups often make the initial contact through front groups – that is,
supposedly independent structures that exist as the public face of the more secretive,
closed inner group. The front groups are, however, closely controlled by the inner
group. The Unification Church, commonly known as the Moonies, has hundreds
of front groups including academic and professional groups, schools, businesses and
a variety of cultural, political and educational groups that perform functions from
recruitment, to fundraising, to political power-brokering.[16] The Church of Scientology organization, as another example, is noted both for its inner organization,
the Sea Org, and for its many organizations such as the Sterling Management corporate training arm or the Narconon drug rehabilitation program,[17] both of which
also perform recruitment and money-making functions. The right-wing, allegedly
anti-Semitic Lyndon LaRouche group has fronts ranging from the LaRouche
Youth Movement[18] to the Fusion Energy Foundation.[19]

   Front groups hide the true agenda and goals of the inner group and offer a
seemingly harmless initial contact point for the recruit. Want to help raise money
for poor people? Why not gather used clothes for a charity shop as the group
Humana Tvind does? The money, though, will go to the leader's bank account and
you may end up working for free for years to come.[20] Want to make some extra
cash? Why not try Amway? – although it will likely leave you with shattered family

relationships and financial ruin.[21] Want to do amateur theater? The Newman Tendency will happily help you out as it did for Steven Stewart who only broke away 12 years later, socially isolated and in serious debt. When it comes to recruitment, there really is something for everyone.

Engulfment and isolation

Once the initial contact has been made, and the new recruit is now in the sphere of influence of the group, what does the next phase of a planned, coordinated recruitment process look like? There are as many variations in this process as there are cultic groups. But the two key elements remain: position the group as the safe haven and isolate the group member from prior relationships. This sets the recruit up for the later brainwashing or indoctrination phase where the individual internalizes the mission of the group and becomes a deployable agent – at least until (and if) such a time as they can escape.

Here's how it worked in the Newman Tendency, depending on the channel through which the initial contact was made. When therapy was used as the recruitment channel, the individual started in individual therapy and then was rapidly moved to, first a single-sex "grouplet," and then to a larger, mixed-gender therapy group – usually within only one or two months. While some therapists were licensed psychologists, many others were not – notably, therapist-in-chief Fred Newman. Gillian, a former social therapist trainee I interviewed, reported providing services as an unlicensed therapist in a state in which this was illegal. She stated that this was a common practice in the Newman Tendency.[22]

Therapy patients were strongly discouraged from staying in individual therapy. Some therapy patients then remained in group therapy for many years, being involved in the "periphery" only and never progressing to the inner cadre circle but providing a useful source of income for the organization. But others were targeted for recruitment to the inner, secret organization. Juliet describes how she was moved along in the process and drawn in to other Newman Tendency activities involving their other front groups:

> I was in the grouplet for a while and as I say, they moved me out of individual into a group. So I had the group with Z. and N. and the grouplet with just N. and sometimes Y. would visit, would sit in on our sessions – our grouplet sessions. But the receptionist, G., she used to like ask, "Could you leaflet? Could you give out these leaflets?" Or, you know they would sell tickets to things, raffles . . .
>
> There would be literature all over the place for different upcoming events and both political and non-political, both therapeutic and New Alliance Party[ii] events. So she'd just, you know, she was very nice and she'd just ask you in a very innocent way, "Could you just give out a couple of these?"

ii The New Alliance Party was a front group of the Newman Tendency.

or, "We're petitioning. Could you gather a couple of signatures for us?" Or, you know, there was always something going on, like a fundraiser, "Could you come?" And as I got into the grouplet and then the group, I started to meet people, other patients who were there and we'd do this as an activity – we'd go to a fundraiser together . . . because they were starting to become friendly.

Some therapy groups included a combination of full-time cadres, new recruits and non-members, while others were strictly internal, for cadres only. In the more public groups, the focus was on individuals' problems, but involved a gradual shift to the political and "developmental" viewpoint of the Newman Tendency. Celia, a former member, gives us a glimpse into how social therapy discouraged ties to anyone outside the group:

> Some people were very new like I was, and some people were, I would say, "plants," you know, more advanced . . . There was another patient who was more advanced – she had been around maybe a year – so she was probably in already, but I didn't even know that existed. She came in one day into the group and she was upset because . . . her lover was upset about her losing so much time with her work with this group and she wanted help with her relationship. So basically what we came to the conclusion was that her lover was inhibiting her develop- ment, her lover was oppositional to her development, her lover was being, you know, was not good, was standing in the way of her development of her – you know, all that stuff, and that she was concentrating too much on "doing family," and that that brings you down and inhibits your growth and your development, so people in your life should be supporting you, growing, development . . .

For the sake of one's "development" it became necessary to leave behind those friends and family who were holding one back.

In a planned progression, then, the group's therapists encouraged followers to become more deeply involved, to develop friendship ties within the group, while discouraging external ties. The group became the sole source of support for the recruit – the new safe haven – having edged out the recruit's prior support system. The therapy groups were well-suited to this function, being an environment where people were both physically and emotionally available to form such ties, and to listen to relational advice from therapists and other group members. Activities – preferably with these newfound "friends" – with other Newman Tendency front groups were also encouraged.

On the other hand, for those whose initial contact was through a political chan- nel, an important step was to get them involved in therapy. Grace describes how she was recruited through the presidential campaign of high-level Newman Tendency member Lenora Fulani:

> So not only did I become involved in her campaign, I remember getting involved in the feminist group and the gay group [unrelated to the Newman

Tendency] . . . I ended up joining them all. So it became a part of all of that and not necessarily the only thing I was doing. . . . The difference was after I started, at some point after I met Fulani, I was told that they have a therapy center and a therapist who was seeing people. So what ended up happening was myself and T. and a couple of other students from college, including my roommate E., ended up going into social therapy and seeing this therapist.

So, regardless of how recruits first entered the Newman Tendency, they all wound up immersed in the same set of situational conditions: a combination of social therapy, left-wing (later "independent" and "progressive") political activities, and a new and increasingly dense social network. Their preexisting relationships were discouraged, and their emotional involvements became centered within the group.

Isolation increased as the schedule and activities of the group started to engulf the recruit leaving little time to continue preexisting relationships. This monopolizing of the recruit's time is typical of totalist groups. Here it is reflected in 17-year-old Londoner Ed Husain's account of recruitment to first the Young Muslim Organization, and then to Hizb ut-Tahrir, two extremist Islamist groups. In an account eerily similar to my own experience, Ed Husain describes how his time was taken over by the group. Early in his recruitment, he writes:

> Brother Falik had given me an A4 sheet of paper with 'YMO Daily Routine' written across the top. Listed on the sheet were activities I had to report on every day, including how many of the five daily prayers I had read in congregations at a mosque; how much of the Koran I had recited; how many pages of Islamic books I had read; how much time I had spent with family; how many hours I had dedicated to the movement; how many new members I had targeted for recruitment.[23]

I too had a form – the PS03 – to fill out on a weekly basis. In my group we used color-coding to shade in the different areas of "practice." The categories were: work, programmatic work, study, summary, household chores, eating, sleep and even sex. Thus were we monitored and not-so-subtly pressured to increase our group "practice." Generally this method is explained as helping the new recruit to become more "efficient," holy or self-aware. But the effect is to ensure that every element of the recruit's life is monitored and any empty gaps are filled with group activities.

Sometimes there may be a physical isolation in the early recruitment phase. The Unification Church was known for its recruitment sessions where unsuspecting recruits, having accepted an invitation to a "friendly dinner," were bussed far from the city to an isolated farm in northern California. Many so-called "personal growth" groups have intensive workshop events lasting several days where the nearly round-the-clock schedule prevents any private time to get away for quiet reflection at the end of the day or to contact persons outside the group.

And there is often the beginning of secrecy – these same personal growth groups (also known as large group awareness training programs or LGATs) enjoin recruits who have attended the initial training to keep the content of the workshops secret in order not to "spoil" the experience for the next wave of recruits they are then instructed to bring in.[24] In many political groups, such as my own, "security" is the reason given for high levels of secrecy and centralization. Such groups operate on the "need to know" principle, supposedly to protect the group from the enemy (the State, other groups and, in fact, anyone not supportive of the group in question). Secrecy is a powerful control mechanism in many areas of group life, but in the recruitment phase it functions particularly well to establish isolation early on.

These various isolating tactics mean that the only people with whom the new recruit can reflect upon their (often unsettling) experience are those already in the group or undergoing the same training. They are, in effect, forbidden from sharing and reflecting upon their experience with persons outside the system. Thus they lose the benefits of checking in with their preexisting support figures, who are likely to reflect and remind them of their prior beliefs and values. How handy, then, that the totalist group is ready to supply its own belief system and its very own claque – the new safe haven – to reflect and validate it.

Propaganda: Disabling critical thought

As Newman Tendency recruits were drawn in to therapy or to other activities through the various front groups, so they were also gradually introduced to the group's ideology and its use of political language and analysis. Juliet, who had not previously been political, said:

> They asked me to start petitioning and that's when the group started to talk about more political issues, issues about who we were in the world, and working class versus middle class, classism, this type of thing. . . . We were all friends, so afterwards, like on Saturday night we'd all get together and we'd all accuse each other of being this or that and we had no clue what we were talking about – it was just flinging out these words 'cause we were just learning them. Actually we became unbearable – it really was like a very strange time. . . . But these words – these other words started to pop up: "sexism," "racism" – the "isms," the – you know, and it was hard because I had no understanding of what that meant or what it meant in relation to me – I just really didn't know.

The belief system, or ideology of the group, supports the isolating relational shifts. The totalizing ideology of the cult establishes and encourages the division between Us and Them, and gives the theological, political or other ideological rationale for breaking ties with family, friends and other preexisting attachment figures. This is often already evident in the recruiting propaganda, which is how the recruit first encounters the group's ideology. For example, under the guidance of the Young Muslim Organization (YMO), Ed Husain studied the writings of the extremist group Jamat e-Islami's Abul ala Mawdudi who "taught that there were 'partial Muslims' and 'true Muslims'." Husain's recruiters criticized his parents suggesting they were not "true Muslims" and so encouraged the growing rift between them and Husain.[25]

Propaganda is the smooth advertising that belies the oppression of life within the group. It is the bunch of flowers presented by the future batterer with which he woos his new romantic partner. Put simply, it is the set of lies put forward by a group to present itself as acceptable or even attractive. Few would willingly join an organization that ends up controlling every element of life, but many might be interested in charitable works, or developing themselves spiritually, politically or socially. Few women would deliberately enter a relationship in which they are to be beaten. They are wooed into it. Propaganda serves this initial wooing function.

Apart from the important cases of those press-ganged or kidnapped, propaganda plays an important role in what we might call "voluntary" recruitment. (It is important, however, to remember that people do not join totalist organizations, they join causes they believe in or think will do them or others some kind of good.) Propaganda consists of the ideas, messages, images and narratives that are used specifically to communicate with the outside world. It is often delivered through the front groups that form the outer shell and entry point for many totalist groups. Front groups serve as transmission belts[26] between the internal world of the cult and the external world, and propaganda is the message carried along these transmission belts.

Propaganda is not indoctrination, though it may be the first step towards entering a process of indoctrination. Indoctrination is what happens during the subsequent process of brainwashing within an isolated context. Importantly, those to whom propaganda is directed are not yet isolated or are only partially so. They still have some points of reference in the outside world.[27] They may still have friends or family or colleagues with whom they can check out their impressions. The much more intense process of indoctrination to extreme beliefs occurs when the new recruit has been successfully separated from their external contacts. Then they can begin to be broken down, to lose their own sense of reality, their own common sense, and they can eventually be pressured to take on new and often dangerous or damaging ideas and behaviors. This part of the process can sometimes take years. Propaganda can be seen as the softening up process that gets the recruit to the point where indoctrination processes can start to be implemented.

Propaganda must be believable enough, must have some kind of hook into the real world so that potential recruits will follow the thread and not simply be repulsed immediately. Certainly they are not to be scared off with promises of suicide missions, 20-hour work days, forced marriages, divorces, pregnancies or abortions, or other threats to their close, loving relationships. At the time of Masoud Banisadr's recruitment he would never have considered divorcing his beloved wife or abandoning his children for the cause of the Iranian Mojahedin. He had to be brought to that point first by responding to the propaganda appeal of the recruitment process and then by the years of indoctrination once isolated within the group.[28]

Kerry Noble, searching for Christian fellowship and a community in which to pursue his Bible studies and learn how to "worship the Lord in spirit," responded to the propaganda put forward by Christian Identity leader Jim Ellison who preached the way "out of Babylon" and "into the realm where Jesus walked."[29] Kerry wrote:

> For as long as I could remember, I wanted to live and work with Christians and raise my family in a truly Christian environment. Not a churchy environment, full of hypocrisy and church politics, but where Christianity was a lifestyle, not a set of stuffy doctrines and traditions.[30]

Ellison said "Learn to let God do that which is right in His own sight, Kerry, and you will learn to have peace and trust . . . no one will ever die here, as long as we trust Jesus and do what is right in His own sight."[31] But eight years later Noble was a lieutenant of Ellison's right-wing paramilitary organization under siege from the FBI's SWAT team – certainly not the goal he started out with.

Thus totalist groups have one brand of discourse – propaganda – that is outer-directed and recognizable to the outside world, and another – indoctrination – which is a different language and set of ideas directed solely to members within the group. Persons outside the inner group are rarely privy to the language and ideas of indoctrination.

In the Newman Tendency the outer-directed, propaganda form of social therapy, appears, at first glance, like any typical contemporary therapy, addressing problems of depression, relationships, anxiety and so forth. The back cover for Newman's book, *Let's Develop: A Guide to Continuous Personal Growth*, promises a kind of pop psychology, and enthuses:

> Let's Develop! will show *you* how to achieve continuous personal growth . . . transform your life . . . rid yourself of emotional pain . . . Dr. Fred Newman has discovered that *we can reinitiate our development* – at any age and at any stage in life! What's more, says Dr. Newman, *development is the cure*.[32]

As Louisa, a social therapy patient who was never recruited to the inner group, told me:

> It was just therapy. It was purely just therapy, as far as I could tell: growth and development, and that somehow – they always use that word [development] – really, performing your life better, to help people with their suffering.

During the recruitment process, the Newman Tendency social therapy propaganda was couched in terms of therapeutic care for personal problems that clients presented to the group. It is from these real personal problems that "the lies of totalitarian propaganda derive the element of truthfulness and real experience they need to bridge the gulf between reality and fiction."[33] In this way the language and ideas of Fred Newman's propaganda serve as the "bridge of normalcy" between the real world and the "fictitious world"[34] of his one-man show where arranged marriages, forced abortions and endless hours of unpaid labor comprised the secret, unhappy lives of full-time cadres.

Similarly, in my own group, propaganda linking the closed, oppressed world of life in the group to the outside world included the application of pseudo-scientific analytical "Tools" to promote everything from child development in our scruffy public childcare center to the commercial bakery we ran with below-minimum-wage labor.[iii] The discussion of the superiority of our analytical "Tools" permeated our work, both in our interactions with the outside world, and in our own intense self-criticisms internal to the group. The difference was that no mention of social change, nor of the inner group linking these disparate front groups, was made in its external, public usage, whereas internally we understood that we were applying the "dialectical-materialist tools" to transform ourselves into effective revolutionaries of an underground political party.

As recruits enter more fully into the life of the group the language and messages change. In Mormon recruiting practices telling new recruits one thing and consolidated followers another is justified as the need to give "milk before meat"[35] to the new believers: new recruits are seen as babies – they are not ready yet for the hard stuff. The Unification Church refers to the same thing as "Heavenly Deception" – it's fine to deceive new recruits and hide the less salubrious elements of church life from them since the ultimate goal is their salvation. Yet even in the recruiting propaganda elements of the later indoctrination language are introduced. Newman Tendency recruiting materials referred to language such as "development," "growth," "community," "doing family" – all of which became important later symbols in the indoctrination stage.

In the recruitment stage, one of the tasks of the group is to begin to disable the target's critical thinking. Social psychologists Petty and Cacciopo[36] describe two ways in which people process information and become persuaded: the central and peripheral routes of persuasion. A key purpose of propaganda is to begin to edge new recruits away from the central, critical route into a primarily peripheral mode of processing information about the group.

Central route – or systematic – processing involves careful evaluation of information and requires quality information, sufficient time and the ability with which to think about a problem or question. In deciding to join a specific group a potential member engaging in central route processing would take time to gather information from a variety of sources and make careful comparisons and an evaluation of the pros and cons of this commitment before reaching a decision. They might do background research on the history of the group, talk to current and former members, and seek out both critical and positive information.[iv]

iii These "tools" however were not adequate to vanquish the rats who inhabited our bakery (and this despite the 13-year-old daughter of a group member being made to clean the entire place every weekend with no pay).
iv Unfortunately, as my friend and colleague, Doug Agustin, explains to those he trains in how to resist persuasion attempts by dangerous groups: "People are more likely to spend time researching an electronic gadget than a group to which they are making a lifetime commitment."

Peripheral route – or automatic – processing, on the other hand, involves being persuaded by cues and rules of thumb that are logically unrelated to the actual content of a persuasion message – they are "peripheral" cues, focusing on surface attributes of the message or messenger. A person deciding whether to join a particular group using only peripheral route processing might feel rushed by a sense of urgency: "One time offer! Sign up now!" They might find the recruiter attractive, be inundated with testimonials, or have participated in a highly emotional group "peak experience," among many other types of peripheral persuasion cues. Peripheral route processing results from rapid decision-making under time constraints, a quantity of weak arguments, rapid presentation and distractions, such as strong emotional arousal. In this way decisions are made based on peripheral, rather than central, characteristics of the question.

Groups that wish to persuade potential recruits of their benign intent, and need to hide their internal practices and beliefs, rely on recruiting people by making use of the peripheral route of persuasion to begin to derail critical thinking. Steve Hassan described the early intensive phase of his recruitment to the Moonies – the Unification Church – when he attended a workshop of several intense days of highly structured activities with no time to himself and little sleep:

> Each evening we had to write feedback. At the end of the last day I remember writing: 'I am too blown away to write anything now.' My mind was exploding.[37]

In just a few pressurized days and constant high levels of stimulation the UC had successfully hobbled his ability to think critically.

The group's propaganda must serve to prevent the recruit from examining too closely its actual practices and history and instead must sway them through overwhelming their critical thinking with superficial and emotionally arousing information and experiences. Through deception it engages recruits by presenting the group in a non-threatening light. It begins to introduce the language of indoctrination in preparation for consolidating the recruit as a group member. And, finally, it begins to justify the isolating strategies of the group in order to remove the recruits' prior attachment relationships.

Undue influence mechanisms in recruitment

A variety of other social influence techniques are employed in the recruitment stage. They include: obedience to authority, as demonstrated in Milgram's famous electric shock experiments;[38] Festinger's theory of cognitive dissonance;[39] the majority effect shown in Asch's "lines" experiments;[40] and ingratiation techniques such as flattery, similarity and making use of the principle of reciprocity.[41] These and other scholars have defined a variety of ways in which we, as humans, conform, comply and obey – all features necessary to group living, but behaviors that can also be subject to manipulation.

Undoubtedly Marina submitted to obedience to the authority of her therapist when agreeing, against her will, to leaving individual therapy to join the therapy group. She responded to flattery when told what great comments she'd made during therapy and at meetings. Cognitive dissonance is the uncomfortable state one experiences when holding two beliefs (or feelings) that are inconsistent – Festinger's theory holds that in such a state one will try to resolve the inconsistency by changing one of the beliefs. Marina describes below a therapy session with Newman and how she resolved her dissonant beliefs about him in favor of a positive evaluation:

> We were made to wait outside, you know, after the appointed time of our, you know, sessions. We had group sessions and we would just be sitting outside fidgeting and waiting and then his secretary would come and say "He's ready now," and we'd all go in and he'd be sitting there eating a pastrami sandwich and, you know, or she would bring it to him and we'd have to wait for him to eat and I remember feeling – starting with every, almost every group where this kind of happened – starting out feeling extremely pissed off, but by the end of the group, I was so elated and happy and thankful for the wisdom that I thought he had imparted and it was like, you know, dependent on whether he picked me to make a point or asked me a question or said "Yes, you're right!" you know, kind of thing or something I had said, and those were the moments of, you know, elation in therapy where – where I did something right or I said something right or I got it. . . . I just remember that – that by the end of the group, I – I mean, those feelings of uneasiness in the beginning would turn into feelings of guilt. Why are you feeling this way towards him? Look at what he's saying or doing. You know, and that would turn into feelings of love and euphoria for our – the work we were doing. It was just this weird roller coaster ride . . .

These social psychological processes are used to great advantage by totalist groups. They are very important to understand, but they are not the focus of this book. Writers such as Cialdini, Lalich, Singer, Hassan and Zimbardo[42] have described these well and studying their work results in a tremendous pay off in terms of protecting one from making poor decisions based on rather universal human vulnerabilities.

Who is vulnerable? It's situation, not personality

An extensive ethnographic study of a variety of Nazi skinhead groups including Youth Corps (the youth wing of the KKK), the Aryan Youth Movement (the youth wing of WAR) and Volksfront (an Oregon Nazi skinhead group) found that:

> Nazi skinheads can serve as "big brothers" or "friends in need" to frustrated boys whose fathers have been laid off or who have been harassed by minority peers. Like the members of cults, skinheads provide a sympathetic ear, a critical explanation of the problem, and an action program that appears to (somewhat) resolve the problem.[43]

The social-psychological pincer movement of becoming the target's new best friend while introducing the propaganda of White supremacy is key to recruiting new soldiers to the race war – some of whom will go on to join right-wing militia groups.[44] Regardless of the specific ideology then, a two-fold immersion process engaging both emotional and cognitive elements is necessary to draw recruits further in to these charismatic and authoritarian-led groups.

The search to find "who is vulnerable" to totalist recruitment is destined to continued failure. Cult recruitment is primarily the result of *situational* vulnerabilities not *personality* vulnerabilities (or what social psychologists call situational as opposed to dispositional factors). What are these situational vulnerabilities? Singer, who counseled thousands of former cult members, described a key vulnerability as being in a normal life "blip."[45] That is, some recent, yet developmentally normal, change in life situation such as a recent move to attend university, a divorce or other relationship breakup, perhaps a death in the family, or a change of job or housing. War, natural disasters or social upheavals – such as the breakup of the former Soviet Union, or the current collapsed states of Syria or Somalia – can contribute to weakening family and community ties leading to increased social fragmentation and isolation. Simply living in the contemporary developed world, with fewer neighborhood ties and more dispersed families, means most of us live in increasingly vulnerable social networks.

Social isolation or atomization is an increasingly generalized situational fact of contemporary life. It is insufficient, therefore, to state that totalist groups "mainly attract people who are socially isolated or lonely."[46] This makes social isolation a dispositional (i.e. a personal) characteristic or weakness rather than a generalized situational one that affects nearly all of us at some point or other. *Any* group attracts those who wish to affiliate with others – and those who seek affiliations often do so to overcome social isolation. It is, in fact, a healthy response to atomization to seek to join up with others. As humans we are social animals. We have a fundamental need to join with others to seek solutions to the problems of survival. The danger arises if, in that effort, one encounters a totalist group that seeks to isolate and control its members – then one's own survival, and potentially that of others, is put at the gravest risk.

In my study comparing former members of the non-totalist Green Party with the highly controlling Newman Tendency, I found few differences in social isolation between the two groups of members prior to entry. Both had average (according to the US General Social Survey)[47] numbers of close friends and relatively similar family relationships, although what happened to those friendships and family ties *during* their group tenure differed drastically.

Therefore, rather than stating that prior isolation and weak social connections are a situational vulnerability, it would be more accurate to say that contemporary conditions of social fragmentation may lead people to seek out group membership generally. Whether they find a totalist or non-totalist group to satisfy this need to belong may be strictly a question of luck, or, as Crenshaw put it, they may run into the totalist group by accident.[48] What *is* a differentiating factor is what happens to a person's social networks *after* they join a group. The Greens kept nearly all their friendships throughout their membership while the Newman Tendency members dropped their friendships and family ties and only repaired a few of those after they finally left the group. The totalist group thus further isolates a person from prior relationships, while the non-totalist one is likely to have no effect at all on the person's previous relationships.

For over half a century, then, scholars of totalism from Arendt to Zimbardo have found that there is no personality profile of a potential recruit to a totalist or extremist group. The latest UK government report has come out, confirming yet again that "researchers concluded there was no 'vulnerability profile' to help identity those at risk of becoming radicalized without creating an 'unmanageable number of false positives'."[49]

As these studies show, it is unhelpful to continue looking for a profile of a "typical" terrorist or cult recruit – most of us could become vulnerable given the right conditions, the right group and the right time. A far more fruitful approach is to understand the profile, methods and operating (perhaps we should say "hunting") grounds of the *organizations* to which people are recruited, and to be able to distinguish effectively between open and relatively benign organizations from dangerous, totalist organizations that are capable of exerting extreme levels of control over their members. Developing a profile of such organizations would enable societies to begin to educate and protect the public from such recruitment and indoctrination attempts. Beginning efforts in this direction exist in France, Belgium and Germany, where processes of "mental manipulation" are being defined and criminalized. Some government-sponsored information centers and public awareness campaigns also exist.[50] But much more work is needed.

Hammaad Munshi, according to a family friend, was "a normal boy," "a good little boy who did listen to his parents." But he was a teenager, in a normal life stage of questioning and defining his identity – Singer's life "blip." He ran into a totalist group who proceeded to systematically recruit him. Marina Ortiz was in a life blip too – she had broken up with her partner and was depressed. She had the accidental bad luck of finding the wrong therapist. Kerry Noble, seeking a bucolic Christian life, encountered the racist, gun-loving Christian Identity Movement.

By the end of the recruitment phase the recruit (whether voluntary or involuntary) has been pulled away from prior attachments. They are being taught that these attachments are holding them back (or they have simply been removed from their attachment figures as in the case of child soldiers). The leader and group have been established as the sole available source of comfort and knowledge, the new safe haven. Recruits are becoming busy and engaged with their groups, and they are increasingly exposed to the groups' totalist propaganda. Cognitively the person's independent thinking has been disrupted by a variety of social psychological persuasion pressures, as well as by the loss of their prior social sources of reality verification. The recruit's prior emotional and cognitive structures that have been part of their means of survival and adaptation to life are now effectively removed or neutralized.

Our new recruits are within the crosshairs of their respective groups. Now that we have seen the various ways totalist groups go about recruiting new members, and how the initial softening-up occurs, we move on to the next step: indoctrination, the step where the disorganized attachment bond is formed. In the next chapter we see how, with the recruit in range, the trap, now set, is sprung.

Notes

1 Crenshaw, Martha. 2011. *Radicalization and Recruitment into Terrorism*. Paper presented at the Processes of Radicalization and De-Radicalization, April, Bielefeld, Germany.
2 McVeigh, Karen. 2014. "Peer Pressure Lures More Britons to Syria Than Isis Videos, Study Finds," in *Guardian*, November 6, 2014. London: Guardian.
3 Jones, Celeste, Kristina Jones and Juliana Buhring. 2007. *Not without My Sister*. London: Harper Element.
4 Wall, Elissa and Lisa Pulitzer. 2008. *Stolen Innocence*. New York: William Morrow.
5 "Midnight's Children: Could the Lord's Resistance Army's Horrific Practices in Africa Soon End?" *The Independent*. Retrieved November 18, 2012 (http://www.indpendent.co.uk/news/world/africa/midnights-children-could-the-lords-resistance-armys-horrific-practices-in-africa-soon-end-6297943.html).
6 Jal, Emmanuel. 2009. *War Child: A Boy Soldier's Story*. London: Abacus, p. 76.
7 Lifton, Robert Jay. 1961. *Thought Reform and the Psychology of Totalism*. New York: The Norton Library.
8 Schein, Edgar H. 1961. *Coercive Persuasion: A Socio-Psychological Analysis of the "Brainwashing" of American Civilian Prisoners by the Chinese Communists*. New York: W.W. Norton.
9 Demick, Barbara. 2010. *Nothing to Envy: Real Lives in North Korea*. London: Granta.
10 Ibid., p. 39.
11 Crenshaw, *Radicalization and Recruitment into Terrorism*.
12 For example, see Sageman, Marc. 2004. *Understanding Terror Networks*. Philadelphia: University of Pennsylvania Press.
13 Hansen, Chris [Director]. 2004. *In Pursuit of the Almighty Dollar: Dateline Investigation: Inside Story of Business That Attracts People with Promise of Easy Money*. NBC.
14 Press Association. 2011. "Internet Help to Al Qaida 'Limited'," in *The Guardian*. London.
15 Stevens, Tim and Dr. Peter R. Neumann. 2009. *Countering Online Radicalisation a Strategy for Action*. London: International Centre for the Study of Radicalisation and Political Violence.
16 For a fascinating and extensive list see: http://www.freedomofmind.com/resource-center/groups/m/moonies/front_groups.htm
17 Atack, Jon. 1990. *A Piece of Blue Sky*. Seacaucus: Carol Publishing Group; Singer, M.T. and J. Lalich. 1995b. *Cults in Our Midst: The Hidden Menace in Our Everyday Lives*. San Francisco: Jossey Bass.
18 McLemee, Scott. 2007. "The Larouche Youth Movement," *Inside Higher Ed*, July 11.
19 King, Dennis. 1989. *Lyndon Larouche and the New American Fascism*. New York: Doubleday.
20 Henley, Paul [Director]. 2002. *Denmark's Tvind*. British Broadcasting Corporation.
21 Brown, David. 2007. "Marketing Group Merely 'Selling a Dream'." *Times Online*. Retrieved December 15, 2011 (http://www.rickross.com/reference/amway/amway120.html).
22 Interview with Gillian, October 2004.
23 Husain, Ed. 2007. *The Islamist: Why I Joined Radical Islam in Britain, What I Saw Inside and Why I Left*. London: Penguin, p. 38.
24 Singer, *Cults in Our Midst: The Hidden Menace in Our Everyday Lives*.
25 Husain, *The Islamist*, p. 37.
26 This is Hannah Arendt's helpful term. See Arendt, Hannah. 1948/1979a. *The Origins of Totalitarianism*. Orlando: Harcourt Brace.
27 Ibid.

28 Banisadr, Masoud. 2004. *Masoud: Memoirs of an Iranian Rebel*. London: Saqi.
29 Kerry Noble. 1998. *Tabernacle of Hate: Why They Bombed Oklahoma City*. Prescott, ON: Voyageur Publishing, p. 31.
30 Ibid., p. 27.
31 Ibid., p. 49.
32 Newman, Fred and Phyllis Goldberg. 1994. *Let's Develop!* New York: Castillo International, Inc.
33 Arendt, Hannah. 1948/1979a. *The Origins of Totalitarianism*. Orlando: Harcourt Brace, p. 353.
34 Ibid.
35 Mormons refer to this as "Lying for the Lord." The Unification Church (commonly known as the Moonies) has a similar phrase: "Heavenly Deception," which is used to justify lying to recruits not yet ready for the full message: Hassan, Steven. 1988. *Combatting Cult Mind Control*. Rochester, VT. Park Street Press.
36 Petty, R.E., and J.T. Cacioppo. 1986. *Communication and Persuasion: Central and Peripheral Routes to Attitude Change*. New York: Springer/Verlag. For a similar, highly readable overview of research and application of these two different systems of thinking, see Kahneman, Daniel. 2011. *Thinking, Fast and Slow*. London: Allen Lane.
37 Saner, Emine. 2012. "'I Was a Moonie Cult Leader'," in *The Guardian*. London: Guardian News and Media.
38 Milgram, Stanley. 1974. *Obedience to Authority: An Experimental View*. New York: Harper & Row.
39 Festinger, Leon. 1962. *A Theory of Cognitive Dissonance*. Stanford, CA: Stanford University Press.
40 Asch, Solomon E. 1951. "Effects of Group Pressure Upon the Modification and Distortion of Judgements," in *Groups, Leadership, and Men*, edited by H. Gvetzkow. Pittsburgh: Carnegie Press, pp. 177–90.
41 Cialdini, R. 1984. *The Psychology of Influence*. New York: William Morrow.
42 Ibid.; Hassan, *Combatting Cult Mind Control*.; Lalich, Janja. 2004. *Bounded Choice: True Believers and Charismatic Cults*. Berkeley: University of California Press; Singer, *Cults in Our Midst*; Zimbardo, Philip and S. Andersen. 1993. "Understanding Mind Control: Exotic and Mundane Mental Manipulations," in *Recovery from Cults*, edited by M. Langone. New York: Norton, pp. 104–125.
43 Blazak, Randy. 2001. "White Boys to Terrorist Men: Target Recruitment of Nazi Skinheads." *American Behavioral Scientist* 44(No. 6, February 2001):982–1000.
44 Ibid.
45 Singer, *Cults in Our Midst*.
46 Baumeister, Roy F., and Mark R. Leary. 1995. "The Need to Belong: Desire for Interpersonal Attachments as a Fundamental Human Motivation." *Psychological Bulletin* 117:497–529, 522.
47 McPherson, Miller, Lynn Smith-Lovin and Matthew E. Brashears. 2006. "Social Isolation in America: Changes in Core Discussion Networks over Two Decades." *American Sociological Review* 71(3):353–75.
48 Crenshaw, *Radicalization and Recruitment into Terrorism*.
49 Press Association, "Internet Help to Al Qaida 'Limited'."
50 See Mutch, Steven. 2011. "Cults and Public Policy: Protecting the Victims of Cultic Abuse in Australia," in *Cult Information and Family Support*. Canberra, Parliament House (http://www.cifs.org.au/protecting.php); and also Kropfeld, Mike. 2008. "A Comparison of Different Countries' Approaches to Cult-Related Issues." *ICSA E-newsletter* 7(1) (http://www.icsahome.com/articles/countryapproaches).

4

TOTALIST INDOCTRINATION
Isolation in a crowded place

> It has frequently been said, and it is perfectly true, that the most horrible aspect of [totalitarian] terror is that it has the power to bind together completely isolated individuals and that by so doing it isolates these individuals even more.
>
> Only isolated individuals can be dominated totally.
>
> Hannah Arendt, *Essays in Understanding*[i]

The two elements of isolation of the follower and positioning of the group as the new safe haven as discussed in the previous chapter, have prepared the follower for indoctrination into the totalist system. There is continued, and now, nearly complete, isolation from prior friends and family (unless they are in, useful to or conforming to the group). The follower's life becomes almost totally swallowed up by the group. And finally, with the follower isolated from prior sources of support, the group arouses threat, fear or stress in some form. This sequence is not necessarily a linear process, and can take many forms – all, however, can result in a relationship of disorganized attachment and the chronic dissociation that is at its heart. Whatever form they take, these three elements – isolation, engulfment and fear arousal – are fundamental to the brainwashing process.

This process takes place within a totalistic organization, and so, to understand it, the organization as an entity, an organism itself – its structure, the processes that keep it going, its birth and its death – must be understood. And at the same time the experience of the follower who is subjected to brainwashing, their journey into

---

i *Essays in Understanding, 1930–1954* by Hannah Arendt. Copyright © 1994 by Hannah Arendt. Reprinted by permission of Georges Borchardt, Inc., on behalf of the Hannah Arendt Bluecher Literary Trust.

and through the organization, must also be understood. There are, then, these two interrelated processes to grasp. It is at the nexus of these two entities that the core mechanism of brainwashing takes place: the action of the organization upon the follower to induce a relationship of disorganized attachment whereby the leader can gain and maintain control of followers.

When the process of brainwashing or totalist indoctrination by the group is successful there is a threefold outcome. The followers' feelings are disrupted and an attachment to the group and/or leader is formed. Their thinking, and in particular their ability to *think* about their *feelings* and attachments, is in turn disrupted. Finally, followers can then become deployable – that is, able to be directed to engage in actions regardless of their own survival interests. Deployable followers lose their autonomy of thought and action.

Isolation and engulfment

To take the first two elements of the brainwashing process: as the group consolidates the isolation from friends and family that began in the recruitment stage (if there was one) they simultaneously engulf the follower in group activities, surrounding the recruit with other group members. Juliet describes her experience of this in the Newman Tendency. For example, her new obligations and schedule meant she became, as she told me, "totally unavailable" to her mother to whom she had previously been very close. Similarly she lost contact with her friends, telling them: "I'm really busy, I'm working on this thing, I can't get together with you." She continues:

> I did make attempts. I think I invited people to a talent show that I was working at in the hopes of having them come see what I'm doing now, 'cause I was so excited about what I'm doing now … and spending some time with them but of course I got … um … I got put on security and I couldn't spend any time with them. I don't remember feeling angry about it. I was a bit disappointed that I didn't get to spend time with them but then, like, I was getting closer and closer to the people in the organization and I had less and less in common with people outside of the organization. There was less to talk about um, I think I almost felt, not superior but … like, I, oh, I can't talk about these mundane things like you know, your problems with your boyfriend or, you know, what I mean. I'm doing, I'm doing revolutionary work here, you know [laughs].

In order to more completely isolate the follower and ensure they become focused on the group, the group controls the follower's time, their communication with others and the communications they receive. In Juliet's case she became a full-time staff member of the Newman Tendency's political arm, the New Alliance Party, working in Harlem. She said, "I was busy working, working, working – no time to think, you know. There's no sleep. I mean really, I was so exhausted." Juliet goes on to describe the engulfment:

> Well, I mean the thing with that was that while I was in the organization, you didn't, everything you needed was there, was . . . within the organization. You had a whole community of people, a whole community of friends. You know, there was the doctor, Doctor D., you know, if you were sick you'd get an appointment right away. There was . . . the legal team, if you were having an issue you could talk to them. I mean . . . it, it's, it felt like you know, you, if I, if I think about it, it was a very very large family, even though we weren't family but . . . they, it was . . . like you didn't really, I didn't really associate with anybody outside of the group at that point, you know. I associated with people only inside of the group and in that sense, it felt like a safety net.

Her use of the term "safety net" reflects how the group had managed to make themselves the new safe haven for her. Why worry about your lost friends and family if everything you need is within the group? They will take care of all your needs.

Emmanuel Jal became a child soldier in the Sudanese Peoples Liberation Army (SPLA) at the age of 9, recruited while in a UN refugee camp in Ethiopia and far from his family. The SPLA sent Jal to a training camp with other young boys. Every day they worked in the camp: fetching water, cleaning the soldiers' boots and other camp maintenance tasks. Before and after this work they trained for hours in basic drills. Night after night the army trainer woke the small boys and made them run into the darkness. "My head ached, my back hurt and as soon as we got back into bed, he'd wake us up again and we'd have to start jogging. I felt as if I'd never slept."[2] The war had already separated Jal from his family and friends – but after being sent to the training camp any new close friendships the boys might form were forbidden and punished severely, friends sometimes being made to beat or whip each other to end the friendship. In this extreme way the boy Jal's isolation was cemented and the SPLA became his entire world. When he had completed his training his commander said again: "Always remember: the gun is your mother and father now." Jal wrote in his memoir: "I looked at him. I had a family, a home again."[3] Having been uprooted from his own family and his village, and then removed from the refugee camp, now this 9-year-old's only remaining safe haven was this brutal army.

Miriam Williams became both isolated and engulfed in the bible-based cult the Children of God (aka The Family), a group she encountered when she was 17. After she moved to their camp in New York state, the process of indoctrination began. Each day started early in the morning with an hour of prayer and proceeded through long hours of bible classes, followed by "time to memorize verses, always with an older brother or sister to guide us, and then to read the Bible silently, but not alone." After dinner came "inspiration, which included a few hours of singing and then a message from our leader."[4] Never being left alone, having no time and having no money, she was not able to call her family – her "flesh family" as the group referred to it. When she did finally go to see them it was with a group member, Hosea, as chaperone, and the purpose of the visit was to pack up "everything from my personal possessions that Hosea thought the Family could use."[5]

Miriam was later paired with an "older sister." Many groups use this type of buddy system – in the Newman Tendency members were each assigned a more experienced "friend" to guide them. Ruiz described the process thus:

> Whenever you joined the inner party, you get assigned a friend. And the friend is kind of somebody that's been in a long time, that can guide you through things, that's somebody you can talk to if you need to, or whatever. B. was my friend. And, there's no kind of end to the friend you know? His assignment kind of ended, but it was unclear, you know, when the friend ended. But, yeah, so he would guide you through things and talk to you.

In the notorious Heaven's Gate cult, which ended in the horrific mass suicide of 39 of its members, each member was continually in the presence of a "check part-ner" who monitored the other and reinforced their commitment to the group.[6] Similarly, young Mormon missionaries are always assigned a companion (formerly unknown to them) and the Missionary Handbook instructs them that for the two years of their mission they must:

> Never be alone. It is extremely important that you stay with your companion at all times. Staying together means staying within sight and hearing of each other. The only times you should be separated from your assigned companion are when you are in an interview with the mission president, on a companion exchange, or in the bathroom.[7]

This chaperoning system serves two functions. It keeps the follower (and, for that matter, the buddy) from ever being alone and thus having some autonomy to, for example, contact former friends or family, or simply to have quiet time in which to reflect. The buddy also monitors the follower's behavior and provides a model and guidance about the new group norms the follower is to observe.

Part of the isolation process is to remove elements of the follower's identity – this becomes what Agustin[8] refers to as "isolation from the self." Often the cult member is given a new name. Members of Heaven's Gate were given new names, which all included the suffix "-ody." For example "Stlody" or "Anlody" denoting, said the leader, Applewhite, a "young member of the Kingdom of God . . . a young 'un, a child of the Next Level."[9] In the Children of God, Miriam was given the name Jeshanah. Her own clothes were taken away and she was instructed to dress from the communal supply.

In my case all written communications to me were to my code name of "Claire," or, alternatively to my code number "NB25." This had the effect of distancing my prior identity and sense of self from my dealings with the group. And though I did not dress from a communal supply, I did begin to dress in the same manner as other group members – leaving behind my jeans and flannel shirts and taking on the "smart casual" clothing norms of the group.

Sometimes a formal process marks the completion of the stage of removing prior attachments and replacing them with the group. For example, in the Newman Tendency, after accepting the invitation to fulltime cadre status, induction to the party took place. This was marked by a ritual, complete with sacred objects, whose purpose served to now reinforce the boundaries between those in the group and those outside.[10] Grace describes her induction:

> I was invited to a reception that Fred was present at. I was invited to a reception at somebody's apartment when I was brought in – a number of people were brought in at the same time and we were given books, a bookmark – some sort of communist bookmark, when we came in. And then we had our first class. It was sort of, you know, it was very formal, . . . so in a sense I became a member of the entering class of new members, so there was like six or seven of us that were the new class. And we came in and started classes . . . the process was extremely secretive. Oh, D. in that meeting, one of the things she made very clear to me was that I was entering a secret organization. She made it clear that it was a revolutionary organization so that it could never be spoken about to anyone.

In the Church of Scientology, the induction process famously involves signing a billion year contract – one's commitment is therefore cemented for all possible future lives. This induction ritual is visited upon old and young alike. Jenna Miscavige Hill, born into the church, reports that she was made to sign this document when only 7 years old.[11]

Isolation and engulfment, then, go hand in hand. On the one hand, one's trusted or, at least, known friends and family are edged out, as with Miriam and Juliet, or have already gone as in Jal's case. And on the other, the group fills every waking moment with group activities. Some followers, however, may be allowed, or even encouraged, to continue certain external activities – most commonly their means of earning income – in order to support themselves and donate to the organization. For example, former Scientologists Luis and Rocio Garcia built up a profitable printing business while in the group and so were able to donate hundreds of thousands of dollars.[12] Similarly, followers may be allowed limited, and closely monitored, connection with those outside the group (including even former friends and family) as long as those contacts have an organizational purpose, that is recruitment, fundraising or other types of support for the group.

But fundamentally the combination of isolation and engulfment results in a situation that the philosopher Hannah Arendt describes as people being "pressed together" so tightly that there is no space between them, "so that the very space of free action – and this is the reality of freedom – disappears."[13] The space between people, she says, is what makes up the "world." It is in the space between people that conversation, speaking to one another, occurs by which "everything that individuals carry with them innately becomes visible and audible."[14] In other words our difference and individuality, our different experiences and different views only become real, in a sense, when we are in conversation with others across this space that separates us, that allows us this difference. Arendt sees this conversation as the essence of real friendship.

But in a totalist system, no differences are allowed – all are pressed together and compelled to have a single set of beliefs, goals and behaviors. With only a single view, a single, absolute "truth" allowed, then no conversation is needed – after all, in such a case we already agree on everything, we already (apparently) experience everything in the same way. What then, is there to talk about? In fact, what is key in totalitarian groups is a constant monitoring to ensure nothing "worldly" (this is the very word used in many bible-based cults) is talked about. And certainly nothing "anti-organizational" – as it was called in my group – may ever be discussed. Indeed, in our case, being accused of anti-organizational talk, thinking or behavior was considered the greatest crime.

The buddy system, described above, aids in this pressing together of people so that there is no space of free action between them, and no possibility of conversation. Of course, sometimes the system might fail and real friendship may develop between buddies, or between any followers, but if this is found out then punishment and separation are the inevitable result. In my group, although there was not physical punishment, any friendships that dared to develop were labeled "bourgeois" and based on "social exchange value." In-depth self-criticisms were extracted to determine the source of such anti-organizational behavior. Thus did the group make friendship a risky proposition. On the other hand, turning in anyone who happened to be close – as I did when I wrote up a formal criticism of my husband in the group – was sure to bring a rare word of praise.

Contrary to the stereotype of cult life, followers are isolated not only from the outside world, but in this airless pressing together they are also isolated *from each other* within the group. They cannot share doubts, complaints about the group or any attempt to attribute their distress to the actions of the group. At the same time as this isolation from other people – either within or outside of the group – is occurring, there is also a deep loneliness and isolation from the self. The time pressures, sleep deprivation and the erasure of the individual mean there is never any opportunity for solitude – that creative and restful state where contemplation, thinking and the space in which changes of mind might occur can take place. As there is no space between people, neither is there any internal space allowed within each person, for their own autonomous thought and feeling. Thus there is a triple isolation: from the outside world, from others in the group and from one's own self.

The creation of fright without solution

Now the follower's social life and time are under the control of the organization. The group has removed other close attachment relationships – either actual or potential – and established itself as the remaining, and only, safe haven. But isolation and engulfment alone are not enough. To brainwash a person – so that they will do your bidding regardless of their own survival-interest – the group must lock in their control of that person's emotional and cognitive life. This is the essence of totalist indoctrination. To isolation and engulfment must be added a third ingredient: threat. Any kind of threat will do, so long as the isolation and engulfment has already been fairly effective and the group has been successfully established as the only safe haven.

Jessica Stern says in her study of terrorism that the deliberate inculcation of apocalyptic fear often predicts cult violence. For example, Jim Ellison, leader of the heavily armed right-wing Christian Identity group, the Covenant, Sword and Arm of the Lord, described the coming apocalypse in gory detail, simultaneously demonizing entire populations:

> It will get so bad that parents will eat their children. Death in the major cities will cause rampant diseases and plagues. Maggot-infested bodies will lie every-where. Earthquakes, tidal waves, volcanoes, and other natural disasters will grow to gigantic proportions. Witches and satanic Jews will offer people up as sacrifices to their gods, openly and proudly; blacks will rape and kill white women and will torture and kill white men; homosexuals will sodomize whoever they can.[15]

But the deliberate inculcation of fear does not only *predict* cult violence, it is, in fact, an *essential ingredient* of the totalistic control of followers. The arousal of feelings of fear can take many forms – from sheer physical fear to fear of the outside world, or from the fear of being expelled by the group to being put on the "hot-seat" in group criticism sessions. It can also be created through various types of physical stress, deprivation or exhaustion.

As a child soldier, Emmanuel Jal lived in a world of constant threat. He hardly had need of its deliberate arousal. Nonetheless, the army trainers constantly beat, kicked and whipped the boys at the same time as keeping alive in their minds the fear of the enemy, the *jallabas*, who had driven them from their villages.[16]

Mark Juergensmeyer describes how Takeshi Nakamura was initiated into Aum Shinrikyo, the Japanese apocalyptic cult led by Asahara. In 1997, Asahara ordered group members to release sarin gas in a crowded Tokyo subway killing 12 people and injuring thousands of others. Nakamura's initiation started with a period of increasing isolation, after which he attended a four-day induction ritual. Initiates wore robes and diapers, were sworn to secrecy and silence about their treatment, primed to think about their own deaths, and then given a drug believed to be LSD:

> Then actors came into the room, disguised as what Nakamura described as "terrible" and "peaceful" gods. They told the initiates that they were in hell

and challenged them to think about what they might have done to warrant such a predicament. Nakamura confessed to being frightened by the experience, but a woman who was a seasoned member of the movement was at his side, assuring him that if he continued to trust in Asahara, he would survive.[17]

This example shows how, after deliberately inducing threat, the leader, Asahara, was positioned as the only safe haven to whom to turn when fearful.

At perhaps the other end of the scale of possible threats, Juliet describes how in the Newman Tendency, in addition to the stress of exhaustion:

> Well you didn't get hurt physically but a tongue lashing was enough and you didn't want that – you didn't want a tongue lashing. . . . Our whole staff was getting our butts kicked because we're not organizing right, we're not raising enough funds, we're not working hard enough, we're not bringing in enough signatures required. One time I came in without my full quota of signatures and I got in trouble. . . . Yeah, they could be as nasty as anybody else in the world – believe me.

When I asked her if she had been frightened or worried during her time in the group she replied, "All the time. All the time, yeah." Along with her fears of harsh criticism she was also afraid the FBI had a file on her due to her membership in a group that conducted weapons training.

Sometimes fear or a sense of threat can be aroused simply by creating intense levels of stimulus and arousal through fatigue, noise, hunger or forcing people to review real or imagined traumas in their past.[ii] Creating a feeling of intense stress is one of the many functions of the sleep deprivation that is seen in nearly all totalist groups. Along with this stress, sleep deprivation also reduces the follower's cognitive resources and thus their ability to understand either the causes, or the effects, of the chronic exhaustion and other stressful conditions to which they have been subjected. Thus fear can be aroused either through provoking stress internally through conditions such as hunger, fatigue and so forth, or through creating a sense of fear of external threats, such as the apocalyptic scenarios Jim Ellison dreamed up.

Fear on its own is also not sufficient. We all experience fear – fear usually works to keep us safe. As a rule it is highly adaptive. When we experience fear we seek ways to escape it, to remove the cause of it, to resolve it in some way to ensure our survival. What happens in totalist groups (or for that matter in a variety of abusive, controlling relationships) is the inculcating of fear where the follower *cannot* resolve the threat. Where the follower is helpless to resolve the threat fear then becomes terror. Terror is the state that attachment scholars call "fright without solution,"[18] and it is the state that can produce post-traumatic stress disorder

---

ii See the old but excellent film: *Captive Minds: Hypnosis and Beyond* (Pierre Lasry, 1983), for examples of this.

(PTSD) in those who have experienced it. The preceding isolation and engulfment ensures that under threat the follower has nowhere to turn except to the source of threat itself: the leader or group. In this way fear under conditions of isolation becomes terror.

Remember, as Bowlby said, fear is not just about running away, but it is about running *to* someone for protection, or, in the case of cults or totalist systems, *to* the group.[19] And of course we can see, along with the deliberate inculcation of fear, the group positions itself as the supposed safe haven – even though *it is the group* itself creating the threat. This inculcation of fright without solution, of terror, creates a crisis in the follower. But after the crisis – created by the group – lo and behold! the group itself is there to save the terrified, broken person, to pick up the shattered pieces. Thus the group contains both the "hard cop" who terrifies and the "soft cop" who "comforts" and provides the only remaining safe haven. Nakamura is told to turn to the leader Asahara when frightened. For Jal, the army becomes his "mother and father." For Juliet and others in the Newman Tendency, the leader, social therapy sessions or the "friend" are in place to turn to when stressed or frightened.

Once in this state of terror or fright without solution, even small gestures on the part of the group begin to feel benevolent and caring, increasing the sense that it is the group that will protect one, the group who will save one from the threat. Miriam Williams was malnourished, ill and exhausted, and the Children of God group had convinced her of the dangers of the outside world – "the Systemites" – warned of the soon-to-come end-times and told her that her family were her "foes." She must, they instructed, love the Lord more than her worldly, flesh family. She broke down under the strain and cried for days. Finally one of the leaders came to her and arranged for her to call her mother. In her memoir she says: "This calculated act of apparent kindness probably kept me in the Children of God . . . pathetically, I was touched by their love and concern for me."[20] She continues, "The lessons they had been teaching me, such as to beware of natural inclinations, to rebuke the devil, and to seek godly counsel, became clearer."[21]

I, too, remember calculated acts of "apparent kindness." In her book *Trauma and Recovery*, Judith Herman insightfully refers to these as the "capricious granting of small indulgences."[22] In the confusion and unhappiness of the oppressive life within the closed world of the O., these acts were powerful. The momentary lifting of pressure resulted in feelings of gratitude as well as some guilt about my own often-rebellious behavior. But beyond that they made me feel as if the leader – who remained unknown to me – was, indeed, benevolent, perhaps even loving and tender. As in the Stockholm Syndrome, thus does the abuser become the perceived safe haven – a person or an entity to whom one can turn for help, mercy, forgiveness, comfort.

When the group creates a sense of fear and threat, the isolated and engulfed participant seeks out the group as a perceived safe haven for protection and comfort. But as the group itself is the source of threat, this is a failing strategy. This failed strategy results in, first, the creation of a strong emotional tie to the group, and second, the participant disorganizes cognitively with consequent confusion, dissociation, disorientation and cognitive lapses.[23]

Why is a strong emotional tie created through this cycle of threat and apparent, promised comfort (or what Zablocki calls a "cycle of assault and leniency"[24])? Let's look first at how the follower's feelings are disrupted by this process, and how the follower becomes attached to the leader and/or group. An attachment theory analysis helps to explain this.

The emotional power of a disorganized attachment bond

An attachment bond is defined as one to a specific other figure (not anyone will do) from whom loss or separation causes great distress. Attachment behavior is behavior that is activated on separation from the attachment figure, or when under stress or threat, and its goal is to regain closeness to that figure for the purpose of protection. As Coan puts it, such a bond is "characterized by a high frequency of close proximity to the putative 'attachment figure,' especially during times of emotional stress."[25] From an evolutionary point of view the purpose of attachment behavior is for the individual to seek protection from a variety of threats to survival. Ordinarily, organized forms of attachment behavior are functional and protective, promoting both engagement and autonomy.

Under normal circumstances attachment behavior operates as a homeostatic system, seesawing in a dynamic but self-balancing way between, on the one hand, comfort and protection-seeking behaviors and on the other, exploratory outward-moving behaviors. This is a balancing act between two systems: the arousal system and the comfort system. When a person's stress levels are aroused their levels of cortisol rise and they may engage in attachment behaviors and seek out an attachment figure, a safe haven (or, particularly in adults, this may occur even internally, just in their thought processes)[iii] to find comfort. Physiologically this comfort causes the production of cortisols to shut down and levels of endogenous opioids (opiates released internally in the body) to rise. We feel good and safe in our bodies when able to experience this comfort, or "felt security." But once the attachment behavior has achieved the goal of gaining this comfort – physically attaining an optimal level of endogenous opioids – then the attachment behavior is terminated.[26]

Feeling safe, and with his or her attachment behavior successfully terminated, the person can then return to exploratory, stimulating activities away from the attachment figure. At this point the attachment figure is providing a "secure base" from which to explore. This exploratory behavior involves the arousal system and

---

iii In fact, this process of "internalizing" one's attachment figures and the relationships with them is part of normal child development and is also ongoing throughout life. Bowlby refers to this as developing an "internal working model" of attachment, or an IWM. In the securely attached, this IWM can provide an internal sense of comfort and a safe haven during times of stress.

increased cortisol production along with shutting down the production of endogenous opioids. But when arousal levels get too high (when we experience too much excitement or stress) and the body produces too high a level of cortisols and, relatedly, opioids drop too low, then once again the person will engage in attachment behavior and seek the safe haven of their attachment figure in order to regain a sense of felt security. In this way they can regulate the level of arousal (cortisols) and bring back up their levels of comfort (opioids).

But, in the case of disorganized attachment the attachment behavior cannot be terminated in a normal way through satisfying the need for comfort and thus balancing cortisol production with opioids. In fact, approaching the fear-arousing attachment figure will instead cause a *further* increase in arousal and cortisol production rather than comfort. A positive feedback loop is created of increasing anxiety leading to increasing need for proximity to the attachment figure in the hope of attaining felt security. This, however, is never fully attained in order to terminate the attachment behavior. Cortisols stay at high and increasing levels, with increasing anxiety, and attempts to gain comfort through proximity also increase. Trying to simultaneously approach and avoid the fear-arousing attachment figure results in the attachment system remaining activated.

If other safe havens were available the person would be able to turn to them, turn away from the fear-arousing figure and resolve the fear and gain comfort elsewhere, thus regulating their arousal levels. Allowing other, mitigating attachment relationships – which I call escape hatch attachments – would therefore defeat this disorganizing mechanism by providing comfort elsewhere and thus attenuate the group member's state of hyperarousal. The structure of totalist isolation prevents alternate attachments, thus setting in place a feedback loop of unresolvable anxiety and need for proximity.

In isolation and the absence of any alternate trusted attachment figures, the participant remains in a state of hyperarousal, constantly seeking comfort from the only available source, and never fully achieving it. Similar to victims of domestic violence,[27] the attachment figure thus acts as a safe haven (promising protection and comfort), but not as a secure base (completing the act of protection and comfort, and thus enabling further outwards exploration). It is this process of unresolved fear arousal – chronic anxiety and hyperarousal of cortisols – that causes the strengthening of the bond to the group.

The "apparent acts of kindness" described earlier help maintain the positive feedback loop by holding out the promise of (never-to-be-attained) comfort like a carrot in front of the hyperaroused follower. This keeps alive the image of the group as safe haven, while never providing the reliable comfort and resulting adequate levels of opioids in the body. In attachment and physiological terms, the brief lifting of pressure gives a momentary experience of comfort, a fleeting infusion of opioids, only to be followed swiftly by the physiological reminder of threat and stress caused by the leader or group in the form of hyperarousal and overproduction of cortisols. The follower's gratitude, then, is an emotional, physiological response to the temporary lifting of pressure, not a carefully considered cognitive evaluation.

The result of this process, in many cases, is that an attachment bond to the attachment figure – in this case the group – is formed. So the group becomes the new, and only, attachment figure available to the follower. The attachment bond is, by its nature, a strong one: remember, an attachment bond is characterized by extreme distress on loss and by attachment to a specific other – this *particular* person, leader or group, and no other. We see then a paradoxical effect where disorganized attachment results in diminished relatedness to others and diminished autonomy.[28]

Although there are the two simultaneously active and competing systems of approach and avoidance in disorganized attachment, Main and Solomon found that in disorganized babies the preference is for approach, for physical proximity with the fearful figure, and this preference for proximity tends to override avoidance of that frightening figure.[29] Whether this is also the case with adults is unclear, but certainly this seems to take place with those who experience life in a totalist group or nation. Unless there is an alternate safe haven available, avoidance or leaving the group usually appears to the follower as the riskier option, and the thought of leaving feels even more terrifying than staying.

This is why inducing a relationship of disorganized attachment makes it so difficult for people in such a relationship to leave, to escape. This disorganization resulting in unterminated attachment behaviors is the emotional glue that sticks people – not irrevocably, but certainly strongly – to a damaging and controlling relationship. In fact I suggest that this is the primary mechanism trapping people in these dangerous relationships – it is a physiological and psychological lock that is created with the disruption of a more functional homeostasis of opioids and cortisols, of comfort and exploration.

To create this locking effect, the totalist leader *must* remove or detach competing attachment figures, potential escape hatch safe havens. In the next chapter we will look at the wide variety of ways in which totalist groups achieve this, replacing close attachments with a dense network of "replaceable others" – replaceable, that is, except for the leader, who is represented as the only true safe haven.

The effect of disorganized attachment on cognition

Disorganized attachment to the source of threat affects followers' thinking, their cognitive abilities that might otherwise help them in finding their way out. When first experiencing threat or stress a person may attempt to engage in either fight or flight to escape the fear. But when unable to escape – as in the situation of "fright without solution" characteristic of a relationship of disorganized attachment – then, in order to conserve resources in an attempt to ensure survival, a person may engage in a passive, freeze response – a state of "metabolic shutdown" that is "detachment from an unbearable situation," "the escape where there is no escape."[30] In this state, both the arousal systems and comfort systems are hyperactivated – that is, again, the individual is seeking to both approach and flee from the source of threat. Unless some way out of the fear-inducing situation is found, this state of unresolved hyperarousal leads eventually to dissociation. Perry describes the process in this way:

> The arousal continuum starts with being calm, then showing increased levels of vigilance, progressing through anxiety and distress to fear, with terror being the most extreme. If adults or children sense a life threatening danger (real or perceived) from which they are unable to defend themselves and from which they have no hope of being rescued, they will experience psychological trauma, the degree depending on their level of distress.[31]

This psychological trauma – resulting in dissociation – can engender a passive "defeat" or learned helplessness response where the person disengages from the external world. In studies of disorganized infants, the result of this type of chronic relational-induced trauma "is a progressive impairment of the ability to adjust, take defensive action, or act on one's own behalf, and blocking of the capacity to register affect and pain, all critical to survival."[32]

Of course, members of totalist groups are not infants, and may not have had a history of disorganized attachment (I believe most will not have). But they do share this experience of chronic relational-induced trauma and the consequent cognitive paralysis and inability to advocate for their own survival. That is, in the situation of unresolvable fear – terror – most people will freeze, dissociate, engaging in "psychological flight," a way of "playing dead" as a kind of last ditch effort to survive by conserving metabolic resources. But there are extreme and serious costs to this and these costs are paid by the brain: in loss of cognitive function and in the long-term effects, even after the terrifying situation has come to an end, effects that we know as complex PTSD.[33]

Let's now briefly put the brain back into brainwashing. Current neuroscience research has given us a good idea of what is happening in the brain during the dissociation experienced in psychological trauma.

The brain is divided vertically into three areas: the brainstem region, the limbic area and the cortex. The brainstem evolved first and communicates directly with the body, receiving sensory inputs and regulating instinctual behaviors and such things as our heart rate and respiration. The limbic area, which evolved after the brainstem, includes the amygdala and hippocampus. It regulates emotions and hormonal activity, such as the production of the "stress hormone" cortisol. And it forms part of the system of creating "implicit" memory – that is, memories of feelings, learned behaviors, habits, reflexive actions and skills such as, for example, riding a bicycle. The brainstem and limbic areas function together in the fight/flight/freeze response to threat. The cortex evolved last and takes these very basic survival signals and functions and makes much more complex meaning-making and functioning possible. "Explicit" memory – such as memories that can consciously be brought into mind such as facts, or, for example, remembering an appointment or recalling a poem – is stored here.

As most of us know, the brain is also divided into two hemispheres, the right and the left. The right brain is the "older" area, in evolutionary terms. The right brain develops earlier in children, and is more directly connected to the older limbic region, and therefore to emotional processing, to implicit memory and to the physiological fight/flight/freeze responses. The right brain is involved in more holistic, image-based thinking, is non-verbal, and is the location of autobiographical memory and of unmediated emotional responses. The left brain, which develops later both evolutionarily speaking and in children, is more analytical and is the seat of logic, language and linear thinking. It is more closely linked to explicit memory. As Siegel says:

> The right hemisphere is more directly connected to the subcortical areas of the brain. Information flows from body to brain-stem to limbic areas to right cortex. The left hemisphere is more removed from these raw subcortical sources – from our physical sensations, our brainstem survival reactions, and our limbic feelings and attachments. . . . Normal life weaves these right-dominant activities into the equally important, but different, left-dominant information flow.[34]

This weaving together of the left and right sides of the brain takes place during REM sleep, and during conversation with others, or with oneself when engaging in internal dialog, and during other collaborative, language-based communication such as telling stories. This creates what Siegel calls bilateral, or horizontal, integration.

Importantly for our understanding of what happens in dissociation (and thereby disorganized attachment, which is a relational cause of dissociation), one of the key parts of the brain that connects these two halves is the *orbitofrontal cortex*. The orbitofrontal cortex sits at the top of the limbic area and is known as the "thinking part of the emotional brain." It has an "executive control function for the entire right brain, the locus of the emotional self."[35] This part of the brain performs a vital connecting function between the right and left sides of the brain, and thus between the raw feelings and emotions of the "older" part of the brain with the later developing conscious reasoning and logical left part of the brain. The orbitofrontal cortex helps us be aware of our feelings and to consciously decide how to act on them. In times of stress it helps regulate our feelings and links our emotional response through to the conscious and reasoning left brain to decide how to act. It is "a master regulator for organization of the brain's response to threat"[36] and so is critical in the organization of responses to social situations and, importantly, situations threatening survival. When working effectively it contributes to "judicious, adapted behavior."[37] The orbitofrontal cortex is also involved in a person's ability to experience empathy.[38]

Dissociation is seen primarily as a dysfunction of the right brain and, in particular, of the integrating function – integration of the "feeling" right brain with the "thinking" left – of the orbitofrontal cortex. The dissociation caused by the terrifying, disorganizing relationship means that emotions, especially those connected to that social and threatening relationship, remain unprocessed, unable to be thought about in conscious, reasoned and "judicious" ways.[39]

Thus disorganized, or traumatic, attachment is a form of chronic trauma that causes a failure of the orbitofrontal cortex to function as the "master regulator" responding to threat. This failure means that the individual is unable then to interpret and act on signals from the body and from the external world in order to marshal an appropriate response to a "social situation, or situations involving survival."[40] Instead of integrating the sensory signals that are perceived through the lower levels of the right brain, and thus allowing these signals to be thought about by this "thinking part of the emotional brain" and then acted upon in ways that increase chances for survival, a passive, dissociated response takes over which conserves the person's resources. This dissociated response fails to integrate consciousness, identity, memory and perception.[41]

A lack of functioning of the orbitofrontal cortex and related brain structures (such as the language-producing Broca's area[iv] and the hippocampus) is seen in persons with PTSD and other dissociative disorders, and in those whose early development was marked by disorganized attachment. The physical development of the right brain bears the scars of chronic relational trauma; the right brain and, in particular, the orbitofrontal cortex, suffer adverse consequences of experiencing ongoing terror.[42] This is relevant for those born and/or raised in totalist systems. But it is also relevant for those recruited into such systems as adults, regardless of their earlier attachment experiences.[v] Given that the brain remains malleable throughout life, adult-onset disorganized attachment also causes changes and loss of function in this area. The symptoms of dissociation involve "numbing, avoidance, compliance and restricted affect."[43] All of these can be seen in followers traumatized by totalist groups. Further, followers often show a (group-enforced) lack of empathy to others (to put it mildly), both inside and outside of their groups. The group-induced isolation from both self and others discussed earlier is also reinforced by the dissociative state: "dissociatively-detached individuals are not only detached from the

---

iv Trauma scholars have shown that when reading narratives of their traumas back to PTSD sufferers, the amygdala and related areas (implicit memory storage) were activated in PET scans, as well as the right visual cortex – reflecting the visual reexperiencing of their traumas. The Broca's area – which is the area where experience is processed by language – was "turned off." "We believe that this reflects the tendency in PTSD to experience emotions as physical states rather than as verbally encoded experiences. Our findings suggest that PTSD patients' difficulties with putting feelings into words are mirrored in actual changes in brain activity," van der Kolk, Bessel A. 1996. "The Body Keeps the Score: Approaches to the Psychobiology of Posttraumatic Stress Disorder," in *Traumatic Stress: The Effects of Overwhelming Experience on Mind, Body, and Society*, edited by B.A. van der Kolk, A.C. McFarlane and L. Weisaeth. New York: Guilford Press, pp. 214–241.

v Once again I need to reiterate that, although a person's early attachment experiences may make them more vulnerable to later poor attachments, early secure attachment does not offer blanket protection against later problems. Similarly, just because a person had early secure attachment, this does not make them immune to cult recruitment, or to compliance within a totalist system. Observers often fall victim to the "fundamental attribution error" that, in short, states that a person's behavior can be largely explained by their internal disposition or personality, and fails to take note of the situational factors facing that person. This is the source of the comment made by many observers that "this could never happen to me," a dangerous assumption.

environment, but also from the self – their body, their own actions, and their sense of identity."[44] However, the very fact that the brain does remain malleable throughout life also gives hope for those who leave totalist systems. Later secure attachments can provide the context in which it can become possible to regain both emotional and cognitive balance and function, although, granted, not without some losses and costs.

Dissociation, the lack of integrative function of the orbitofrontal cortex, explains the inability of followers to comprehend and to act on the source of the threat – namely, the group. In this passive, frozen and dissociated state, with the inability to process and evaluate the fear-arousing stimuli coming from the group's own actions, a gulf of attribution is opened up. The follower cannot interpret what is going on. They cannot accurately attribute cause and effect. If the group can succeed in disorganizing the individual, resulting in dissociation, they can then control that person's interpretations of his or her feelings. Now the group can seize hold of the follower, offering up an opportunistic interpretation to substitute for the follower's own lack of evaluative function, and consolidate the follower as a deployable resource. In other words: listen to the group, they will tell you what the trouble is. Unable to interpret the meaning of events? Don't worry, the group will do it for you. Follow what they say, that will show a way out of the terror. Commit even more fully and all shall be well.

Outsiders are often confounded and confused when observing followers and the numbed, restricted emotions, inability to protect their own survival and lack of empathy that they demonstrate. Observers can also be confused by the inappropriate or rigid emotions of members of cults or totalitarian states. Which emotion is presented depends on the demands of the group. In many religious cults, followers may present a "happy face" that masks the dissociation and terror that followers are not able to act on, nor perhaps even be aware that they are feeling.[45] Or, as in the group I was in, a serious, committed and studious expression was deemed suitable for our task of building the revolution.

It can also be confusing to observers – and for that matter, to former members trying to understand their experience – that brainwashed followers who seem so unable to understand the damaging nature of their commitment, who appear so "stupid" in that domain, are often able to be highly competent in other areas. This makes sense, however, if we understand brainwashing as dissociation caused by a disorganized relationship with a particular attachment figure. It is not a global dissociation. It is specific and targeted to the group, its leader and relationships controlled by the group. The left brain, for example, can continue to be highly functional – as long as it is not having to rely on messages from the orbitofrontal cortex regarding the interpretation of emotional signals to do with the situation of "fright without solution" established by the disorganizing group relationship.

In my own case I functioned at a high level during my cult tenure as, first, a fairly skilled machinist, and then a senior computer analyst. My intellectual capacities were, in fact, a resource that the cult sought to deploy (as it did with all the cult members). A cult certainly has no use for the unproductive! My left brain carried on learning and refining new skills, and in fact had a great capacity to do so under intense time pressure, lack of rest and all the other stresses of cult life. But ask me to think about the O. or some of the glaring contradictions related to my experience in the group and I simply couldn't. I remember well, for example, a former member contacting my husband and I and telling us that the O. was a "cult of personality." We forwarded his letter to the leadership, as a helpful warning that this person was a "security risk." It was only years later, when I was finally on my way out, that I remembered, and could begin to think about this communication. At the time I simply could not approach the thought.

The dissociation of disorganized attachment means one cannot enter into the process of thinking about such things, and critical thinking is kept out of consciousness – but, again, *not globally, but in relation to the group*. Followers literally can't think their way out of the problem. If they should try to think about the group, the terror associated with it causes dissociation and the shutting down of the orbitofrontal cortex, the "master regulator" of the brain's response to threat, which normally would allow the left brain to assess and act upon the fear experienced by the right brain. Thinking about the source of threat itself becomes terrifying with no way to logically work out the cause of the fear. And in fact the follower may not even be able to recognize that they are feeling afraid or stressed – the physical arousal of feelings of threat may be attributed to any number of causes. Followers may be able to think about other things quite clearly, but not about the traumatizing, disorganizing and dissociating relationship.

Controlling and deploying the disorganized follower

Now you have a person who is locked into an attachment relationship with the group and who cannot think clearly. The follower's cognitive deficit is handily filled by the group's ideology, which offers a path out of the confusion: "Don't worry, we will do your thinking for you." Here is where the control of information and the indoctrination (rather than the earlier, and more public, propaganda) component of the ideology become important – the organization's ideas will explain everything to you. As Fred Newman, the charismatic, authoritarian leader of the Newman Tendency wrote:

> The social therapeutic approach tries to teach people how to think as creators and transformers of everything that there is and all there is – in other words, as makers of history.[46]

Newman promises to explain everything to his followers, covering "the seamless historical totality that has no beginning, middle or end, no starting point."[47] This becomes the basis for his control of, in fact, everything in their lives from providing sexual favors and free labor to accepting mandatory breakups from loved partners and forced abortions.

The follower accepts (or is forced to accept) these more extreme, and often incoherent, ideas as a kind of lifeline through the dissociated confusion that the group has induced. With neither an emotional nor a cognitive escape hatch, they cling on both to the group, as the only safe haven, and to the ideas presented by the group as an island of (seeming) logicality in their sea of confusion. But this very clinging deepens and consolidates their dependency. The ideology insists that everyone "out there" "in the world" is evil, has the wrong line, or is in some way destructive to the cause, so the follower searches less and less for alternative relationships, internalizes the ideology and promulgates it.

Having first created an attachment deficit – providing the illusion of a safe haven but no secure base from which to autonomously explore and operate – and second having created a cognitive deficit, now the group can exercise the third and final element of this process: that is, to deploy the follower in the interests of the leader. With the group providing alternative explanations – as part of the indoctrination – for whatever the follower is experiencing, they now can be told what to do. But human beings are complex and layered. So this still has to be managed carefully. The group must be sure that the follower is ready for a given task. A skilled cult leader will know who can be called upon to do what, when.

In my own group, shortly before I joined (and unknown to me until my departure ten years later), the leader, Theo Smith, had killed a man. Smith fled the state and Debbie,[vi] one of the group's lieutenants, helped him run from the crime and enter an underground existence that lasted for several years. I later came into possession of a box of evidence to do with the killing that Debbie had saved. There are several notes she had written detailing a version of the events that apparently the leader had dictated to her immediately after, explaining away his actions. Along with these is a poignant note of her own where her dissociation and confusion is evident as she puts herself at risk for abetting this fatal crime. She writes: *I get clarity when it's put out, explained, but don't sustain it when get in the real conditions.*[48] She is unable to think clearly about what has happened. She is trying to find a way to accept the story she's been given, to work out her role: *I get clarity when it's put out . . .* An intelligent woman, Debbie struggles with her doubts – she is having trouble "sustaining" her "clarity." But the leader, Smith, has successfully created a dependency, derailing her ability to think about him and what he is capable of, and in that vacuum she can be deployed to save his skin by putting her own at risk.

In a more terrible example, Arn Chorn Pond, a child soldier in Pol Pot's murderous regime in Cambodia in the 1970s, was forced to participate in the mass killings that eventually took the lives of one-quarter of the population. Like Emmanuel Jal in the SPLA, Chorn Pond had no choice as a child but to obey the army leaders with whom he lived. Pol Pot eradicated all traces of family life under his regime, at the same time as declaring that all should call him Brother Number One. The only loyalty allowed was to him, and to Angkar or "the Organization" that now controlled the country. "Every day I had to kill my own heart in order to endure," says Chorn Pond. As he relates this part of his life, in the moving film *The Flute*

vi Not her real name.

Player,[49] his ongoing dissociation, the long-term after-effects, which we know as PTSD, become apparent. He stands alone in the killing fields, by a tree against which babies were battered to death. He cannot finish his sentences; his previously articulate speech collapses as he is thrown back decades to that moment. As a survivor, Arn Chorn Pond has shown himself to be the most empathetic, generous, loving and articulate of people – and he has had to come to terms with the horror he witnessed, caused and survived. He has done this through speaking about it, through working with other refugees and now through bringing back the traditional music to Cambodia – the music that Pol Pot banned during the Khmer Rouge regime. Yet still, years later, he can be thrown back into dissociation induced by the isolation, engulfment and terror of his previous life as a child soldier. His right-brain memories overwhelm his left-brain ability to speak as he tries to explain this history – the ongoing effect of that early "escape where there is no escape" into dissociation between the thinking and feeling sides of his brain.

In 1996 I interviewed several mothers from cults and gathered their stories of how the cults had abused their children and controlled the mothers' relationships with them. This control of the mother-child bond, generally seen as the strongest attachment bond one can have, shows the power of successfully disorganizing the follower and creating emotional and cognitive dependency on the leader leading to deployability. Jill was in a cult that blended fundamentalist Mormon teaching with Native American rituals. The group lived in a remote and primitive encampment in a Midwestern state, supposedly "to escape the Russians." While in the group Jill had two children with another follower. At one point the leader took her baby away, giving the child to another couple. Jill told me how she felt when this happened:

> I thought, I don't want to do this, but I will if that's what's *best*, if that's God's will. The leader took the place of God so I thought he'd only do what was best. To me, I needed Chrissie, but he said otherwise.[50]

Despite her unwillingness, Jill allowed this wresting away of her child. The other couple finally returned the child after six months, delivering her back in a wheelbarrow.

As a teenager, Helen joined a bible-based group led by a man from India, who, like Pol Pot, was known as "Brother." At 20 years old she was in an arranged marriage with a man in the group and had her first child. The leader forbade birth control and by the time she left, ten years later, she had seven children. Helen recounted this incident:

> Once when my twins were less than a year old and they were holding onto the hem of my skirt – it was in front of a whole group of people – Brother told me over and over to kick them away, and first I just wiggled, but he insisted that I kick them away and so, finally, I did. Even though it violated my sense of Mother, of Human Being, of the notion of loving the Lord.[51]

Her children suffered considerable physical abuse during their tenure in the group: "Brother said it was the Holy Way. He took so many liberties with my children and told me to consider it an honor."

Both these mothers eventually escaped the cults they were involved in and proceeded to develop positive and caring relationships with their children – in other words, neither of them had an internal, or dispositional, problem as mothers. It was in the context of being coerced through brainwashing within a cultic environment that caused them to be deployable – to uncritically follow the orders of the leader – and thus become unable to protect their children adequately, and to act in their own or their children's survival interests.

In all these examples there is still a struggle – people try to resolve what they feel is wrong. But under the constraints of isolation, engulfment and terror, they are unable to maintain their sense of right and to effectively resist. Many do try, but even those who are able to resist initially may end up just as deployable as those who enter more easily into the process. The fact that a person may attempt to resist is not what is key. What counts is whether those attempts are successfully overcome. What counts is whether the person finally breaks, the moment of eventual surrender – that inability, finally, to hold on to their own relationships and their own thought processes about what is happening. Totalist leaders are experts at moving people through their attempts at resistance – if they were not they would have no followers.

So here is where we see the core mechanism at work. Once that break or surrender has occurred, where the isolated follower's thought processes are dissociated and the group's reasoning becomes accepted, the indoctrination has been successful. But this situation must be maintained: the totalist leader must keep at bay any escape hatch relationships that might provide comfort leading to a subsequent termination of attachment behaviors and a return to exploration and autonomy. The leader must control, contain and confine any spaces in which followers might reorganize their thoughts. This is consolidated and institutionalized in rules, rituals and norms that determine what it is to be a good soldier, a good group member, pure, righteous, on the side of the poor, of Jesus, of Allah, of the True Race or of whatever the cause may be. People are not robots or Manchurian Candidates[vii] who can be sent off as sleeper agents and deployed remotely years later. One way or another they must be kept in the isolated and terrorized state – their dissociation must be maintained.

The way out: Fright with solution

Brainwashing is not a foolproof process. People do get out in different ways and at different points depending both on their own internal resources and experiences,

---

vii *The Manchurian Candidate* was a 1959 novel by Richard Condon about a prisoner of war who was brainwashed by Communists to become a political assassin.

and on the situations they encounter. Although some people do eventually just think their way out of the totalist system, it is much more likely that an alternate, escape hatch attachment relationship is the key to breaking free. If there is such a relationship available, then that allows a resolution to the state of terror, of "fright without solution," and a consequent reintegration of thought processes.

Shin Dong-hyuk was born and grew up in a concentration camp – Camp 14 – within the totalist state of North Korea. At the age of 13, starving and having been systematically separated, both emotionally and physically, from his family, he informed on his mother and brother's escape plans, hoping for extra food as a reward. His mother and brother were arrested and executed, and Shin, instead of being rewarded, was imprisoned and tortured in yet another, deeper layer of North Korea's punishment system. It was in this prison within the concentration camp that he had his "first exposure to sustained kindness" thanks to the care of his cell-mate, a middle-aged man who asked Shin to call him "Uncle." Uncle nursed Shin's wounds, shared his food and told him stories. In a short time he became closer to Uncle than he had ever been to his own parents. This relationship "lifted, if only slightly, a curtain on the world beyond the fence."[52] Later another friendship with an older cellmate in another prison led to his eventual escape from the prison and across the border. These close relationships allowed him to begin to understand and to act on his situation – while those with his own family had been so utterly detached and steeped in deprivation that he saw his betrayal of them only in terms of an extra portion of food. It was only in the later relationships where attachment, protection and care developed, that he could begin to understand Camp 14, not as the whole world, but as a cage that, in order to survive, he needed to escape.

In order for the follower to think clearly about the totalist relationship, an escape from the chronic terror is needed. And that escape can most readily take place with an alternate attachment relationship. Other ways out are possible – some finally give in to exhaustion and see the repetition of failed promises, but this is usually only after many, many years. For some, being temporarily out of reach of the group and in touch with caring others – even if not close attachment figures – allows clear thinking about the relationship.

When we experience high levels of fear arousal we tend to prefer to seek comfort from attachment figures rather than just thinking about how to cope with the fear-arousing situation. As Smith and Stevens have noted: "there appears on average to be an innate advantage in preferring attachment over cognition for managing anxiety."[53] This preference is because physiologically the arousal of anxiety is regulated more quickly through the "lower" limbic and brainstem regions than through the "higher" cortex regions managing cognitive functions. As we grow older most of us develop cognitive approaches based in our memories and internal representations of attachment figures (Bowlby's internal working models)[54] that enable us to self-comfort. But these cognitively based methods operate less quickly and efficiently than the direct presence of an attachment figure. Attachment to a (more or less) secure other is thus a more effective means of regulating arousal and so in more extreme conditions of anxiety and cortisol arousal, we will often seek out our actual attachment relationships for comfort. Once that comfort has been attained, then the cognitive functions can kick in and the dissociated person can begin the process of reintegrating their thought process: the emotional with the cognitive. I suggest, therefore, that an alternate close relationship that is not disorganizing is therefore the principal means of breaking out of dissociation.

Attachment theory provides the link between social relationships and the brain. The brain *is* affected in brainwashing. The combination of isolation, engulfment by a frightening "safe haven" and the resulting "fright without solution" means that the functioning of the orbitofrontal cortex is deactivated: washed out, paralyzed by chronic trauma and dissociation. In thus separating or dissociating the feeling from the thinking side of the brain, these disconnected realms can now be colonized by the totalist leader for his or her own purposes.

The totalist system creates a dissociated follower with a disorganized attachment to the group, their attachment needs stimulated but not satisfied by the group. The result is a deployable follower whose skills, resources and time can be used to suit the purposes of the leader. The rigid boundaries of the engulfing group maintain the isolation of the follower. The total or absolute ideology supports and justifies the position of the leader and the closed nature of the structure of the group. The ideology provides explanations for the follower's distress and reasons to act on the group's orders. Processes of brainwashing rest on the creation of stress or threat with no escape other than to the apparent (un)safe haven of the group. This results in a state of terror that causes a dissociative state resulting from a disorganized bond to the leader, or group as proxy. The hyperobedient and hypercredulous[55] deployable follower existing in this airless world gripped by an iron band of terror can be asked to engage in acts they would not have previously done, nor, once out of the group, would they do in the future.

I remember when I was in the O. and an FBI agent came to the door, looking for the leader, who was unknown to me. I refused to let him in or to talk to him. "You'd talk to me if you knew there'd been a murder in this house!" he'd shouted through the door I had just closed on him. I stood on the other side. Though I believed abstractly that sometimes violence was needed in self-defense or for the oppressed to achieve freedom over despots, in reality I abhorred and feared violence of all kinds. But my critical mind was by then totally disengaged. I would never believe the word of an FBI agent – and particularly not when it came to the Organization. I remember to this day the feeling of hearing the words and pushing them away. It was like pushing a hot pan to the back burner of the stove. It was an almost physical feeling of pushing the thought back: No, I cannot think about that. In this way I neutralized the thought. Then I contacted my superior in the O., reported the incident and later, obeyed the various instructions I received to clear the house of any O. materials. Still I did not think there could be any connection of the O. to this crime. Literally, *I did not think*. I obeyed efficiently. But I could not let the information come to the "front" of my mind for examination or evaluation. Isolation, engulfment in the O., exhaustion, stress and fear had effectively caused me to dissociate, to be unable to think about the O. critically, to deactivate the judicious reasoning of my very own orbitofrontal cortex. I would instead simply do as I was told, and do it to the best of my ability.

After the London Tube bombings in 2005, Anne Singleton spoke about her earlier experience in a political cult she had been recruited to while at Manchester University. She had cut off her parents and her friends, and burned all her diaries, as ordered by the Mojahedin-e-Khalq, known as the Iranian Mojahedin. She became a full-time member of the group, breaking off with her boyfriend (who had introduced her to the group in the first place) in the process. She became fully immersed in the group, undergoing isolation from her previous life and engulfment in the new.

> I didn't question anything. I was shown a film of a female suicide bomber blowing up an ayatollah in Iran. It was horrific, and very shocking, at first, but I was shown the film many times, and each time I was less distressed. Eventually, I didn't bat an eyelid . . . If the leader had said 'kill yourself', I would have killed myself.

Later she was sent to their camp in Iraq for military training. There she surrendered her passport to the group: "You have no human rights, no nationality, you are simply a Mujahed." She went on:

> Psychological manipulation can happen to anyone, any time. If you're lucky, you end up with a timeshare. If you're unlucky you end up blowing yourself and innocent people up on the Tube.[56]

As Jill said, when she gave up her small child: "I don't want to do this, but I will if that's what's *best*, if that's God's will."[57]

Notes

1 Arendt, Hannah. 1994. *Essays in Understanding: 1930–1954 Hannah Arendt.* New York: Harcourt, Brace & Co, p. 356.
2 Jal, Emmanuel. 2009. *War Child: A Boy Soldier's Story.* London: Abacus, p. 80.
3 Ibid., p. 94.
4 Williams, Miriam. 1998. *Heaven's Harlots: My Fifteen Years as a Sacred Prostitute in the Children of God Cult.* New York: William Morrow, p. 36.
5 Ibid., p. 44.
6 Lalich, Janja. 2004. *Bounded Choice: True Believers and Charismatic Cults.* Berkeley: University of California Press.
7 Intellectual Reserve Inc. 2006. *Missionary Handbook.* The Church of Jesus Christ of Latter-day Saints, Salt Lake City, p. 30. Retrieved January 28, 2013. (https://missionary.lds.org/missionary/Missionary%20Handbook.pdf).
8 Doug Agustin, personal communication.
9 Lalich, *Bounded Choice: True Believers and Charismatic Cults.*
10 Durkheim, Emile. 2001. *The Elementary Forms of Religious Life.* Oxford: Oxford University Press.
11 Hill, Jenna Miscavige and Lisa Pulitzer. 2013. *Beyond Belief: My Secret Life Inside Scientology and My Harrowing Escape.* New York: William Morrow.

12 Childs, Joe and Thomas C. Tobin. 2011. "Scientology Couple Who Gave $1.3 Million: Church Mission 'has been Corrupted.'" *Tampa Bay.* (http://www.tampabay.com/news/scientology/scientology-couple-who-gave-13-million-church-mission-has-been-corrupted/1201187).

13 Arendt, Hannah. 1948/1979a. *The Origins of Totalitarianism.* Orlando: Harcourt Brace, p. 342.

14 Arendt, Hannah. 1955/1968. *Men in Dark Times.* New York: Harcourt, Brace & World, p. 10.

15 Stern, Jessica. 2003. *Terror in the Name of God: Why Religious Militants Kill.* New York: Ecco, p. 21.

16 Jal, *War Child.*

17 Jurgensmeyer, Mark. 2000. *Terror in the Mind of God: The Global Rise of Religious Violence.* Berkeley: University of California Press, p. 109.

18 Main, M. 1999. "Second-generation Effects of Unresolved Trauma in Nonmaltreating Parents: Dissociated, Frightened, and Threatening Parental Behavior." *Psychoanalytic Inquiry* 19(4):481–540, p. 484.

19 Hesse, Erik and Mary Main. 2000. "Disorganized Infant, Child, and Adult Attachment: Collapse in Behavioral and Attentional Strategies." *Journal of the American Psychoanalytic Association* 48:1097–127.

20 Williams, *Heaven's Harlots*, p. 43.

21 Ibid., p. 44.

22 Herman, Judith. 1992. *Trauma and Recovery.* New York: Basic Books, p. 82.

23 George, C., N. Kaplan and M. Main. 1996. *Adult Attachment Interview Protocol*, 3rd Ed. Unpublished manuscript, Berkeley: University of California.

24 Zablocki, Benjamin D. 2001. "Toward a Demystified and Disinterested Scientific Concept of Brainwashing," in *Misunderstanding Cults: Searching for Objectivity in a Controversial Field*, edited by B.D. Zablocki and T. Robbins. Toronto: University of Toronto Press, pp. 159–214.

25 Coan, James A. 2008. "Toward a Neuroscience of Attachment," in *Handbook of Attachment: Theory, Research, and Clinical Applications 2*, edited by J. Cassidy and P. Shaver. New York: Guilford Press, pp. 241–65.

26 Bowlby, John. 1973. *Attachment and Loss, Separation*, Vol. 2. New York: Basic Books; Bowlby, John. 1980. *Attachment and Loss, Loss*, Vol. 3. New York: Basic Books; Bowlby, John. 1982. *Attachment and Loss, Attachment*, Vol. 1. New York: Basic Books; Smith, Thomas S. and Gregory T. Stevens. 1999. "The Architecture of Small Networks: Strong Interaction and Dynamic Organization in Small Social Systems." *American Sociological Review* 64:403–20.

27 Lyons-Ruth, K. and D. Jacobvitz. 1999. "Attachment Disorganization: Unresolved Loss, Relational Violence, and Lapses in Behavioral and Attentional Strategies," in *Handbook of Attachment: Theory, Research and Clinical Applications*, edited by J. Cassidy and P. Shaver. New York: Guilford Press, pp. 520–584.

28 Main, Mary and Judith Solomon. 1986. "Discovery of an Insecure-Disorganized/Disoriented Attachment Pattern," in *Affective Development in Infancy*, edited by T.B. Brazelton and M.W. Yogman. Norwood, NJ: Ablex Publishing, p. 117.

29 Ibid.

30 Schore, Allan N. 2002. "Dysregulation of the Right Brain: A Fundamental Mechanism of Traumatic Attachment and the Psychopathogenesis of Posttraumatic Stress Disorder." *Australian and New Zealand Journal of Psychiatry* 36:9–30, 23.

31 Perry, B., 2000 in Bowlby, Richard. 2007. "Babies and Toddlers in Non-Parental Daycare Can Avoid Stress and Anxiety If They Develop a Lasting Secondary Attachment Bond with One Carer Who Is Consistently Accessible to Them." *Attachment & Human Development* 9:307–19.

32 Schore, "Dysregulation of the Right Brain: A Fundamental Mechanism of Traumatic Attachment and the Psychopathogenesis of Posttraumatic Stress Disorder."

33 Herman, *Trauma and Recovery.*

34 Siegel, Daniel J. 2010. *Mindsight: Transform Your Brain with the New Science of Kindness.* Oxford: Oneworld publications, p. 107.

35 Schore, "Dysregulation of the Right Brain," p. 14.

36 Scarr in ibid., p. 20.

37 Cavada, et al., in ibid., p. 15.

38 Decety, Jean and Philip L. Jackson. 2004. "The Functional Architecture of Human Empathy." *Behavioral and Cognitive Neuroscience Reviews* 3:71–100.

39 Schore, Allan N. 2009. "Attachment Trauma and the Developing Right Brain: Origins of Pathological Dissociation, " in *Dissociation and the Dissociative Disorders: DSM-V and Beyond*, edited by P.F. Dell and J.A. O'Neil. New York: Routledge, pp. 107–41.

40 Lipton et al., 1999 in Schore, Allan N. 2002. "Dysregulation of the Right Brain: A Fundamental Mechanism of Traumatic Attachment and the Psychopathogenesis of Posttraumatic Stress Disorder." *Australian and New Zealand Journal of Psychiatry* 36:9–30, 15.

41 Schore, "Attachment Trauma and the Developing Right Brain: Origins of Pathological Dissociation."

42 Ibid.

43 Ibid., p. 111.

44 Allen et al., 1999 in ibid., p. 117.

45 Steve Hassan in BBC. 2013. "London Slavery Case: Suspects 'Former Maoist Activists'." BBC News London. Retrieved December 18, 2013 (http://www.bbc.co.uk/news/uk-england-london-25084830).

46 Newman, Fred and Phyllis Goldberg. 1994. *Let's Develop!* New York: Castillo International, Inc, p. 236.

47 Ibid., p. 234.

48 Stein, Alexandra. 2002. *Inside Out: A Memoir of Entering and Breaking out of a Minneapolis Political Cult.* St. Cloud: North Star Press of St. Cloud.

49 Glatzer, Jocelyn. 2003. *The Flute Player.* PBS.

50 Stein, Alexandra. 1997a. "Mothers in Cults: The Influence of Cults on the Relationship of Mothers to Their Children." *Cultic Studies Journal* 14(1):40–57, 47.

51 Ibid., p. 47.

52 Harden, Blaine. 2012. *Escape from Camp 14.* London: Mantle, p. 84.

53 Smith, Thomas S. and Gregory T. Stevens. 1999. "The Architecture of Small Networks: Strong Interaction and Dynamic Organization in Small Social Systems." *American Sociological Review* 64:403–20, 110.

54 Bowlby, John. 1982a. *Attachment and Loss, Attachment.*, Vol. 1. New York: Basic Books.

55 Zablocki, "Toward a Demystified and Disinterested Scientific Concept of Brainwashing," pp. 159–214.

56 Briggs, Billy. 2007. "My Years of Slavery with the Terrorists." *Yorkshire Post.* January 31.

57 Stein, "Mothers in Cults: The Influence of Cults on the Relationship of Mothers to Their Children."

5
FAMILY AND FRIENDS
Not as close as Chairman Mao

Father is close, Mother is close, but neither is as close as Chairman Mao.
Popular song from Mao's China[1]

As a child growing up during China's Cultural Revolution, Anchee Min loved her pet chicken, Big Beard. Big Beard slept under the kitchen sink on a bed of straw and even produced the occasional egg. But then the local Party committee launched a Patriotic Public Health Campaign with the slogan, "Do not raise duck and hen in the city!" As head of the neighborhood's Little Red Guards, Anchee Min was forced to kill her pet chicken as a show of commitment and loyalty to Mao. Even a child's love of a pet was forbidden. This scene from Min's 1994 autobiographical account *Red Azalea* is reflected again when Min later falls in love with her female commander at the Red Fire Farm labor collective. But the bonds of affection and attachment, this time between the two women, now serve to help each of them survive in a situation where love of anyone or anything but Mao and the Party was considered counterrevolutionary and treacherous.[2]

The formation of attachments – even imaginary or internal attachments – is a fundamental threat to the emotionally and cognitively disorganizing attachments that totalist systems impose. Stepping outside of the framework of the totalist attachment system and finding a (more or less) reliable source of comfort can give the follower a pathway to resolve the fright without solution created in the system; to therefore be able to integrate thought and feeling, and to see and evaluate the world in which they are living with a more accurate interpretation than that provided by the utterly distorting lens of the totalist ideology. Perhaps a more intelligent life form than a chicken would do this job better – particularly from the cognitive aspect – nonetheless the repression of Min's love for her pet shows how seriously a totalist system takes any competing attachment. Isolation from loved ones and engulfment in the system must be maintained in order to control followers.

This chapter details the specific ways the range of attachment relationships are affected and controlled by totalist groups. Although the means may differ widely, the effect is the same: to remove trusting, close relationships (even if such a relationship exists only in a person's internal world, such as with Min and her chicken), leaving the follower dependent on the group. A totalist ideology alone – without the element of control of relationships – cannot lead to brainwashing and deployable agents. In fact, as we shall see in a later chapter, a key element of the totalist ideology itself is its function in supporting and justifying this limiting and control of attachment relationships. It is vitally important therefore to give close attention to how these groups manage and control close relationships – both those to others within the group as well as to people outside of the group.

Seemingly opposite policies in different groups result in the same attack on close attachments. For example, some groups, such as the Iranian Mojahedin, might decree celibacy and rupture existing relationships.[3] The UFO cult Heaven's Gate took this to even more of an extreme when several men were castrated.[4] But the same result – preventing the formation of close relationships – is also achieved through enforced polygamy, promiscuity, pedophilia, arrangement of relationships (where not a cultural norm, and conducted by the group rather than by the family), ordering of separations, forced abortions or the opposite: banning of contraception or abortion. The goal is, above all, to prevent alternate safe havens and non-group alliances from developing in personal relationships.

Totalist groups therefore seek to curtail all forms of attachment relationships other than that to the leader or group. Molly Kronberg, whose husband was allegedly driven to suicide[i] by excruciating levels of stress within the group, illustrated this succinctly when describing her experience in the Lyndon LaRouche extremist political group:

> So the order of things in the LaRouche organization was: Break with your parents and your past, your jobs and your schools; maintain loveless, "political" relations with your husband or wife, making sure that any heterodoxy is intervened on by the leadership; destroy your own children; avoid contact with the "outside" world. "Lyn is Your Father."[5]

It is notable that, like Lyndon LaRouche, many totalist leaders take on identities that reflect family roles, and followers are then required to use that name when referring to the leader. David Berg, head of the Children of God/The Family, was known alternately as Father David, Dad or Grandpa. Jim Jones of the deadly

---

i In fact, the leader Lyndon LaRouche suggested that "Baby Boomers" – his term for the older (and original) members of the group – commit suicide: King, Dennis. 2007. "Lyndon Larouche and the Art of Inducing Suicide." Retrieved December 09, 2013 (http://www.lyndonlarouche.org/suicide.htm).

Peoples Temple was called Father or Dad. David Koresh told the children in his compound at Waco "to call their parents 'dogs'; only he was to be referred to as their father."[6] Elizabeth Clare Prophet of the Church Universal and Triumphant considered herself the "World Mother" and followers addressed her as Mother.[7] Pol Pot, the leader of the Khmer Rouge, was called Brother Number One. Maryam Rajavi, of the Iranian political cult the Mojahedin-e-Khalq, acted as a kind of front for the leader, Masoud Rajavi, and was known as the group's "Ideological Mother."[8]

Families of origin

New members of cults are predictably pulled away from their families of origin (unless the group can also recruit other family members or exploit their resources) and in fact this is often the first time people become aware of cultic activity – when their son or daughter becomes estranged from the family. Of course, young adults, who are stereotypically the subject of cult recruitment attempts, are often at a developmental stage when they are moving away from their families as they develop independence, and so it may not always be obvious that their further separation is a result of cult manipulation. However, to the families there can be a clear difference – changes in personality, habits and a rejection of contact that exceeds normal signs of growing independence.

Free Domain Radio (FDR) is an internet-based group led by Stefan Molyneux, whose homepage claims it is "the largest and most popular philosophical conversation in the world."[9] It has become known for its practice of forcefully encouraging its new recruits to "deFoo" – that is (to translate the FDR language) to reject their family of origin (Foo). A newspaper account describes one such case:

> When Barbara Weed's 18-year-old son, Tom, was right in the middle of his A-levels, he abruptly left home. "Dear Family," said the note he left on the doormat. "I need to take an indefinite amount of time away from the family, so I've moved in with a friend. Please do not contact me. Tom."
>
> He has not been in touch with any of his relatives since. But Tom is not a missing person. His family know roughly where he is. It's just that he won't talk to them and they suspect he never will. "He got hooked in by an online cult," Barbara says. "The website convinces vulnerable people that they should hate their parents and should leave their family."
>
> Even the wording of Tom's letter is from the website. Its founder says, "The letter should buy you six to 12 months before your family come looking for you and that will give you time to get used to living without them."[ii][10]

---

ii Hilpern, Kate. 2008. "You'll Never See Me Again," in *The Guardian*, November 15. Copyright Guardian News & Media Ltd 2016.

Similarly, in totalitarian societies, allegiance to family must come second to allegiance to the leader. The previously mentioned story of Shin Dong-hyuk reveals how far the totalitarian state goes to disrupt family attachment. His connection to his family was so broken (in fact, it had hardly been allowed to develop in the first place, such was the neglect and abuse he had suffered) that even after being forced to watch his mother and brother's execution, he still believed they deserved to die as traitors to the state.[11]

There are many such stories of children being set against their parents and other elders in totalitarian systems. In Cambodia, for example, children were separated from adults and put in children's work camps. Loung Ung reported how the Khmer Rouge cadres would shout out:

> You are the children of Angkar! [the Khmer Rouge organization] In you lies our future. The Angkar knows you are pure in heart, uncorrupted by evil influences, still able to learn the ways of the Angkar! That is why the Angkar loves you above all else. . . .
>
> The Angkar will protect us if we give it our total loyalty. This means we must report to the Angkar suspected infiltrators and traitors. If we hear anyone at all – our friends, neighbors, cousins, even our own parents – speak things against the Angkar, we must report them.[12]

Later one of the female Khmer Rouge camp leaders tells Ung: "Children must be taught to follow orders without hesitation, without question, and to shoot and kill even their traitor parents. That is the first step in the training."[13]

Sadly it is only too common for children in totalitarian systems to be tormented with these orders. John Garang, leader of the Sudanese Peoples Liberation Army (SPLA), told his child soldiers: "If your mother is against us, you kill her; if your father is against us, you kill him. The SPLA is your family now."[14] And we now know that child soldiers in ISIS/Daesh training camps are also being told their "parents were unbelievers and that our first job was to go back to kill them."[15]

In totalitarian societies then, distrust within families is mandated, with severe punishments on hand if a family member's suspected disloyalty is not immediately reported. Even in cases where physical separation from family members is not enforced, these threats make it extremely difficult and dangerous to share any doubts and perceptions about the system with those who normally might be one's closest allies.

This imposed rejection or distrust of the family of origin removes a fundamental source of support for people. Granted not all families are able to provide useful support, but in those more or less secure or organized (in attachment terms) family relationships, at least some type of support is likely to be available. This support can be emotional – where the family acts as a safe haven to which a person can turn when under stress. Or the support can be practical, helping with financial or other material support to allow independence from the totalist system. And importantly the family can also be a primary source of reality-checking. The family of origin, in most cases, obviously has an understanding of an individual's history and social context and can provide verification and support for one's cognitive appraisals of other relationships, belief systems, experiences and interpretations of world events. But in totalism, it is only the organization, its leader and the supporting ideology that one may turn to for reality verification – and there one finds, not reality, but what Hannah Arendt refers to as fiction: the distorting hall of mirrors that is totalist ideology.[16]

Romantic relationships

As with family of origin relationships, romantic relationships must also be closely monitored. However, as opposed to the family of origin, where, perhaps, independence and pulling away might be more easily fit into a "normal" narrative of the life course, independent adults are generally expected to find and settle with a sexual partner. The intimacy of such relationships can create trusting "islands of resistance" that threaten the total domination by the cultic system, and so a variety of methods have been created by leaders to interfere with the creation of secure – or at least organized and predictable – adult romantic relationships. As a general rule, people entering cults will eventually be separated from their partners unless that partner can also be recruited. But even if both persons are in the group, the relationship must still be controlled.

Enforced polygamy, as in the Fundamentalist Church of Latter Day Saints (FLDS) led by the now-imprisoned Warren Jeffs, is one way to prevent such more or less secure or at least predictable[iii] attachments to a romantic or sexual partner. For the women, these polygamous relationships are usually set up when they are very young – in the FLDS this is often when the women are underage (hence Jeffs's prosecution for arranging marriages between adult men and underage girls, and finally, his 2011 conviction for child sexual assault).[17] Such marriages, where one man may have dozens of wives, are unlikely to provide the safe haven and secure base of "good enough," organized attachment.[18] At the same time as locking girls and young women into these arrangements, the young men who become extraneous as a result of this uneven distribution end up literally dumped outside of the group's compounds and left to fend for themselves in a hitherto unknown world.[19] These "lost boys," as they have become known, struggle to integrate in the outside world, cut off from everything familiar to them. Without adequate support many succumb to addiction, mental health problems or suicide.[20]

---

iii Even if a person's attachment in a relationship is not secure, if it is one of the other organized forms
    (i.e. preoccupied or dismissing) then it is at least predictable: the partner may be predictably clingy or
    predictably unavailable. The advantage of these organized forms of attachment status is that they are
    consistent and therefore a partner can adapt and plan around these predictable dynamics. But with
    disorganized attachment behavior is unpredictable.

Fred Newman's method of controlling adult intimate relationships was to con-
flate sexual relationships with "friendship" in his concept of "friendo-sexuality"
where, as a former member of the Newman Tendency explained to me:

> he was a "friend-o-sexual." It's really very self explanatory [laughs] – some
> have sex with men, some have sex with women, some have sex with bulls and
> some have sex with trees, but he has sex with friends [laughs].
>
> (Grace)

Not only did Newman have sex with friends as well as with his therapy patients,[iv]
but he extended this doctrine to the rest of the group as well, which resulted in a
group norm of "bed-hopping":

> Most adults share beds and relation – they swap – like they fuck like bunnies,
> okay? So yeah, they don't have boundaries. Therapy in the 70s, I understand,
> was to become, performed, you know, nude sometimes, sexually other times.
> They come from that generation, you know, and I mean, if that's cool with
> you, you know . . .
>
> (Celia)

Whether or not this was "cool" with followers, having a "private" relationship
was scorned and there was heavy pressure for people to engage in "friendo-
sexuality."[21]

At the other extreme, a total rejection of sexual relationships serves the same
purpose of preventing the close attachment between two persons that might
interfere with the total domination of the leader. In the Heaven's Gate cult, eight
of the men, including the leader, became castrated "to combat sexual urges"[22]
and all other members developed genderless identities and took vows of celibacy.
After the ritualistic deaths by what is rather inappropriately called "suicide" of 39
Heaven's Gate members, a group member (who also killed himself shortly after)
stated their deaths were in order for them to "move into bodies that had been

---

iv See also Newman's interview on NY1:

> Newman calls them his dearest loves, the women he lives with in his West Village townhouse. He
> admits some of the women initially came to him for psychological help. Newman treats patients
> in Social Therapy, his self-created field of psychology. "Some of them were in therapy, yeah," he
> says. . . . "I think that people's sexual relationships should be something very personal between
> the people who are engaging in it, and I think if people love each other, care for each other, are
> attracted to each other and decide together that they want to have sex, they should," he says.
> "[Does it matter that it's a patient and a therapist?] I think sexual relationships are relationships
> between human beings, not human beings under certain descriptions or in certain categories.
> I believe that people should fall in love as they so desire, and if they want to include in that sexu-
> ality, they should include that."

Nissan, Rita. 2005. *"Psychopolitics": Inside the Independence Party of Fred Newman.* November 3, NY1.

prepared for them, physical bodies of a finer nature, androgynous, sexless. It's an evolutionary step . . ."[23]

In between these two extremes, cults may arrange marriages or relationships, require members to seek permission before entering into an intimate relationship (both of which occurred in the O., the group in which I was a member) and/or simply break up any relationship that threatens to become too close, developing trust within the private realm of the couple greater than that of the group. Some may use more subtle methods than threats and simply suggest that a given relationship may be "holding you back." The effect, however, is the same – denigrating one's chosen relationships and engineering relationships that support the goals of the group. Even when a relationship does manage to achieve some level of security or predictability, this will be strictly conditional – it is still the leader who is in charge, and should any disloyalty become apparent the relationship will be swiftly terminated.

Similar phenomena are observable in totalitarian states. Barbara Demick reports that, despite his own early adventures as a "playboy," North Korean leader Kim Il-sung "melded traditional Korean conservatism with the Communist instinct to repress sexuality,"[24] discouraging marriage before 30 and disallowing any other form of romantic relationship. In many cases it is now Communist Party functionaries who have taken on the traditionally family-based role of arranging marriages. Demick describes the long but illicit courtship between Mi-ran and Jun-sang – a couple who were of different rank and status and whom the state would never allow to marry. Even in this case, where Mi-ran considered Jun-sang the love of her life, she could not share with him her deepening despair about the North Korean regime, her utter loss of belief in the propaganda and, finally, her family's plans to defect:

> Neighbors denounced neighbors, friends denounced friends. Even lovers denounced each other. If anybody in the secret police had learned of their plans, her entire family would have been carted away to a labor camp in the mountains.
>
> "I couldn't risk it," she told me. "I couldn't even say goodbye."[25]

The sad reality was that her beloved Jun-sang was also disillusioned and dreaming of escape. But he too knew how dangerous it was to talk politics with anyone, even with his girlfriend. Both eventually did defect, but separately, and by the time they finally found each other again in the south Mi-ran had already married and had a baby with another man.

Close friendships

As with family of origin and romantic relationships, so it goes with close friend-ships. On entering a cult, the recruit must eventually give up non-cult friendships. In my own case I remember in my first year with the group, having moved thou-sands of miles from my previous home, and now in a recent cult-approved marriage to another member of the group, I sat down to write a letter to one of my oldest and closest friends. My husband saw me writing and asked me what I was doing. When I explained he said, in a kindly way, "Why are you doing that?"

"Well, she's my friend, I'm just staying in touch."
"What kind of development are you getting from that relationship?"

I couldn't reply. I had never, of course, thought of my friendship with Terry in that way – as a source of "development." He continued, speaking quietly, "If there is no development, then it is just social exchange, and it will only hold you back."

As we shared a room and I had no private space of my own, and since his tone was so reasonable, and given I was exhausted from 20-hour work-days, my pen remained in mid-air for a few seconds until I set it down by the unfinished letter, which I later discarded. I did not communicate with Terry again until nine years later when I finally emerged from the cult and searched her out, along with my other old friends who I had also discarded in the manner of the unfinished letter.

Close friendships can also become islands of resistance, where the emotional support and conversation between friends provides both a safe haven and a shared view of the reality of the oppressive situation, thus potentially defeating the deceptive totalist interpretation of what is going on. So these relationships, like other close ties, must be controlled by the group. In the Newman Tendency even the word "friend" is retooled for use as a control mechanism, as each recruit is assigned a "friend" in what is essentially a supervisory role to ensure compliance with the new regimen (similar to the Heaven's Gate "check partner," or the "contact" in my group). Just to add to the confusion, in the Newman Tendency a "friend" is also anyone who can be seen as a potential sexual partner in conforming to Newman's "friendo-sexuality" doctrine. Either way the idea of a friend as a close and trusted confidante is eroded.[26]

A world away, Emmanuel Jal tells how the Sudanese Peoples Liberation Army on the one hand forbade the boy soldiers from fighting with each other – stating that they must be loyal to each other, to their "brothers" – while on the other hand the children were equally forbidden from forming friendships. Nonetheless, Jal did form an illicit friendship with another boy, Malual. When this was discovered they were made to whip each other, and after they were finished the army trainer said softly to them, "Well done." Jal reported: "Now he was the one with smiles in his eyes. 'You two friends are finally becoming soldiers.' He laughed."[27] The concept of friendship becomes distorted entirely and real friendship is labeled as weakness, a waste of time or frankly disobedient.

Reproduction and children[28]

The totalist system controls the bond between parents and their children in multiple ways: through control of conception and pregnancy, discouraging the parent-child bond, control of time spent with the child, actual or threatened removal of the child from the parents, monitoring and judging the parent/child relationship, and generally directing child-rearing practices. The control often starts well before pregnancy by controlling the parents' relationship through an arranged marriage as described above. Once the child arrives: "parents in essence turn over the custody of their children to a third party, so that the leader or the group becomes the actual custodian of the children."[29]

There is much evidence that the choice to have or not to have children is highly controlled in cults and totalitarian systems. As Molly Kronberg explains it from her experience in the Lyndon LaRouche political cult:

> Another phenomenon created and institutionalized by LaRouche's Beyond Psychoanalysis was that of forced abortions – forced, if not physically, at least psychologically, on almost every woman in the organization who became pregnant. To have a child was to be ostracized, shunned, driven out.
>
> Why? Because those who had children then had a higher loyalty and a higher responsibility than their loyalty to LaRouche. When Ken and I had our son in 1984 – two National Committee members having a baby! – it was seen as a tremendous act of betrayal of LaRouche.[30]

Similarly, forced abortions have been reported from organizations as diverse as the elite Sea Org formation of Scientology[31] and the Newman Tendency. A former member described how Fred Newman forced his "frontwoman," perennial presidential candidate Lenora Fulani, to have an abortion.[32] While publicly portrayed as a model of a powerful black woman, Newman nonetheless subjected Fulani to the same kinds of control as other followers. Others in the group were instructed by either Newman or their therapists (Newman's homegrown therapy being a key element of the control mechanism employed by the group) to have abortions if they became pregnant. As Grace told me:

> The woman that I lived with, she had to ask permission to keep her child when she got pregnant. She also had to ask permission to get married. Most people were ordered to have abortions when they got pregnant ... There was also a very general sense that the organization didn't want children and that they were a burden on the organization.

Women were told that children would get in the way of the group's work. One former Newman Tendency member observed that few of the "lifers" – long-term leadership members – have children. Most of these lifers are women who are now in their 50s and past child-bearing age. Thus they have sacrificed their fertile years to the demands of the group. Within the group this is seen as a noble act, necessary for the success of the revolutionary project.[33]

In the organization of which I was a member, followers were also required to seek permission to have children. Depending on how the leader determined it was best to control the follower, permission was either granted or withheld. One woman waited years before receiving permission to have a child. She said: "I really want children, but I know I'm not ideologically developed enough yet."[34] On the other hand, control can be exerted by ordering women to become pregnant. In my case I was sent a memo telling me to have a child. This was a way of cementing my tie to the group, and of asserting authority over me as I was exhibiting rather too much of my rebellious and independent streak and threatening to leave the group.

Another way to control reproductive choice is, of course, to prohibit contraception. This is a cornerstone of many right-wing and fundamentalist religious groups, serving not only to control women within the group, but also as an ideological plank in the political realm used to mobilize followers and gain new recruits.

The control of reproduction in totalitarian states is well known. In Nazi Germany it was an important – and early – element of Hitler's genocide. The Nazi eugenics program included forced sterilizations and forced abortions for non-Aryans and others carrying "life unworthy of life."[35] At the same time the regime prohibited abortions and drastically limited access to contraception for Aryan women.[36] There was a two-fold effect of these policies. On the one hand the genocide of the Holocaust demonized and destroyed the "out-groups" of Jews, Roma and other groups, but on the other, the close control of personal relationships and reproduction also affected the "in-group" – Aryans – and was an intrinsic part of the control system cementing loyalty to Hitler. This element is part of the overall pattern of interrupting the general population from having autonomy in the private realm of family life.

Although the control of reproduction has many causes and functions in different societies and groups, it is important to understand its role in totalism as a specific case. It is not necessarily simply to control women (although clearly this is part of it), but is a way to control attachments in general, to control attachments of parents to children and is a fundamental step in forcing followers to relinquish the control of family life to the leader.

From the point of conception to ongoing aspects of pregnancy the totalist system exerts its influence. As former political cult member Laurel said, "It was clear to me that this child was going to be a guaranteed recruit – it was by inheritance."[37] In such cases the mother may be encouraged to feel proud of her role, as was true with Aryan mothers under Hitler's regime. Unfortunately, this esteem does not usually translate into actual privileges such as adequate rest, nutrition and prenatal care, all of which are notoriously absent, certainly within most cults.[38] During her time in a bible-based cult Helen described herself as: "being pregnant and looking like walking death – I was emaciated."[39] She both fasted and nursed during pregnancy (members of her cult ate full meals only two or three times a week, living on bread the rest of the time). She had prenatal care only during her first pregnancy, and for ten years after that neither she nor any other cult member went to a hospital or clinic. In other cases, when a woman miscarries the cult may blame her for "ideological murder"[40] or, as in a Christian cult member's case, for not being "faithful" enough.[41]

The rights of children in cults and totalitarian states are few, and their existence can be perilous. The problem of how to protect children in these conditions is extremely serious and complex. The secrecy and closed nature of these systems makes it very difficult for outsiders to know what is going on and to intervene.

If the parent's relationship with their child has been controlled from the point of reproduction, then the very foundation of the relationship with the child is subject to the authority of the group. In some cases the mother may never, then, be fully able to attach and form an independent bond with her child, free of the dictates of the totalist leadership. The effects on the treatment of children are likely to be hugely destructive. These can range from frequent – even total – separation of parents and children to extreme physical and sexual abuse. In milder cases the effect may be limited to chronic neglect or hypercontrol of the child's environment and belief system.

Mothers are often discouraged from having a special bond with the child. In my cult we were told, "Children are not your private property" or "You have too much value in your children." Deikman, in *The Wrong Way Home*,[42] describes cult members saying to Clara, a fellow member, "Your family is the whole world . . . [your son] David is just one of the many children you are responsible for." In some cults, such as the Branch Davidians[43] or the earlier Slaves of the Immaculate Heart of Mary,[44] children barely know who or what parents are.

Mothers may spend very little or no time with their children due to the demands of the cult. In the early years of the group I was in, parents only saw their children an hour or less a day. The rest of the time children were in the group childcare center. Fellow cult member Mary said:

> It was like being a workaholic with meetings and fundraising and political work day and night. It consumed our lives. I knew the children would never understand – nor did I want them to. It was assumed that we would give a hundred percent.

A former Christian cult member said:

> I decided I should wean him early because that would leave me freer to be involved in the group. There was pressure to be right and faithful and to give one hundred percent.[45]

In many cases the child is physically taken from their parents. Nancy, a child raised in my cult, spent four of her early teen years away from her parents, living with other 'cadres.' Jill, who was in a cult that blended Mormon and Native American rituals, was persuaded to give her 6-month-old baby to a childless couple in the group (the leader's brother and sister-in-law). This was to supposedly "help her" while she recovered from a breakdown induced by the stress of cult life. The leader secretly promised the couple that the baby would be theirs forever and assured them that Jill would never get well. Six months later when Jill was living in the cult's primitive encampment the couple wheeled the baby back to Jill in a wheelbarrow. The surrogate mother told Jill that she realized Jill and the baby were bonded and the child could never really be hers.

Mothers' behavior towards their children is carefully monitored. This monitoring may be in the name of science, devotion to God or personal development. However, the purpose it serves is to control the relationship between the mother and child. In my group we had Observation Forms on which we were to record the child's behavior, the less-than-scientific results of which were later entered into a digital spreadsheet. Helen reported that, "We had to be careful not to be too kind to a child if that child had been in trouble – or we'd get criticized. You had to keep track of which children were in disfavor." Parents can be 'turned in' for their behavior towards their child: I was reported to leadership for letting my four-year-old play with Ninja Turtles and engage in "unproductive free-play."

While there is, on the one hand, an abundance of 'supervision' over parenting, on the other hand there is no real support. Many mothers in cults report isolation or condemnation, rather than any help in dealing with parenting problems. Further, mothers may live with the heavy fear that, should they make too serious a mistake, their children may be taken from them. Laurel told me: "Becky once said she was afraid of having a second child because she saw Libby's kid taken away."

The mothers' position in the cult may be judged by the behavior of their children, or by the processes of pregnancy and birth. Laurel reported that: "The only time I was ever praised was when I sent a memo saying I'd figured out that J. was born with a birth defect because of my anxiety and tension during the pregnancy – in other words, it was my ideological problem." Janie was criticized for "being into attention" with her child:

> If you showed any interest or affection to your child you were really trying to draw [the leader's] attention to you. I was exhausted with breast-feeding all the time and I felt I was a bad Christian and a bad example.

The mother must often participate in 'child-rearing' or reproductive practices that may range from abuse and neglect to ridiculous pseudo-science. These practices are well documented in the cult literature.[46] In my own research I listened as Helen told her story:

> My kids have been physically hurt by every adult in the cult: slapping, kicking, pulling hair. But only Brother was allowed to use the cattle prod . . . I laughed because everyone laughed, but on the inside I was feeling absolutely sick . . . 'Desperate Discipline' was needed to save their souls.[47]

Preventing the bond of parents to their children is not an easy task but it is critical if the totalist leader is to maintain control. When the leader is successful in defeating this primary human bond it is one of the most shocking and damaging elements of cultic or totalitarian systems.

As Molly Kronberg stated, failing to control parents' attachment to their children risks the parent developing "a higher loyalty and a higher responsibility"[48] to their children, rather than to the cult. And without adequate control by the totalist system this loyalty and responsibility to their children – this attachment bond – can create a mitigating or escape hatch attachment, which may allow the parent to reintegrate their thought processes. Providing a safe haven for their children, activating the caregiving system (as it is called in attachment theory), can, given the right conditions, trump the disorganized attachment bond to the group or leader. Once another attachment bond is in play the parent's thoughts may then be able to circumvent the disorganized dissociation set in place by the chronic trauma of life in the totalist system. The need to protect the child can sometimes allow the perception of reality, and reintegration of the thinking with the feeling part of the brain, to regain the upper hand. It is unlikely, however, that this happens without other forms of support, a break in isolation or alternate information sources about the group.

Helen described what happened to her:

> I started seeing inconsistencies – I wasn't judging, but I was aware. When the thought processes kicked in they were acute, keen. I started journaling. . . .
>
> I wept over Jonah when he was born because . . . I knew what was in store for him. One of the brethren had held a gun to one of my twin's face, and pulled the trigger – my child didn't know it was unloaded. But this is why I wept for Jonah . . . The last straw was when a woman kicked him when he was a year and a half old – because he was wiggling around. It was over and I knew it. I had no fear of what anyone thought for the first time. We were all in the church and I got all my kids. I said 'Get your blankets' and they got their stuff and we left.
>
> I thought – you can hurt me, but . . . not my kids, not anymore.[49]

Born and raised in totalist environments

As of this writing, three women have escaped from a 30-year enslavement within a remnant of a UK political cult with the unlikely name of the Workers' Institute of Marxism-Leninism-Mao Zedong Thought. One of the women was born in the group – now down to five people, living in seclusion within a densely populated area of South London. Her whole life has been within the extraordinarily narrow world circumscribed by the leader – who is also her father. In a message she was able to get out to an outsider whilst still captive she said she felt like a "fly trapped in a spider's web" and described her life as "unspeakable torment."[50] One cannot imagine the process of integrating into an open world that this young woman now faces. But this is the task of thousands of young people who were born and/or raised in cults who, if able to, emerge in adulthood. They face phenomenal obstacles, and without the right support may fail to transition effectively, with far too many of these young people turning to self-harm and suicide.

For many of these adults born or raised in totalist groups,[v] leaving the oppressive world of the cult, in which many of them suffered long-term physical and sexual abuse, also means leaving those family members who stay in the group. The cults

---

v A recent term used in cultic studies literature for those born or raised in cults is "Second Generation Adult" or "SGA." However, as many are third, fourth or more generations from the initial member this term is not totally satisfactory.

then prevent or greatly limit further communication with those still inside result-ing in shunning the former member. Often the adult may have to leave their entire family behind in the cult. Thus we come full-circle to the children, the next genera-tion, who while freeing themselves are now cut-off from parents and siblings – their family of origin who remain entrapped.

In yet another tragic twist, sometimes parents are forced to leave young chil-dren in the cult when they themselves are expelled. Peter Frouman was born and brought up in the Children of God/The Family. He has documented the story of his family, one where the cult tried to keep the children even after the parents had left the group. This too is a common situation – the leaders of these groups want to maintain control of these young people, both in order to keep members and to maintain their total control. Peter's father left the group in 1979, but his mother and siblings remained. But when his mother, suffering from breast cancer, tried to leave the group with her younger children she was forcibly detained in the group until she agreed to leave her children behind. Peter recounts:

> Next to the house in Corrientes [in Argentina] was a large two-story ware-house that was being converted into living quarters using 2x4s and sheets of wood panelling to construct walls. According to one of my siblings, both he and my mother were held in this warehouse for weeks while they were on a strict program of correction that included being required to fast and read Mo Letters [the leader's writings]. . . .
>
> For weeks, they tormented her and did everything they could to destroy and weaken her mind, her body and her will to fight back. Finally, on July 18th, 1987, they decided that the almost 16 years of her life (total life-time: 37 years, 5 months and 12 days) she had given the Family was not enough. They wanted her children as well. . . .
>
> Not long after my mother returned to the United States, her three younger children went to Montevideo, Uruguay with Stuart Baylin. At the time, I and my older brother Manoli were living in the "Teen Combo" in Buenos Aires run by Susan Claire Borowick (aka Borowik) and her husband, Cacho. As an ex-member, my mother was not allowed to know the address or the phone number of the houses where her children were living.[51]

At the age of 13 Peter finally decided to leave when:

> Stuart Baylin told me that I should forget about ever seeing my mother again, that she was a backslider and that I should burn the few pictures of her and letters from her I had.[52]

In any case the group kept most of the letters she had sent and never gave them to the children. After his escape from The Family, Peter had a few years of what he called "a normal childhood," but it took years for three other brothers to leave, and one remained.

Peter is now among a group of second-generation-adult cult leavers who have become active in trying to protect the rights of children in cults and to help young people after they get out. Their stories illustrate the extent to which totalist systems will go in controlling and destroying close ties between family members.

Replaceable others

What then are the attributes of the relationships that *are* allowed within the totalist system? They are a strange hybrid – neither attachment relationships nor what are termed affiliative relationships (i.e. looser friendship or collegial ties). The relationships among peers within totalist groups are on the one hand intense and close in certain ways but on the other they lack the defining features of attachments – true attachment (though disorganized) is reserved for the leader and the group as a whole. The rather unusual closeness found in the other relationships among members of totalist systems has several aspects: conditional material and instrumental support, mutual confession and breaching of boundaries of personal space, and the closeness of "comrades" that derives from long hours spent together engaged in group tasks.

One may be able to call upon a fellow member (sometimes any member) for help if that help is required to further the goals of the group. Should one get a flat tire that might impede completing a group task then another member may be quick to respond and get one back on the road, back being a productive member of the group. However, if a member gets sick and cannot contribute, they may often be ignored completely. This happened to Masoud Banisadr when he was hospitalized for several weeks while on a mission in London. No one from the group came to see him. The unintended consequence of this, from the group's point of view, was it finally allowed Masoud to break free. While he was in the hospital, this group's lack of empathy and support contrasted with the simple exposure to

> normal relationships of people with each other. There was a guy beside who had an accident and I was helping him to shave his beard, or to feed him and so on, and this revived my individuality and my humanity and self-confidence.

This experience became a key turning point for Masoud where this newly formed emotional connection to an outsider, along with time to think, allowed him to begin reconsidering his commitment.[53] So, although certain kinds of material and instrumental support are readily available from fellow members, the nature and type of support they offer is highly conditional.

Another element of the close aspect of cultic relationships has to do with the principle of confession that is common to all totalist groups: one's innermost thoughts must be exposed to the group. In Lifton's seminal study of reeducation and prisoner of war camps in Mao's China and North Korea, he refers to this as the "cult of confession."[54] Regardless of whom one might actually feel close to, this confessional mode is expected to be engaged in with any group member when ordained by the system. In the Newman Tendency this exposure of one's inner self usually took place in the "social therapy" sessions, which, unlike in more standard therapies, were far from confidential. In fact, as one cadre put it: "If I wanted to share it with the world, I'd take it to therapy" (Juliet). Thus, therapy, rather than being a "safe space" in which to explore personal issues and problems, became the location of public confessions and of placing members on the "hot seat," pressured by other group members.

Although the follower is encouraged to expose their doubts and weaknesses of belief, and confess their failings, such confessions are then used by the group and turned against the follower. Any actual critique of the group's practices, on the other hand, is strictly forbidden. Thus, even between a couple, or close friends, it is a dangerous practice to try to criticize the group, and especially the leader, in any way. This risks punishment, up to and including expulsion, which will result in the follower being shunned. In the Newman Tendency former members reported to me that they could not freely share doubts about the group to anyone – they were aware that this risked punishment. The former members of the non-cultic Green Party, on the other hand, constantly and freely shared doubts and complained about a variety of aspects of party life – this was almost central to their experience. In fact we can say that the freedom to doubt is a hallmark of an open, democratic society.

But in totalist groups doubts are seen as dangerous disloyalty, and any that might be shared are expected to be reported to leadership. In this way privacy does not really exist. So in confiding with others, one is always potentially "confiding" with the whole group – eliminating the very notion of both privacy and confidentiality. This is what Schein refers to as the elimination of the private,[55] and Arendt refers to as collapsing the private and the public together thus annihilating both.[56] As there is no public space in which to discuss differences (other than to confess one's sins and failings) so there is no private realm in which to turn over with a trusted other the issues and problems one might wish to contemplate. All is grist for the totalist mill.

An ersatz closeness can also be created by long hours spent working together, group living and sharing of the daily chores and other matters that might normally occur in a family or between close friends. And similarly, the confusion of sexual and other forms of intimate boundaries adds to the intensity of within-group relationships. Thus these ties are not simply the friendship or collegial affiliative ties of non-cult life – they have an added tightness and strength: one is a comrade, a soldier-in-arms, marching together for the greater good and subsuming any petty personal needs.

In the Newman Tendency former members described being close to everyone in the group – all 500 members – showing this kind of interchangeability of relationships rather than attachments to specific others. Grace, for instance, stated:

> The people that I was particularly close with? Well I was friends – with most of the people in the IWP. In other words I, I describe the group as a

close-knit group. We were in therapy together, we knew each other, we, we had to be, you know, "non abusive" in the way that we relate to each other, we were very – intimate with one another.

In totalist settings these replaceable others are often abundant – the follower must be enmeshed within a tight engulfing network. In my research Newman Tendency members listed twice as many "close" friendships during their group tenure as did members of the non-totalist Green Party. Green Party members' friendships were not noticeably changed during or after their tenure in the party. Newman Tendency members, on the other hand, gained totally new "friends" on entering the group, and lost all of those connections on leaving, given the ubiquitous process of shunning that takes place when followers escape totalist systems.

When people do leave a totalist group and are shunned, remaining members are not to express grief at the loss of that person. This is particularly painful for those born or raised in the group who, if they leave, may leave behind their entire families. Their parents who remain in the group are forbidden from grieving the loss of their grown-up child whom they may rarely or never see again. Similarly, if a potentially close person should be redeployed to a far-off location then those they leave behind are not to complain or miss the one who has left as they are clearly doing "God's work" or whatever other justification is stated.

The strange and hybrid closeness – which one might call boundaryless – found in totalist groups is not the closeness of attachment. Attachment relationships are defined as first, being to a "specific other" and second, causing extreme distress on loss (through any rupture of the bond, from a break-up to death). This type of close attachment relationship – in the maladaptive form of disorganized attachment – is reserved for the leader and the group as a whole, not for individual relationships within it. In fact, the within-group relationships are to *replaceable or undifferentiated* others.[57] This is one reason cults may move members around frequently, and certainly act to break up relationships that appear to be becoming too close: to prevent any alternate attachments forming to specific others.

The totalist system must walk a fine line: intensive interpersonal interaction is required[58] in order to keep the follower tied into the system and to break down interpersonal boundaries. Yet these relationships must not be so close and trusting that followers can find individual escape hatch safe havens within which they can gain comfort, lower their arousal levels and share their honest perceptions about the system together. If followers were able to do so, and gain both a feeling of safety and social support for their perceptions of reality, they risk reintegrating their thought processes and therefore being able to think and feel their way out of the cognitive and affective trauma bond. They may also form dissenting minorities, or "islands of resistance," to threaten the system. To prevent this, then, the intensive interpersonal interactions must be ritualized, constrained within the narrow limits of what the group allows members to feel and think,[59] rather than functioning in informal, spontaneous and private ways in order to give comfort and feedback about the reality of the situation. Thus we see the predictable organizational control of personal life, including close friendships, family relationships, sexuality and reproduction.

These undifferentiated, replaceable, densely networked relationships tie the new member to the group, but do not provide a safe haven nor a secure base from which the member can move out to explore the external world. They are pseudo-attachment relationships, merely front relationships for the new and disorganized fundamental relationship with the group that is now in place. In this way, multiple, dense, weakly differentiated ties to other group members and a lack of external ties result in a primary tie or attachment to the leader or group as a whole, rather than to individuals within it.

In order to be able to control followers the leader needs to isolate the follower from alternate attachments (or even the internalized representation of such attachments), as part of creating a situation of "fright without solution" and thus creating a follower with a disorganized attachment to the group, and resulting dissociation and deployability. The leader must create a closed and rigid structure that is supported by an equally closed and rigid ideology in order to both remove and prevent any potentially mitigating escape hatch attachments. It is to the leader's pathological need for control and the totalist structure as the expression and means of that control that we turn next.

Notes

1 Chang, Jung. 1991. *Wild Swans: Three Daughters of China*. New York: Simon & Schuster, p. 263.
2 Min, Anchee. 1994. *Red Azalea*. New York: Pantheon Books.
3 Banisadr, Masoud. 2004a. *Masoud: Memoirs of an Iranian Rebel*. London: Saqi.
4 Lalich, Janja. 2004. *Bounded Choice: True Believers and Charismatic Cults*. Berkeley: University of California Press.
5 Kronberg, Molly Hammett. 2009. *Pawns of His Grandiosity: Psychological and Social Control in the Lyndon Larouche Cult*. Paper presented at the Speaking with Forked Tongues: The Rhetoric of Right-Wing Extremism Today, June 26, 2009, University of Northampton, UK. Retrieved December 09, 2013 (http://lyndonlarouche.org/molly-kronberg.htm).
6 Rimer, Sara and Sam Howe Verhovek. 1993. "Growing up under Koresh: Cult Children Tell of Abuses," in *New York Times*, May 4, 1993. New York City.
7 Pietrangelo, John Joseph. 1994. *Lambs to Slaughter: My Fourteen Years with Elizabeth Clare Prophet and Church Universal and Triumphant*. Tucson, AZ: Author.
8 Banisadr, Masoud. 2004. *Masoud: Memoirs of an Iranian Rebel*. London: Saqi.
9 Molyneux, Stefan. 2013, *Freedomain Radio*. Retrieved December 09, 2013 (http://www.freedomainradio.com/).
10 Ibid.
11 Harden, Blaine. 2012. *Escape from Camp 14: One Man's Remarkable Odyssey from North Korea to Freedom In the West*. London: Penguin.
12 Ung, Loung. 2007. *First They Killed My Father: A Daughter of Cambodia Remembers*. Edinburgh: Mainstream Publishing, p. 160.
13 Ibid., p. 164.
14 Jal, Emmanuel. 2009. *War Child: A Boy Soldier's Story*. London: Abacus, p. 97.
15 Hall, John. 2016. "Isis Is Brainwashing Children to Murder Their Own Parents, Child Soldier Who Escaped from Raqqa Reveals," in *Independent*, January 18, 2016. London.
16 Arendt, Hannah. 1948/1979. *The Origins of Totalitarianism*. Orlando: Harcourt Brace.

17 Pilkington, Ed. 2011. "Fundamentalist Sect Leader Jailed for Life for Sex with Child Brides," in *The Guardian*. August 11. London.

18 Jessop, Carolyn and Laura Palmer. 2007. *Escape*. Random House Digital, Inc.

19 Guiora, A.N. 2010. "Protecting the Unprotected: Religious Extremism and Child Endangerment." *Journal of Law & Family Studies* 12: 391.

20 Jeffs, Brent W. 2010. *Lost Boy: The True Story of One Man's Exile from a Polygamist Cult and His Brave Journey to Reclaim His Life*. Random House Digital, Inc.

21 Stein, Alexandra. 2007. "Attachment, Networks and Discourse in Extremist Political Organizations: A Comparative Case Study." Doctoral Dissertation, Sociology, University of Minnesota, Minneapolis.

22 Lalich, *Bounded Choice: True Believers and Charismatic Cults*, p. 30.

23 Ibid., p. 99.

24 Demick, Barbara. 2010. *Nothing to Envy: Real Lives in North Korea*. London: Granta, p. 81.

25 Ibid., p. 10.

26 Stein, "Attachment, Networks and Discourse in Extremist Political Organizations."

27 Jal, *War Child*, p. 86.

28 Much of this section is taken from my previously published article, Stein, Alexandra. 1997. "Mothers in Cults: The Influence of Cults on the Relationship of Mothers to Their Children." *Cultic Studies Journal* 14(1):40–57.

29 Singer, M.T. and J. Lalich. 1995. *Cults in Our Midst: The Hidden Menace in Our Everyday Lives*. San Francisco: Jossey Bass, p. 261.

30 Kronberg, Molly Hammett. 2009. *Pawns of His Grandiosity: Psychological and Social Control in the Lyndon Larouche Cult*. Paper presented at the Speaking with Forked Tongues: The Rhetoric of Right-Wing Extremism Today, June 26, 2009, University of Northampton, UK. Retrieved December 9, 2013 (http://lyndonlarouche.org/molly-kronberg.htm).

31 Kent, Stephen A. 1999. "Scientology – Is This a Religion?" *Marburg Journal of Religion* 4(1):1–23.

32 Stein, "Attachment, Networks and Discourse in Extremist Political Organizations."

33 Ibid.

34 Personal communication.

35 Lifton, Robert Jay. 1986. *The Nazi Doctors: Medical Killing and the Psychology of Genocide*. New York: Basic Books, p. 21.

36 Stephenson, Jill. 2013. *Women in Nazi Society*, Vol. 35, London and New York: Routledge.

37 Stein, "Mothers in Cults."

38 Singer and Lalich, *Cults in Our Midst: The Hidden Menace in Our Everyday Lives*.

39 Stein, "Mothers in Cults."

40 Personal communication from former political cult member.

41 Stein, "Mothers in Cults."

42 Deikman, Arthur J. 1990. *The Wrong Way Home: Uncovering the Patterns of Cult Behavior in American Society*. Boston: Beacon Press.

43 Perry, Bruce Duncan and Maia Szalavitz. 2007. *The Boy Who Was Raised as a Dog: And Other Stories from a Child Psychiatrist's Notebook: What Traumatized Children Can Teach Us About Life, Loss and Healing*. New York: Basic Books.

44 Connor, Robert. 1979. *Walled In*. Scarborough, Ont: New American Library of Canada.

45 Stein, "Mothers in Cults."

46 E.g., Markowitz, Arnold and David A Halperin. 1984. "Cults and Children: The Abuse of the Young." *Cultic Studies Journal* 1(2):143–55.

47 Ibid.

48 Kronberg, Molly Hammett. 2009. *Pawns of His Grandiosity: Psychological and Social Control in the Lyndon Larouche Cult*. Paper presented at the Speaking with Forked Tongues: The Rhetoric of Right-Wing Extremism Today, June 26, 2009, University of Northampton, UK. Retrieved December 9, 2013 (http://lyndonlarouche.org/molly-kronberg.htm).

49 Stein, "Mothers in Cults."

50 Steve Hassan in BBC. 2013. "London Slavery Case: Suspects 'Former Maoist Activists'." BBC News London. Retrieved December 18, 2013 (http://www.bbc.co.uk/news/uk-england-london-25084830).
51 Frouman, Peter. 2005. *Family Values*. Retrieved January 12, 2013 (http://www.frouman.net/kidnapping/).
52 Frouman, Peter. 2005, *Family Values*. Retrieved December 30, 2013 (http://www.frouman.net/kidnapping/).
53 Banisadr, Masoud. 2004. *Masoud: Memoirs of an Iranian Rebel*. London: Saqi.
54 Lifton, Robert Jay. 1961. *Thought Reform and the Psychology of Totalism*. New York: The Norton Library.
55 Schein, Edgar H. 1961. *Coercive Persuasion: A Socio-Psychological Analysis of the "Brainwashing" of American Civilian Prisoners by the Chinese Communists*. New York: W.W. Norton.
56 Arendt, Hannah. 1948/1979. *The Origins of Totalitarianism*. Orlando: Harcourt Brace.
57 Zablocki, Benjamin D. 2001. "Toward a Demystified and Disinterested Scientific Concept of Brainwashing," in *Misunderstanding Cults: Searching for Objectivity in a Controversial Field*, edited by B.D. Zablocki and T. Robbins. Toronto: University of Toronto Press, pp. 159–214.
58 Lofland, John. 1977. *Doomsday Cult: A Study of Conversion, Proselytization, and Maintenance of Faith*. New York: Irvington Publishers: distributed by Halsted Press.
59 Schein, *Coercive Persuasion*.

6

THE WILL OF THE FUEHRER IS THE PARTY'S LAW[1]

Totalist leaders and the structures they create

> Totalitarian movements are mass organizations of atomized, isolated individuals. Compared with all other parties and movements, their most conspicuous external characteristic is their demand for total, unrestricted, unconditional and unalterable loyalty of the individual member. This demand is made by the leaders of totalitarian movements even before they seize power.[2]
>
> Hannah Arendt: *The Origins of Totalitarianism*[i]

The totalist system is driven by its leader. It is the leader who creates – or sometimes inherits – the system, whose position of power shapes it as a closed and hierarchical system, and who implements its supporting ideology, which both reflects and enables its isolating, top-heavy structure. The totalist organization exists to maintain the undiluted control of the single, totalitarian leader where the will of this leader "becomes the 'supreme law'."[3]

The leader's psychopathology is at the root of the very structure of totalism. The need to control followers, to bind them to him or herself with the combination of terror and "love," flows from the leader's own disorganized attachment. In this chapter I discuss first, the leader's psychopathology and how this is expressed relationally, and second, how these relationships can develop into smaller or larger group structures with the particular attributes required to cement his or her control.

---

i Excerpts from *The Origins of Totalitarianism* by Hannah Arendt. Copyright 1951 by Hannah Arendt. Copyright © renewed 1979 by Mary McCarthy West. Reprinted by permission of Houghton Mifflin Harcourt Publishing Company. All rights reserved.

Charismatic authoritarianism

It is a difficult job to study the psychology or even biographies of totalist leaders. They tend not to want to be the subject of investigation. Their need to be in
control does not lend itself to their being a willing participant of a psychological
interview. Further, they often play fast and loose with how they tell their life stories,
this usually being a key part of the mythology they build up around themselves.
Thus we must piece together a rough picture based on biographical studies, on
reports from those who knew them and on the things they say in their own verbal
or written communications. I do not claim to offer any definitive study of these
leaders, but instead I suggest a way of looking at leaders, a hypothesis, anchored in
attachment theory, of what makes them tick.

Based on what we know of their backgrounds, and the way they conduct their
relationships, it seems clear that totalist leaders themselves are disorganized in their
attachment status with others.[ii] By definition, they have a high need to control
others, and have the psychological means to do so. Further, they do this not through
simple violence alone, as do dictators,[4] for example, but through a combination of
terror and (apparent) love. This combination is expressed in the two characteristics
of authoritarianism and charisma central to the personality of the totalist leader.

Authoritarianism is one face of the totalist leader's makeup. Adorno[5] described
the authoritarian personality as exploitatively dependent and power-oriented. He
found that such persons were the product of a domineering father and punitive
mother and an upbringing involving threats, coercion and threats of withdrawal
of love as a means to induce obedience; in his study, the children of this type of
environment tended to be insecure, dependent, fearful and hostile. These features
parallel Schein's[6] description of totalist leaders as anxious and insecure, requiring
constant reassurance, lacking flexibility in thinking and perceiving, only able to
see their own viewpoint and lacking in empathy. Authoritarians are bullies who
threaten and punish.

Although authoritarianism is part of the totalist leader's personality, it is not sufficient on its own to explain the particular way these leaders entrap and retain followers. Dictators who rely only on violence are only authoritarian. Mussolini, for
example, was a dictator who ruled by simple violence alone.[7] In such authoritarian dictatorships, "[T]he difference between guilt and innocence turned on actual
voluntary conduct . . . People could be intimidated through violence because they
knew what they had to do to avoid it."[8] Subjects must obey, but internally they can

---

ii They may also fit the Cannot Classify status (Alan Sroufe, personal communication), which refers
   to a *global* disorganization – i.e. disorganization that is not limited to attachment relationships but
   is observable in relation to other elements of experience. Persons with this attachment status show
   a global incoherence in the way they talk about both their attachment relationships and their other
   life experiences: Main, M. and R. Goldwyn. 1998. "Adult Attachment Scoring and Classification
   Systems," in *U.C. Berkeley.* For simplicity's sake I will assume both classifications but only refer to
   disorganization in the text.

disagree. But in a totalitarian system there may be no way to know how to avoid punishment, and, indeed, terror is often targeted at the clearly innocent – as we can see, for example, in the imprisonment and violent punishment of the children of political prisoners in North Korea.[9] Unlike the dictator, the totalist leader seeks *total* control, and this requires an inner coercion on the part of their followers: their goal is not mere obedience, but mass loyalty and, as Herman states, "willing victims."[10] Under the rule of the totalist leader one can never be sure of safety, no matter how one follows the rules. This is because an essential part of the system involves the constant arousal of fear leading followers to turn to the leader or group as the only possible source of rescue and "comfort."

To create the impression of this "comfort" or "love" means the totalist leader must also have charisma in their toolkit. There are two aspects to the appeal of the charismatic. First is the initial appeal that draws the follower into the charismatic's sphere of influence. However, the initial appeal to a given cause or organization may not, in fact, be solely due to the personal and charismatic appeal of the leader but can also be a result of social conditions, situational factors and the particular ideological come-on employed.[iii] Second is the role of charisma in retaining followers. The feelings of "love," worship and uniqueness that the charismatic relationship engenders become part of the glue that binds the follower tightly to the leader or group. These feelings may not always be directed at the individual person of the leader, and may in some cases be for the "cause" or the organization, but they are, nonetheless, put in place and set in motion by the charismatic relationship between the leader and at least the core group of followers.

However, charisma on its own is also not sufficient to explain the totalist leader's personality. Charisma describes a bond between leader and follower that involves awe and veneration of the leader.[11] Leaders such as Nelson Mandela, Martin Luther King and Mahatma Gandhi all had charismatic relationships with their followers. But they were not authoritarian: they certainly did not terrorize followers, nor did they exert complete control over the organizations they were associated with. Neither is there any indication they engaged in mental manipulation or bullying of followers. In fact, their goals, and often their practices, were to gain power not for themselves but for their people and in the service of furthering democratic processes.

But when the two powerful attributes of charisma and authoritarianism are merged in one individual this can result in a highly controlling totalist leader who wields an all-encompassing worldview to form a closed and isolating organization. In this way they can remove both alternate attachments and alternate worldviews available to followers, resulting in the affective and cognitive isolation of followers. This organizational, affective and cognitive closure is what differentiates between a

---

iii In fact the initial appeal for recruitment sometimes may not involve the personal charisma of the leader at all – as discussed in Chapter Three, recruitment can take many different pathways where the leader may be entirely absent or unknown (as was the case in my own recruitment).

charismatic *authoritarian* leader such as the Nation of Islam's Louis Farrakhan and a charismatic *non-authoritarian* leader such as Mandela.

Totalist leaders, then, require these two attributes. In attachment terms the two elements of disorganized attachment – the simultaneous "running from" and the "running to" a source of threat – are represented by the two elements of authoritarianism and charisma, or terror and love. On the one hand is the fear that these leaders arouse in followers ("running from"), and on the other is the haven of safety that they create – the "love" that they offer ("running to") – while removing any alternate, competing safe havens from the reach of the follower. Without the charisma/love/safe haven element pure physical force would be needed, but totalist leaders do not rely just on that (although clearly this is often part of the equation). With the charisma/love/safe haven element in place, once authoritarian threat is triggered, the situation is primed for followers to become glued to the system with a disorganized bond to the disorganized leader.

The leader's disorganized attachment

Attachment disorganization predicts controlling and aggressive behavior as well as fearful relationships with peers.[12] It involves intense abandonment anxiety, which is also seen as a "core feature of the abusive personality."[13] There are, however, a variety of types of disorganization, some leading more to aggressive, dominant and externalizing behaviors and some to more passive, subordinate and internalizing characteristics.

In attachment terms, I suggest that the leader has a particular form of this disorganization: that which occurs with a primarily dismissing (known as avoidant in children) subtype. In children this disorganized subtype has been shown to be overrepresented in those with aggressive and controlling, punitive behavior disorders. These studies show that such children have a background of maltreatment – particularly having been subject to controlling physical abuse.[14] This hostile or controlling-punitive form results from violent, frightening, controlling backgrounds, or what has been termed "hostile self-referential parenting."[15] These children respond to this situation by themselves becoming hostile and controlling towards others.[iv] Without any intervening secure or organized attachments this can lead to transmission of the same qualities to the next generation:

> Caregivers who display a hostile interaction pattern appear to be attempting to master unbearable feelings of vulnerability by denying their own feelings of fear and helplessness. This denial may be accomplished through suppression of conscious experience of vulnerable emotions and through

---

iv There are other forms of disorganization – for example the form that results in controlling caregiving – but this has different behavioral expressions and is a more subordinate form. In fact, I would suggest that this passive, helpless, hypervigilant and clingy form is that which is created in followers whilst under the control of the leader.

consistently controlling others in relationships. Behaviorally, parents in this group may reenact discipline by coercion, suppression of children's anger, and premature encouragement of autonomy. In these families, both researchers and clinicians note extreme attempts to control children's behavior, with subsequent chains of reciprocal coercive and negative affectivity between parents and children.[16]

The following brief examples of totalist leaders illustrate this transmission process.

According to a source who had been close to him, right-wing political cult leader Lyndon LaRouche was a "misfit" in his youth who was bullied at school and responded verbally with a "vicious mouth." "His father, Lyndon LaRouche Sr., would fly into terrible rages for small infractions and would then beat Lyn physically." At 17 he ran away from his family after yet another beating from his father.[17] LaRouche himself described his childhood as that of "an egregious child, I wouldn't say an ugly duckling but a nasty duckling."[18] David Koresh, leader of the Branch Davidians, had a self-reported history of abuse as a child, along with a history of early behavior problems and a pattern of aggression.[19] A study of David Berg, leader of the Children of God, details Berg's childhood history of sexual and psychological abuse.[20]

Alice Miller has described the physical and emotional abuse of Hitler's early years. She cites an earlier study detailing just one such episode:

> Years later he told one of his secretaries that he had read in an adventure novel that it was a proof of courage to show no pain. And so "I resolved not to make a sound the next time my father whipped me. And when the time came – I still can remember my frightened mother standing outside the door – I silently counted the blows. My mother thought I had gone crazy when I beamed proudly and said, 'Father hit me thirty-two times!'"[21]

This icy self-control is characteristic of the disorganized/dismissing classification and highly predictive of bullying, relational violence and controlling behavior in adulthood.[22] This cluster of attributes of the disorganized/dismissing leader may then be expressed, given the right conditions, in coercive and violent acts within, or by, the group, as directed by the leader. This set of attributes fits the model of the psychopath,[v] which includes characteristics such as: shallow affect, lack of empathy, guilt or remorse, superficial charm, egocentricity, manipulativeness, deceitfulness, grandiosity, and callousness in interpersonal relationships.[23]

Some idea of what is happening in the minds of such persons can be understood with a concept known as "mentalizing."[24] Those who are securely attached are able to mentalize – that is, as they relate to another person they are able to both understand what is happening in their own minds, at the same time as being able

---

v See Lalich, Janja and Madeleine Tobias. 2006. *Take Back Your Life: Recovering from Cults and Abusive Relationships*. Berkeley: Bay Tree Publishing for an excellent analysis of how cult leaders fit the characteristics of psychopaths.

to imagine what is happening in the mind of the other. "Mentalizing effectively entails simultaneously feeling and thinking about feeling"[25] both about the self and the other. Thus those who are able to mentalize learn to control their emotions and are able to "negotiate rather than fight."[26]

In the case of the disorganized leader, however, and resulting from his abusive background:

> under the combined pressure of needing comfort and escaping abuse from the same person he disrupts his capacity to represent the mental states of himself and others. People become objects or bodies, rather than whole, real, and meaningful individuals.[27]

Totalist leaders, as psychopaths, are unable to understand or reflect on their own mental states. Interestingly, one of the two brain structures involved in mentalizing is the orbitofrontal cortex – that same area that is involved in thinking about one's feelings and which is deactivated in post-traumatic stress disorder and dissociation, and which I have suggested is similarly deactivated by the dissociative process of brainwashing (see Chapter 4).

Yet at the same time as these leaders are unable to think about their own mental states, they do have an acute ability to understand the mental states of others – at least insofar as it allows them to manipulate their followers. They understand the minds of followers not through empathy but as a result of their need to control. Thus they have insight without empathy. As they require guaranteed and unilateral attachment from others, they therefore see others as objects to be acted upon solely for their own needs. From their own backgrounds, where they have been subject to the love/fear "fright without solution" relational dynamic, this is what comes naturally to them in managing their subsequent relationships. Having themselves lacked any secure escape hatch attachment (Miller refers to this as having a benevolent witness),[28] they also understand the need to prevent such secure, safe attachments among and with their followers in order to cement their control.

The leader's intense abandonment anxiety – his or her terror of being alone – causes this need for guaranteed attachments. And it is this need – more than the desire for material rewards – that I see as fundamental in what drives the totalist leader. Cultic and totalitarian leaders gain other resources in the process of controlling followers: financial resources, free labor, political power, sexual resources and so on. But I would suggest that these gains are actually by-products of the fundamental motivation of seeking guaranteed attachments. The need to control others as a means of guaranteeing attachment is the one consistent feature of cult leaders – not all of them seek to increase wealth as a result of their domination of followers.[vi] But

---

vi I am particularly aware of this from my own experience with a leader who appeared to live modestly and at times refused financially beneficial opportunities and offerings. Similarly, it is thought that Jim Roberts, the leader of The Brethren (also known as the Garbage Eaters), did not receive financial benefit, but nonetheless exerted complete control over the group. See: Griego, Evangeline, A.T. Productions. 2010. *God Willing.*

of course, once a leader has succeeded in controlling group members' attachment to him or herself, then these other benefits can accrue as well.

Totalist leaders seek to grasp people to them, to press them to themselves to prevent the terror of their own isolation. One such case was Otto Muehl, the leader of the Friedrichshof "art and therapy" commune and cult in the 1970s and 80s. The cult came to an end in 1991 when he was jailed for seven years for the crime of child rape. Muehl is on film stating that he first started the commune after his divorce when his family "dissolved." He invited people to live in his apartment "so I won't be so lonely . . . It was out of loneliness, pure and simple. Not for some big idea."[29]

But to keep people close, to prevent the terror of loneliness, leaders must also ensure that they are not frightened by those attachments, as they have been in their frightening pasts – therefore it is imperative that they must be the ones in control. As Mao Zedong's doctor described Mao's relationships:

> Mao was a man who had no friends . . . He saw everybody as a subject, a slave. The mistake of those who got purged was to see themselves as equal to him. He wanted everybody to be subservient. [He] was actually an irritable, manipulative egotist incapable of human feeling who surrounded himself with sycophants.[30]

The lonely, disorganized leader-to-be, armed with the twin attributes of charisma and authoritarianism, reproduces the disorganizing processes of love/fear as they begin the process of pulling in the guaranteed attachments they crave. They therefore set in place structural conditions of isolation and engulfment of the follower in order to create the dissociating situation of fright without solution by which the follower becomes subject to their control.

How do leaders learn these methods of control? They learn them, in the first instance, "at their caregiver's knee," within their first disorganized relationship. Later many refine their methods through associations in adulthood where they cross paths with similar figures and further develop methods of coercive persuasion. It is an interesting exercise to trace the organizational affiliations of cult leaders – often they have had experience in other cultic groups and have then split off and formed their own organizations. Werner Erhard, the founder of est (which now has morphed into Landmark Education, a so-called "personal and professional growth" company), was, himself, a former member of Scientology. Many of the terms used in Landmark reflect this previous association, such as, for example, "tools" and "technology." Similarly Fred Newman had an early alliance with Lyndon LaRouche – it is likely each picked up tricks from the other. However, these associations rarely last as a totalist group can only sustain one top dog. On the other hand, leaders by inheritance – such as David Miscavige who succeeded Scientology's founder, L. Ron Hubbard – of course, learn from their previous, late leader's methods. Organizations that outlive their leader over several generations may eventually develop a leadership group, as, for instance, the Governing Body of the Jehovah's Witnesses. These leadership bodies still employ the same methods and embody the two attributes of charisma and authoritarianism.

Relationship zero

Every totalist leader has to start somewhere. And unless they do inherit an organization – like David Miscavige, or James Taylor Jr. and Bruce Hales of the Exclusive Brethren – they need a first relationship. I call this "relationship zero." Some – such as the two-person Washington DC sniper cult led by John Allen Muhammed – never get beyond relationship zero, while others end up in control of entire totalitarian states. But this first two-person, or dyadic, relationship is the beginning of creating the social network – a series of connections of one person to another – that makes up the organization.

Fred Newman's relationship zero was Hazel Daren. According to an early "official" history of Fred Newman's totalist group, Newman, then 33, met Hazel Daren in 1968, when she was 18 and a student of his at the City College of New York. They met at an encounter group that Newman ran under the aegis of the Philosophy department. Newman recounts how Hazel Daren later begged him to return from a hiatus in California, in,

> a beautiful letter, made all the more profound and touching by Hazel's child-like handwriting. Most fundamental, however, was her child-like sincerity and reasoning. 'Don't leave the struggle' was the essence of her message. 'You were made for activism and our people, working people, need you' was the implication.[31]

Hazel was Newman's first recruit and became the first of his group of common-law wives.

In the "O.," the group of which I was a member, Theo Smith's relationship zero was with a young man who had been a left activist for some time. They met at a hippie farm in Wisconsin, leading to discussions about how to organize activists in neighboring Minnesota. From that beginning an organization was formed, culminating in several hundred members, rifts in the leftist community and violent confrontations between O. members and other progressives. The young activist looked up to Smith, became a lieutenant in the organization and, some 40 years later, remains associated with him and the tiny rump group of O. members that remain.[32]

In a one-on-one cult that stays at the level of this first relationship no formal ideology or structure is necessary. The follower must be isolated, but this can be done with declarations of love, threats and informal means of isolating the follower. For example, in relationships of controlling domestic violence the batterer will restrict or prohibit access to the telephone, will control money and the relationships and movements of the victim. There may be impacts on the victim's family, or children, but not beyond that.

However, in a system that grows beyond a simple two-person dyad, more formal means and broader ideological themes may be needed, and rituals, rules, systems and group norms will be set in place to ensure followers' isolation in order to induce and maintain dissociation. After the relationship zero has been formed, additional members can be drawn in and these more formal means begin to develop as the network grows. Often these early members become the core inner circle and the foundation of the lieutenant layer. From the first coerced individual, then, a larger system can be built, one where a culture of obedience is created, where minority dissent is quashed immediately, and where these coerced individuals recruit, monitor and surveil each other, thus strengthening the system.

The growth and trajectory of the group depends on the particular leader and their needs, but also on their historic context – the time and place in which they find themselves. This historic context provides both opportunities and constraints to the development and reach available to the leader. Some may simply become wife-beaters, some may run small or larger religious, political or commercial groups. But, given the right political climate and circumstances, some may be able to start totalitarian mass movements that, in a few cases, eventually attain sufficient power to become totalitarian states. However, regardless of the number of followers, the leader must follow the principles of isolating and engulfing them while maintaining the alternation of terror and love.

The totalist structure: Layers of an onion

As the totalist organization grows, it develops a structure of concentric onion-like layers with the leader in the center providing the driving movement.[33] These concentric circles are a kind of "bird's eye view" of the steep hierarchical pyramid structure of the totalist group (see Figures 6.1 and 6.2). There may be several layers – from the leader, to the lieutenants, to the elite inner circle, to other varying levels of membership, down to mere fellow-travelers or sympathizers. Arendt describes the innermost part of the structure:

> In the center of the movement, as the motor that swings it into motion, sits the Leader. He is separated from the elite formation by an inner circle of the initiated who spread around him an aura of impenetrable mystery which corresponds to his "intangible preponderance". His position within this intimate circle depends upon his ability to spin intrigues among its members and upon his skill in constantly changing its personnel.[34]

Arendt has dissected in detail both the innermost and outer layers within Hitler's Germany and Stalin's Soviet Union. According to her each layer serves a double function: "as the façade of the totalitarian movement to the nontotalitarian world, and as the façade of this world to the inner hierarchy of the movement."[35]

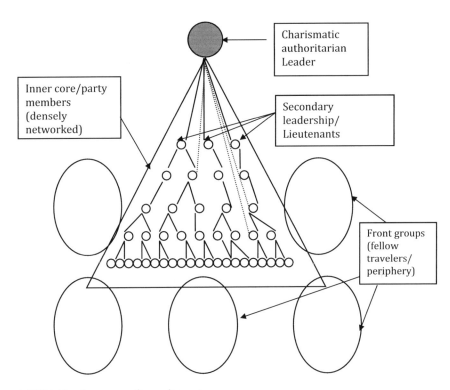

FIGURE 6.1 Structure of a totalist system

In other words, the deeper you go towards the center of the system, the more distant from reality you become as you enter the "fiction" of the closed and secretive totalitarian world. The life and beliefs of the innermost circle are so extreme that the outer circles must be protected from it until they are ready and have moved through the intervening layers, becoming sufficiently conditioned along the way. On the other hand, the inner circle must also be protected from the reality that might burst their fictional bubble. Therefore each layer has the job of both connecting to the next layer further out, presenting a "reasonable" face to that more external layer, and at the same time it must protect the next innermost layer from the truth and reality of the outside world. In support of this structure the group employs secrecy and deception to maintain the separation between layers.

For example, in Scientology the public was typically protected from the most extreme elements of the internal ideology of aliens bursting from volcanoes and inhabiting humans' bodies (this is now widely known since being leaked onto the internet by an anonymous former member in 1994).[36] The group attempted to keep this core belief under wraps so as not to scare off new or potential recruits who they aim to draw in by the more benign promise of personal growth and development. It takes time to move a person sufficiently far into the system until

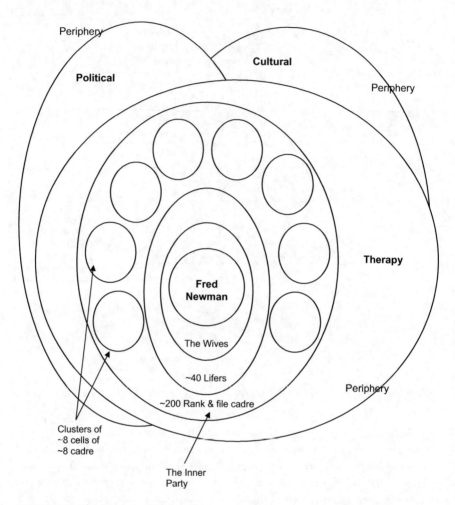

FIGURE 6.2   The Newman Tendency

they become isolated and detached enough from rational thought before the group can afford to unveil these secret ideas.

Similarly, the inner circles must not be exposed too much to the "normalcy" of life outside the closed inner world of Scientology. Too much of this exposure might lead those who have become more fully converted to gain information and relationships that might disconfirm the ideas that uphold the totalist structure. In recent years many senior members of Scientology have left and posted accounts of the life within the group, and this has led to something of a flood of defections. Exposing the inner secrets of Scientology on the internet allowed both the public and, in many cases, current group members to gain a critical view of these ideas and behaviors. In this way the public's often disbelieving and mocking response to the internal theology becomes a potentially dangerous "normal" source of feedback to group members, from which the multiple organizational layers are supposed to protect them.

The inner circles of totalist groups, insulated by a series of these outer layers, are difficult to penetrate and shrouded in secrecy. In the O., for example, rank and file members did not even know the leader's name. We received communications only from the idiosyncratically named "P.O.O." – what that stood for was never spelled out, though later this scatological acronym caused much raucous laughter for former members.

Moving outward from the leader, the innermost circle protects him or her from the masses outside, at the same time as projecting the leader's orders and ideology outward to the next layers. The personnel in this layer may constantly change, depending on the leader's whim. Fred Newman was surrounded by his immediate lieutenants: "The Wives." They were in charge of looking after his personal needs as well as leading the organization on a daily basis. Newman added or discarded wives at his whim. Similarly, Maryam Rajavi serves this function within the Mojahedin-e-Khalq, implementing Masoud Rajavi's wishes and serving as a proxy for him while his whereabouts remain secret.[37] But she, too, will likely be dispensable should he so desire.

Further out from the center, there may be yet another lieutenant layer: the daily leadership of the organization, which may or may not be the same as the innermost circle. The number of layers within a system depends on its size and functions. Arendt[38] details how layers in the National Socialist Party were added as needed as the Nazi organization developed. Adding layers allowed further differentiation between the inner and outer worlds, and more flexibility to promote and demote Nazi party members. Further, the addition of yet more elite layers meant new controls could be established "to control the controllers"[39] – the various ranks of party members had to be kept in line by the innermost, most loyal and elite formations.

Individual members of these secondary lieutenant levels of leadership are frequently promoted, demoted and purged to prevent any possible opposition developing to dilute the absolute and single point of power of the leader – this is readily seen in Stalin's purges and in Mao's regime, particularly during the Cultural Revolution.[40] An important characteristic of totalism is that it is made up of an unstable, fluctuating hierarchy rather than the more stable, rule-bound hierarchies typical of bureaucratic institutions.[41]

Another example of this "fluid" hierarchy can be seen in the Mojahedin-e-Khalq, where Rajavi appoints authority figures in the hierarchy based, not on "expertise, but because of 'ideological rank'."[42] These rankings change on a dime, depending on Rajavi's whim. At one point, in a major "ideological" move, men were removed from any leadership posts and an all-female leadership replaced them (with the exception, of course, of Rajavi himself) – presumably in an effort to keep the men subservient and prevent the development of internal resistance to Rajavi.[43] More recently seven members of Rajavi's inner circle have disappeared and MEK watchers suspect they are likely to have been "eliminated" as no longer being of use and potentially dangerous "because of the information they carry."[44]

After the lieutenant layer may come some form of elite, senior membership. Within Scientology this is the Sea Organization (known as the Sea Org), many of whose members are recruited as children and who, even at young ages, may wield considerable authority over long-term and older members.[45] In Newman's group this layer consisted of 40 or so "Lifers": long-term, highly loyal members.

Further yet from the center, the next layer may be the rank-and-file membership. In Scientology this is the regular membership. In Newman's group this layer consists of about 200 members organized into secret cells of about eight cadres in each. These cadres are, according to former member Marina Ortiz, under group discipline "24/7." Nearly all members are in Social Therapy (which they pay for) and they work in the various internal and public parts of the organization. Members' lives are almost entirely encapsulated within the group. Members find it hard to leave the group, or, in some cases, even to imagine life outside. As one former member I interviewed said:

> There was a mentality, you know, while you were in it, that, that, that you would more or less die if you actually ever became outside of it. So there was a lot of confusion about that, you know, sort of, how am I, how am I no longer in it anymore? I didn't even think that was a possibility.

This is the essence of the trauma bond that is formed in these groups: followers are conditioned to internalize a terror of the outside world – the goal of the system is that followers reject entirely and forever the prior reality and the outside world.

There may be an appearance of close, "comradely" relationships, but these will be instrumental, repressive and highly conditional. Internally members are densely tied to each other in multiple ways, but these ties are replaceable and undifferentiated. This isolation from fellow members is structurally and systematically imposed, as in this example from a description of life inside the Mojahedin-e-Khalq's Camp Ashraf:

> No two people could sit alone and talk together, especially about their former lives. Informants were planted everywhere. It was Maryam's idea to kill emotional relationships. "She called it 'drying the base,'" Afshari said. "They kept telling us every one of your emotions should be channeled toward Massoud, and Massoud equals leadership, and leadership equals Iran."[46]

The Mojahedin also insisted on segregation of the sexes from early childhood, forbidding girls from speaking to boys, and severely punishing children who associated across gender lines.

Life for the rank and file within totalism is stressful and uncertain, as members need to be on high alert should they be sanctioned for misdeeds. The unstable hierarchy is also visible at this level. A striking example of this can be seen in Otto Muehl's cult, the Friedrichshof, shown in a moving film made by Julien Robert, a man who was born and grew up in the group.[47] The film describes the key organizational form of the group: the *Struktur* (the Structure). Called Papa by group members, Muehl reviewed the rankings of his 800 followers daily and pushed various of them up or down the ranks. This included even very small children who would be lined up and ordered according to Muehl's criteria of the day. As Muehl himself said, "The hierarchy is not rigid, but fluid." This kept everyone on their toes: Muehl was the only one who did the ranking and only he was safe. Muehl also set up a sexual hierarchy, starting with his "First Lady," his preferred partner of the moment. As for the rest of the group they were forbidden from foreplay or affection in sex and were "all commanded to sleep with a different partner every night – apart, that is, from Muehl, who can sleep with whomever he wants whenever he wants."[48] Once again, then, the totalist leader has a mechanism in place to prevent any alternate attachment relationships from forming.

Finally, after the layers that exist strictly within the confines of secrecy and absolute closure of the group, come the front groups. These are broader and more open and porous outer circles designed specifically for recruitment or other supportive or strategic functions.[49] They face directly out to the non-totalist world. The double function of the layer mechanism also operates here. Front groups allow rank-and-file members to feel "normal" as they have channels to interact with the outside world – although these interactions are rigidly scripted and controlled. They also present a benign face of the group to the outside world while nonetheless being a way in, a wide-open entry point into the no-exit lobster pot of the group.

In a classic study, Lofland[50] describes the various and many front groups (possibly numbering in the hundreds) of the Unification Church, including academic and professional groups, schools, businesses, fund-raising operations, and a variety of cultural, political and educational groups that perform functions from recruitment, to fundraising to political power-brokering. The Church of Scientology organization, similarly, is noted for its many front organizations, such as the Sterling Management corporate training arm or the Narcanon drug rehabilitation program, which perform recruitment and money-making functions.[51] In the O. we had a health food bakery (as does the cultic Nation of Islam, led by Louis Farrakhan), a childcare center, software companies and even – my personal favorite – Careful Construction, a remodeling company known for its extraordinarily shoddy, and sometimes dangerous, work.

While he was alive, Fred Newman sat on top of a structure whose outermost layers were made up of three overlapping sets of front groups. Several Social Therapy centers were maintained in different cities, offering therapy and training to the public. The well-funded Castillo Theatre (producing plays of which the vast majority were written by Newman) and the All Stars are cultural programs for adults and youth. And the Newman Tendency was active in Independence Party politics, for a time essentially controlling the party in New York City. Inner party members run all these fronts although the fronts have no open ties to the Tendency. As front organizations they serve to bring in new members, money and other resources (see Figures 6.1, 6.2).

While totalist groups may have multiple – sometimes hundreds – of front groups, coalitions with other organizations are, however, infrequent[52] and when they do exist are likely to be tempestuous and short-lived[53] given the need for the leader to exert complete control over his domain. Power-sharing is never going to last long with a totalist leader involved. This is another way whereby the leader maintains complete control and the extreme closure and "self-sealing" nature of the group.[54]

The duplication of societal functions

An important feature of the totalist structure is what Arendt terms "duplication" by which the totalist group gives "the impression that all elements of society are embodied in their ranks."[55] This is particularly so in the pre-totalitarian phase before a group has achieved state power, as well as for groups that are not seeking state power at all. That is, the group, as part of its isolating structure, will set up duplicate institutions within it that claim to serve its members (and sometimes sympathizers involved in front groups) by fulfilling various needs. The Nazis set up fake departments of foreign affairs, education and so forth, which had little professional value but with which "every reality in the nontotalitarian world was duplicated in humbug."[56]

An ISIS/Daesh document was recently unearthed that shows the extent to which they are devising these duplicate systems. The document, titled *Principles in the Administration of the Islamic State*, is described as a civil servant's handbook and comprehensively details the institutions of the state-to-be of the promised caliphate:

> Isis appears to have numerous categories of civil servants including those for statistics, finance, admin and accounts.
> The blueprint then goes on to lay out plans for future departments, including the military, education, public services and media relations.[57]

Cults often do this on a smaller scale. For example, a former member I interviewed described how this worked in the Newman Tendency, listing the medical, legal and, of course, therapy services available within the organization. She felt that she had everything she needed in the Tendency and that, in her words, they provided her with a "safety net."

The more the group can contain all "societal" functions within it, the less members have reason to associate with the outside world. Many religious cults establish their own complex, though low-quality, institutions: the currently vigorous home-schooling movement is often a part of this. Cults may also set up their own schools, as, for example the Twelve Tribes group, which has been accused of abuses relating to homeschooling including group-ordained beating of children and illegal child labor.[58] Recently *The Independent* reported that the British Board of Education shut down an unregistered ultra Orthodox Jewish haredi school, which:

> has operated illegally for 40 years, does not teach children English [and] was failing to meet "minimum" standards. . . . The school, which has more than 200 students, encourages "cultural and ethnic insularity because it is so narrow and almost exclusively rooted in the study of the Torah," inspectors said following an investigation of the school.[59]

This is just one of many such illegal schools that closed groups operate. Preventing children from attending schools independent of the cult allows, again, the group to maintain its isolation, while simultaneously providing sites of indoctrination for the next generation. These duplicate structures create both a fictional total world that promises to take care of all of a follower's needs, along with a constricting and only too real totalist environment by which to exert control.

The simultaneous isolation and engulfment of the follower is ensured by the structure of the group that presses followers so tightly together that they become part of an undifferentiated mass while at the same time erasing any real connections between them. The totalist organization maintains this pressure by keeping followers – and therefore the organization – in constant motion and under constant stress. This non-stop movement in the name of the great cause provides the condition and justification for preventing followers having any time for themselves, time in which they might sleep, dream, think or feel; time to develop any of those crucial and potentially emancipatory real attachments to others.

The attributes of the structure – its closed nature, the fluctuating hierarchy, the highly centralized, onion-like layers, the secrecy and deception, internal and external isolation, duplication, and endless motion – ensure power and control remains in the hands of the leader. Followers must remain subordinate in order to serve the unilateral attachment needs of the leader. Once this structure is in place resources then can flow upwards to the leader: these resources can be emotional, sexual, financial, material and whatever else a ready supply of free and obedient labor can produce.

While resources flow up to the leader, orders and ideology flow down to the followers. (See Figure 6.3.) When members are consolidated in the inner group they must demonstrate uncritical obedience, regardless of their own survival needs. But not all followers need to be controlled entirely as long as they contribute in some way – thus many groups have peripheral members, or fellow travelers, who may give money, time or other resources through the front organizations. As long as they provide useful resources to the group, and remain uncritical, these more distant sympathizers may maintain some autonomy.

The outcome of the totalist structure and the immense power that the leader gains is the extreme control over and superexploitation of followers. In North Korea this control is enforced by punishments for "political crimes" including starvation, forced abortions, infanticide, torture, forced labor, rape and arbitrary execution.[60] The result of this control and the upwards flow of resources can be seen in the leader's opulent lifestyle in stark contrast to the decades of malnourishment of the population.[61] This superexploitation is thinly veiled with the absurd figleaf of fake elections in which 100 percent of votes are cast for ballots featuring only one candidate.[62] It is only now that enough escapees from the regime are telling their stories and being heard, the UN finally has charged the regime with crimes against humanity.[63]

The totalist structure is set in place to isolate, engulf and create ongoing stress in order to keep followers in a state of fright without solution, thus trapping

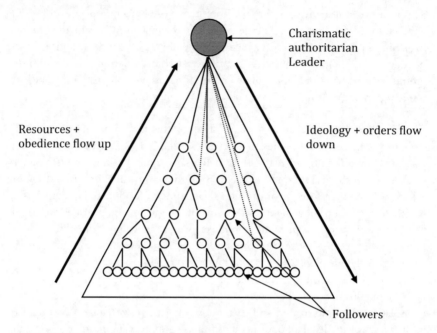

Charismatic
authoritarian
Leader

Resources +
obedience flow up

Ideology + orders flow
down

Followers

FIGURE 6.3   Direction and quality of interactions in a totalist system

them within a disorganized and guaranteed attachment to the disorganized leader. The total, or absolute, ideology, which flows down the steep pyramid from the leader to the membership, is the sheep's clothing that both disguises and justifies the sharp teeth sunk into the follower's neck. Understanding how the ideology supports this structure to serve the pathological needs of the leader is the next task.

Notes

1   Arendt, Hannah. 1948/1979. *The Origins of Totalitarianism*. Orlando: Harcourt Brace, p. 374.
2   Ibid., p. 323.
3   Ibid., p. 365.
4   Arendt, *The Origins of Totalitarianism*.
5   Adorno, Theodor W. 1944. *The Authoritarian Personality*. New York: Norton.
6   Schein, Edgar H. 1961. *Coercive Persuasion: A Socio-Psychological Analysis of the "Brainwashing" of American Civilian Prisoners by the Chinese Communists*. New York: W.W. Norton.
7   Arendt, *The Origins of Totalitarianism*.
8   O'Kane, Rosemary H.T. 1996. *Terror, Force, and States: The Path from Modernity*. Cheltenham: Edward Elgar Publishing, p. 73.
9   Harden, Blaine. 2012. *Escape from Camp 14: One Man's Remarkable Odyssey from North Korea to Freedom In the West*. London: Penguin.
10   Herman, Judith. 1992. *Trauma and Recovery*. New York: Basic Books.
11   Weber, Max. 1968. *Max Weber on Charisma and Institution Building: Selected Papers*, edited by S.N. Eisenstadt. Chicago: University of Chicago Press.

12 Lyons-Ruth, Karlen. 1996. "Attachment Relationships among Children with Aggressive Behavior Problems: The Role of Disorganized Early Attachment Patterns." *Journal of Consulting and Clinical Psychology* 64(1):64.

13 Dutton in West, Malcolm and Carol George. 1999. "Abuse and Violence in Intimate Adult Relationships: New Perspectives from Attachment Theory." *Attachment & Human Development* 1(2):137–56.

14 Lyons-Ruth, Karlen, Betty Repacholi, Sara McLeod and Eugenia Silva. 1991. "Disorganized Attachment Behavior in Infancy: Short-Term Stability, Maternal and Infant Correlates, and Risk-Related Subtypes." *Development and Psychopathology* 3(04):377–96.

15 Ibid.

16 Lyons-Ruth, Karlen, Sharon Melnick, Elisa Bronfman, Susannah Sherry and Lisa Llanas. 2004. "Hostile-Helpless Relational Models and Disorganized Attachment Patterns between Parents and Their Young Children: Review of Research and Implications for Clinical Work." *Attachment issues in Psychopathology and Intervention* 65–94, 79.

17 Hedgehog, Hylozoic. 2009, "Smiling Man from a Dead Planet": LaRouche Planet. (http://laroucheplanet.info/pmwiki/pmwiki.php?n=Library.UnityNow14).

18 King, Dennis. 1989. *Lyndon Larouche and the New American Fascism*. New York: Doubleday, p. 4.

19 Tobias, Madeleine and Janja Lalich. 1994. *Captive Hearts, Captive Minds*. Alameda: Hunter House.

20 Kent, Stephen A. 1994. "Lustful Prophet: A Psychosexual Historical Study of the Children of God's Leader, David Berg." *Cultic Studies Journal* 11(1):135–88.

21 Miller, Alice. 1980. *For Your Own Good*. New York: Farrar, Straus Giroux, p. 156.

22 Lyons-Ruth, "Attachment Relationships among Children with Aggressive Behavior Problems."

23 Hare, Robert D and Craig S Neumann. 2008. "Psychopathy as a Clinical and Empirical Construct." *Annual Review of Clinical Psychology* 4:217–46.

24 Fonagy, Peter, Gyorgy Gergely, Elliot L. Jurist and Mary Target. 2004. *Affect Regulation, Mentalization and the Development of the Self*. London: H. Karnac Ltd.

25 Twemlow, Stuart W., Peter Fonagy and Frank Sacco. 2005. "A Developmental Approach to Mentalizing Communities: I. A Model for Social Change." *Bulletin of the Menninger Clinic* 69(4):265–81, p. 276.

26 Ibid., p. 266.

27 Meloy, J. Reid. 2003. "Pathologies of Attachment, Violence, and Criminality." *Handbook of Psychology*, p. 30.

28 Miller, *For Your Own Good*.

29 Robert, Paul-Julien [Director]. 2013. *My Fathers, My Mother and Me*. FreibeuterFilm.

30 Bernstein, Richard. 1994. "The Tyrant Mao, as Told by His Doctor," in *New York Times*. New York.

31 Newman, Fred. 1990. "The Women I Live with/Maudie and the Men's Club." *Practice*, Winter.

32 Personal communication.

33 Arendt, *The Origins of Totalitarianism*.

34 Ibid., p. 373.

35 Ibid., p. 367.

36 Grossman, Wendy M. 1995. "Alt.Scientology.War." *Wired*.

37 Khodabandeh, Massoud. 2008. *Iran Interlink Special Report from Baghdad: Camp Ashraf and the Mojahedin-E Khalq*. (http://iran-interlink.org/userfiles/File/Camp%20Ashraf%20february%202008.pdf).

38 Arendt, *The Origins of Totalitarianism*.

39 Ibid., p. 369.

40 Chang, Jung. 1991. *Wild Swans: Three Daughters of China*. New York: Simon & Schuster.

41 Arendt, *The Origins of Totalitarianism*.

42 Banisadr, Masoud. 2004. *Masoud: Memoirs of an Iranian Rebel.* London: Saqi, p. 332.

43 Ibid.

44 Khodabandeh, Massoud. 2011, *Prepare for More Mystery Deaths of Mojahedin Khalq (Mko, Mek, Rajavi Cult) Members:* Iran Interlink. Retrieved March 7, 2014 (http://iran-interlink. org/wordpress/?p=3879).

45 Hill, Jenna Miscavige and Lisa Pulitzer. 2013. *Beyond Belief: My Secret Life Inside Scientology and My Harrowing Escape.* New York: William Morrow.

46 Rubin, Elizabeth. 2003. "The Cult of Rajavi," in *New York Times.* New York.

47 Robert, *My Fathers, My Mother and Me.*

48 Margolis, Jonathan. 1999. "The Price of Free Love," in *The Guardian.* London.

49 Arendt, *The Origins of Totalitarianism,* Berger, Peter L. and Thomas Luckmann. 1966. *The Social Construction of Reality: A Treatise in the Sociology of Knowledge.* Garden City, NY: Doubleday.

50 Lofland, John. 1977. *Doomsday Cult: A Study of Conversion, Proselytization, and Maintenance of Faith.* New York: Irvington Publishers: distributed by Halsted Press. See also an updated list at: http://freedomofmind.com/Docs/UCFrontList.pdf

51 Atack, Jon. 1990. *A Piece of Blue Sky.* Seacaucus: Carol Publishing Group; Singer, M.T. and J. Lalich. 1995b. *Cults in Our Midst: The Hidden Menace in Our Everyday Lives.* San Francisco: Jossey Bass.

52 Lofland, *Doomsday Cult.*

53 King, *Lyndon Larouche and the New American Fascism;* Tourish, Dennis and Tim Wohlforth. 2000. *On the Edge: Political Cults Right and Left.* Armonk: M.E. Sharpe.

54 Lalich, Janja. 2004. *Bounded Choice: True Believers and Charismatic Cults.* Berkeley: University of California Press.

55 Arendt, *The Origins of Totalitarianism,* p. 371.

56 Ibid., p. 371.

57 Malik, Shiv. 2015. "The Isis Papers: Behind 'Death Cult' Image Lies a Methodical Bureaucracy," in *Guardian,* December 7, 2015. London.

58 Paterson, Tony. 2013. "In Germany's Twelve Tribes Sect, Cameras Catch 'Cold and Systematic' Child-Beating," in *The Independent.* London.

59 Connett, David. 2016. "Charedi Talmud Torah Tashbar: Stamford Hill Jewish School that does Not Teach English Ordered to Close," in *The Independent,* January 14. London.

60 BBC News. 2014, *UN's North Korea Report: Main Findings:* BBC. Retrieved March 10, 2014 (http://www.bbc.co.uk/news/world-asia-26223180).

61 Knight, Richard. 2012, *Are North Koreans Really Three Inches Shorter Than South Koreans?:* BBC. Retrieved March 10, 2014 (http://www.bbc.co.uk/news/magazine-17774210).

62 BBC News. 2014, *North Koreans Vote in Rubber-Stamp Elections:* BBC. Retrieved March 10, 2014 (http://www.bbc.co.uk/news/world-asia-26223180).

63 BBC News, *UN's North Korea Report: Main Findings.*

7

SECRETS AND LIES

Ideology and language in totalist systems

> The aim of totalitarian education has never been to instill convictions, but to destroy the capacity to form any.
>
> Hannah Arendt[i]

The ideologies of totalist organizations vary from left to right, from a belief in aliens to post-modern therapy, from "peaceloving" to militant, or from apocalyptic to pseudo-scientific – but they all share a set of common formal traits and functions. In this chapter I explain the two purposes of the ideology and the specific use of language in these organizations.

The first purpose is to reflect and justify the absolute control and single point of power of the leader and the isolating structure he or she creates. This is the sheep's clothing that disguises the wolf. The leader strategically presents a series of different faces to the outside world, to new recruits and to different levels among followers.

The second purpose of totalist ideologies is to maintain dissociation. These ideologies aim to separate or prevent the integration of feeling with thinking, of sensory and cognitive processing. In the right-wing Lyndon LaRouche organization, for example, there is the explicit demand that members "COGNATE EVERY-THING and SENSE NOTHING, because 'You can't trust your sense perception'."[1] Other groups take the opposite tack, insisting on feeling only, and giving up thinking or intellectualizing. In either case the result is dissociation to "destroy our sense of reality" and to thereby create a cognitive vacuum that allows the group to

---

i Excerpts from *The Origins of Totalitarianism* by Hannah Arendt. Copyright 1951 by Hannah Arendt. Copyright © renewed 1979 by Mary McCarthy West. Reprinted by permission of Houghton Mifflin Harcourt Publishing Company. All rights reserved.

further introduce the content of its particular ideology as a critical step in creating deployable followers.

This chapter will give examples of how these two purposes are served through the exclusive nature of totalist belief systems, the special private language of the group, the peculiar complexity and often incomprehensible nature of the ideology, and other ways by which thoughtful reflection about the ideology and the reality it conceals is made almost impossible.

What is a total ideology?

Ideologies, says Arendt, are: "*isms* that pretend to have found the key explanation for all the mysteries of life and world."[2] Each total ideology claims to "explain all historical happenings, the total explanation of the past, the total knowledge of the present, and the reliable prediction of the future."[3] It rejects any knowledge from the outside world in order to create a fictitious world within the hermetically sealed totalist system.

As Arendt observed, totalitarianism has, "thanks to its peculiar ideology . . . discovered a means of dominating and terrorizing human beings from within."[4] This ideology and the language it uses in its delivery are fundamental to the ability of the leader to control his or her followers. In his study of prisoners of war in 1950s Chinese Communist prisons, Edgar Schein[5] states that language, rather than physical coercion, was such a core part of the brainwashing methods that some foreign prisoners "forgot" they knew Chinese in order to resist the process.

The total ideology is central to the leader-enforced interpretation of individuals' felt experiences. In creating a situation of fright without solution in followers, and thereby causing them to dissociate and become unable to think about the fear-arousing situation, the group can then further insinuate its own ideology as a substitute for the follower's critical thinking. Once this total ideology gains a foothold through this dissociated window in the follower's mind, it serves to continually reinforce and shore up the initial dissociation. A total ideology allows for no other views, and so, once accepted, provides the cognitive lock for the follower, in the same way as isolation from others and the prohibition of alternate attachment relationships provides the emotional lock.

A total ideology, and what it represents, can be confusing to observers, especially when they take it at face value. An especially difficult problem is that outsiders may assume that the belief system being peddled shares the qualities of belief systems that those in the non-totalist world hold. But this is not so. Both the structure and the function of totalist ideologies are quite different. In point of fact a totalist belief system represents a completely divergent thought system that cannot be understood with an outsider's vocabulary and ways of determining what is true.

Non-totalist belief systems, while they may be strongly held, are *partial*: they do not form the entirety of a person's worldview.[6] A productive scientist may worship a God or multiple gods. A Christian may use the Bible as a guide in many areas of life, yet not believe, as fundamentalist Creationists do, that every word in it is literally true. A partial ideology is exactly that: it is a belief system for part of life, which allows for a mix or complex of other beliefs and sources suited to different aspects of life. But a *total* ideology requires that the belief system, as defined and interpreted by the leader, enter into every last element of life without exception, and regardless of the self-interest of the believer. Totalist ideologies have an "ice-cold logic"[7] and rigidity that includes everything and allows no deviation. It is only the leader who may deviate and it is entirely within their rights (and a right many make use of) to make a 180-degree turn should that suit their goals. The leader of the Children of God, David Berg, for instance, needing to justify taking on a mistress, shifted from an ideology of celibacy to its opposite – enforced promiscuity for all in the group – thus giving him the ideological cover to dismiss wife one and take on wife two, not to mention his sexual abuse of young girls in the group.[8]

Observers may try to grasp the internal logic of a total ideology in order to understand why a follower holds to these beliefs. But this rarely helps as the total ideology cannot be separated from the whole structural system of brainwashing and coercive control.[ii] The individual interest of the member of a totalist system should not be assumed to be represented by their mouthing of the dogma. The follower has been brought to these beliefs by a process of coercion and manipulation, not as a result of independent rational or spiritual discernment. In addition, observers only have access to the external propaganda elements of the ideology – those elements deemed suitable for consumption by the outside world. As Lofland found in relation to the Unification Church, they:

> wanted the entire world to know and accept their ideology, but only certain parts were felt to be appropriate for disclosure to outsiders. Other parts should be held in secret until prospects were sufficiently instructed to understand them properly. The secret portions were controversial and, moreover, they made no sense apart from an acceptance and understanding of the less esoteric sections of the system.[9]

The two faces of total ideology: Propaganda and indoctrination

Another source of confusion for outsiders is the fact that there is a distinction between two functional faces of the ideology: propaganda and indoctrination. The totalist group employs propaganda as it communicates with the outside world, or

---

ii For an example of this confusion in the field of new religions, see Barker, Eileen. 1984. *The Making of a Moonie: Choice or Brainwashing?* Oxford, New York: B. Blackwell. In her attempted deconstruction of the Unification Church's dogma, Barker gets sidetracked by her in-depth, but ultimately unenlightening, analysis and avoids completely the issue of indoctrination, membership and a close look at the internal life of the group. In contrast, Lofland's 1977 *Doomsday Cult* summarizes the UC's total ideology in a few brief pages before moving on to the more salient issues of indoctrination, relationships within the group, recruitment, and faith maintenance.

with supporters and followers who are not fully consolidated.[10] It is the public face of the group's ideology. Thus propaganda must keep certain lines of communication open, despite being, internally, a fundamentally divergent set of beliefs. Propaganda must be somewhat understandable to outsiders, yet it is cloaked in "heavenly deception" (as the Unification Church says) in order not to frighten off potential recruits.[11]

The propaganda of Jung Myung Seok's Providence, or Jesus Morning Star (JMS), cult involves inspirational activities for the young. The ideas presented at this level keep a shaky foothold in the external world, so they can be accessible and attractive to non-members. For example, a JMS event at the University of California, San Diego, included a modeling show featuring young women, titled "Autumn Fantasy: The Spirit of Harvest." The theme of the show was "Developing Beauty from Within," and included dance performances and a videotaped "inspirational message" about perseverance from Jung.[12] Similar events have been held in London, Vancouver, New York and many other cities.[13] Songs sung at the early stages of recruitment to JMS – the propaganda stage – are bland and generic and could be from any mainstream religion:

> This is my Father's world, and to my listening ears
> All nature sings and round me rings the music of the spheres
> This is my Father's world; I rest me in the thought
> Of rocks and trees, of skies and seas; His hand the wonders wrought[14]

Only later in the indoctrination process do the songs reveal that, in fact, Father, the Lord, is Jung himself. The propaganda phase also doesn't tell you that sex with the Father is the way to purge your sins – this is saved for the later in-depth indoctrination of young women. The transition from propaganda to indoctrination occurs via a series of 30 lectures that begin to cast Jung as the "central figure" in the increasingly isolated environment into which recruits are drawn.[15] Jung is currently serving a ten-year sentence for raping four women[16] and over 100 women members have accused him of sexual abuse.[17]

So once the recruit is within the system and the isolation from their previous relationships is well under way, the form of the ideology starts to switch from propaganda to indoctrination. In the Newman Tendency, those recruits who came in through the various front groups and were deemed suitable for further "cadre training" spent a year in study groups reading Newman's writings. This was a transition year, similar to the JMS process of 30 lectures. After that, however, no more formal study took place – the social therapy sessions became the site of indoctrination. The talk within the cadres' social therapy then changed from an initial focus on the individual's presenting problem to a focus on "giving to the group." Marina Ortiz described how the language in group therapy transitioned from the propaganda to the indoctrination function:

> The younger you were [i.e. as a group member], it was more about your personal development, but down the road therapy was more about stripping

your ego and they would say things like – and this was later on when we were full cadre – you couldn't have individual thoughts, you couldn't even want things for yourself, you couldn't talk about yourself, because you were being bourgeois, you were being egotistical, you're thinking of yourself, you're not thinking of others, you're not thinking of the group. . . . If someone were to come into a more experienced group and talk like that [i.e. personally], the response would be something like, maybe by Fred Newman, "What does this do for the group?" you know, "How are we going to build the group? That's what I'm concerned with. Let's talk about that." So that individual and personal things were not even mentioned anymore. I'm talking like once you were all the way in.

Indoctrination is targeted to existing group members and serves the purpose of retaining these members, keeping them controlled and entrapped within the system. But there are overlaps between the two types of ideology – propaganda and indoctrination – as there must be if recruits are to be transformed into loyal followers. For example, some language transfers between the two stages – in the Newman Tendency, the words "growth" and "development" are used in both stages, but later, new words are also introduced such as the concepts of "party cadre" who would be "proletarianized" and work with "organic members" (black and Latino recruits).[18]

Having pulled the recruit away from their prior attachments, and started to introduce them via propaganda – the "safe," more digestible form of the ideology – to the new thought system of the group, and with the beginnings of dissociation in place, more extreme forms of the ideology are now slowly poured into the dissociated space that has been created within the recruit's mind. Propaganda is the thin end of the ideological wedge but the recruit is consolidated through the indoctrination that takes place along with isolation, engulfment and stress, and in the cognitive gap created by the ensuing fright without solution.

The context in which indoctrination takes place is very important to the process. In social therapy the context of small groups of people, previously unknown to one another, meeting together over time and sharing private, personal information fits Schein's[iii] description of the importance of *new* social connections in this reorganized "conversational apparatus."[19] Schein states that when prisoners of war in Chinese camps who knew each other *before* prison would talk to each other they would create a bond of shared hostility to the authorities, and this strengthened their capacity to resist. But when housed in cells with cellmates who didn't know each other and who would then be in struggle meetings together, this would create attachments with the new cellmates (based on the new ideology) and weaken resistance.

iii And also Sageman's 2004 *Understanding Terror Networks* networks of "bunches of guys."

The suffocating structure of the total ideology

The structure of the ideology mirrors and reinforces the rigid structure of the group and the divide between those in the group and those outside. It mirrors the structure by having a single truth as there is a single leader; by its closed absolute-ness in that there is no other way, and it must be adhered to exactly and without dissension; and by having levels and layers of secrecy reflecting the onion-like layers of the group.

If the totalist ideology is the reflection and justification of the leader and his or her controlling relationship to followers, then we can see that the ideology must also reflect the three-fold process of creating fright without solution – this being the primary control mechanism the leader employs. First, the ideology must present the leader/group as the only safe haven. Second, it must label all other potential safe havens (family, friends, the outside world) at worst as dangerous, and at best as ignorant obstacles to "salvation." And third, it must broadcast elements of fear, stress or threat to trigger the traumatic disorganized bond of the follower to the group, and set in place the resulting dissociation that this maladaptive response causes.

One truth, one leader

The structure that the totalist ideology reflects and justifies is a steeply hierarchi-cal one led by an all-powerful leader. As there is one single point of power in the group – the charismatic and authoritarian leader – so there is only one Truth: a single, absolute set of ideas, the one and only, the Theory of Everything, the answer to all life's problems, from the great to the small. In this sense the structure of the ide-ology is more important than its particular contents.[iv] This single truth, the sacred word, is the word of the leader, or that of a deity to whom the leader is the only one to have a direct line (e.g. the Reverend Moon of the Unification Church). All knowledge comes from the leader, and no other knowledge is required. However they choose to say it, the leader makes clear that their beliefs (or their interpreta-tions of other texts, such as, of course the Bible, Qur'an, Das Capital and so forth) are the only True, Sacred, Holy, Correct, Developmental, Effective, Proletarian or Transformative ones. To be saved, one must accept the dogma whole hog: hook, line and sinker.

As Fred Newman explains: "The message here is this: if you want to change anything in your life, you have to change your whole life."[20] No alternate beliefs are necessary when a total ideology exists to explain everything in the past, the present and the future. In Pol Pot's Cambodia even the past was abolished and the calendar changed. When his Khmer Rouge came to power, a former child soldier recounted: "This is Year Zero, they say. Nothing has come before. All past

---

iv For an interesting study on this see Martin, John Levi. 2002. "Power, Authority, and the Constraint of
   Belief Systems." *American Journal of Sociology* 107(4):861–904.

knowledge is illegal."[21] ISIS/Daesh is currently doing the same (as did the Taliban before them): destroying historical artifacts as a way to destroy any history but their own, fictitious one. In his own way, mini-dictator Newman handily also communicates the irrelevance of all other views by announcing "the end of knowing," the title of his book[22] in which he concludes that a person has no need to know anything at all (of course except for what he has to teach).

Anne Singleton, the Yorkshire-born and raised ex-member of the Mojahedin-e-Khalq (MEK), writes of her former leader:

> Rajavi has always said that he is only interested in those people who accept him as their ideological leader. For these people, when they accept an ideological leader, sins mean nothing. What he does must be right and good, rather than as they might interpret it; they aren't capable of knowing what is right or good, only the ideological leader can say this.[23]

Mojahedin members were to "recognise and accept Rajavi's transcendent ideological qualification to lead the organisation from above with reference to no-one but God."[24]

This single truth then, and its supposed genesis in the epiphanies and expertise of the leader, supports their absolute power, which then entitles them to the guaranteed attachments of loyal followers. The leader "owns" the single truth in the same way as they own the organization. The ideology then serves to reinforce this by raising the leader both to god-like omnipotence and to the symbolic position of parent to the group. As discussed in Chapter 5, in many totalist systems the leader has among their titles that of "Dad" (Jim Jones, Peoples Temple, many of the Nigerian Pentecostal leaders, and Phillip Berg of the Children of God), "Benevolent Mother" (Park Soon-ja, of the Paradise cult),[v] "True Parent" (Reverend Moon, Unification Church) or Brother Number One (Pol Pot). These parental or familial titles reflect the dual relationship of both power and attachment.

One "safe haven" attachment

The ideology portrays the leader (and the group as proxy) as the one true safe haven – the comforter, source of all goodness, the infallible one to whom the follower must turn. For example, after the Ideological Revolution that he imposed, Rajavi demanded that MEK followers now love him and become devoted to him – they must not act out of hate for the enemy, but rather out of love for Rajavi. (Predictably this ended up with that "love" being shown by his extraction of sexual favors

v Park Soon-ja was implicated in a fraud investigation and in 1987 she, her 3 grown-up children and 28 others were found dead inside the factory where they had lived and worked. "They had been drugged and strangled in what appeared to be a mass suicide." *LA Times* 08/03/1987 http://articles.latimes.com/1987–08–30/news/mn-4994_1_cult

from many women in the group.)[25] Indian guru Nithyananda titles his book: "Rising in love with the Master: The greatest love affair." These unsubtle, direct suggestions reinforce the idea that the leader is the only safe haven.

The total ideology also reflects and justifies the structural isolation of followers – the removal of any alternate safe havens that might offer an escape from the system. Followers must be kept from the outside world. The dichotomous "Us" versus "Them" thinking "draws a sharp line between those whose right to existence can be recognized, and those who possess no such right."[26] All within the group have the promise of being saved or transformed if sufficiently compliant to the dictates of the leader. Those outside the group are at best lost and ignorant, or, worst case, the evil enemy. Only the leader can determine who has the right to exist and who does not.

Islamist extremists use the term *kuffar* (infidels or unbelievers) to describe these outsiders,[27] while the Children of God called outsiders "Systemites."[28] Jonny Scaramanga describes how the isolating, Christian fundamentalist school he attended drew this line of separation:

> In my first week at the ACE school, the principal preached a sermon called "Birds of a Feather Must Flock Together". This 45 minute rant can be summarised in one sentence: "Don't be friends with non-Christians". So began three years in which I learned to view 'unbelievers' with a mixture of fear and contempt. . . .
>
> There was a second way creationism was used to fend off outsiders. The school claimed that creationism proved the Bible was the Word of God. Biblical authority thus established beyond question, I was forced to live by such Scriptures as Psalm 1:1, "Blessed is he that walketh not in the counsel of the ungodly . . ." My only interaction with sinners was for evangelism.[29]

The total ideology must also justify the isolation that followers experience from trusting and open relationships with others in the group, especially close attachment relationships. As discussed in detail earlier in Chapter 5, the ideology exists to "explain" why followers must not have any other attachments.

Fred Newman's concepts such as "friendo-sexuality" are designed to de-emphasize the emotional intimacy of sexual relationships. "Patients were taught to resent all personal relationships . . . with therapists denouncing partners as engaging in 'coupling'."[30] Maintaining family relationships was referred to derogatorily as "doing family." Family relationships were discouraged as being a distraction from the important work of the group, as "the therapist explained, because they tended to 'alienate' and 'retard' human growth and development."[31] Similarly, while "you weren't told 'You can't be with your kids,'" in a direct way, as Sidney reported, "If there's a conflict between doing political work and taking care of your kids, you do the political work . . . if you love your kids, you'll do the political work."

Nithyananda, an Indian guru currently charged with multiple counts of sexual abuse of young, female followers,[32] tells followers not to have "attachments" (other, of course, than to him) while engaging them in constant volunteer work for his group. His insistence on rejecting "attachments" included instructing at least one follower to have an abortion. His ideological justification is that attachments prevent spiritual growth and enlightenment.[33]

The ideological divorces of MEK involved severing all personal relationships within the group. Spouses were regarded as "buffers" between the leader and members, and that to enhance members' "capacity for struggle" and their ability to unite with the leader, these buffers must be removed.

> Rajavi announced at the meeting that as our "ideological leader" he had ordered mass divorce from our spouses. He asked everyone to hand over our rings if we had not already done so. That meeting was the strangest and most repugnant I had ever attended. It went on for almost a week.[34]

One truth, one conversation

Beyond close attachments, any conversations with others within totalist groups can be monitored and restricted. The only approved conversations are those that take place within the strict and rigid confines of the ideological framework. Other discussions are considered a waste of time, or, worse, toxic and dangerous to one's development. Often talking with others is overtly controlled as in this example from a girls' boarding school run in a cult-like manner in association with Believers Baptist Church in Indiana:

> That brings me to the "talking list". When you first get there you are told that you are only allowed to talk to a handful of girls (the ones who have the privilege of talking to everyone). If you are not allowed to talk to a girl you are not allowed to look at her or remotely in her direction let alone have any contact with her. Now imagine living, eating, sleeping and working with 29 other girls and you can't talk to or look at maybe 25 of them.[35]

In North Korea the consequence of unapproved talk is terrifying: an official slogan painted on the side of a marketplace threatens, "Death by firing squad to those who gossip!"[36] In the O., talk that was not directed to "functional" and "productive" ends was rather more mild, but was considered "exchange value" and subject to severe disapproval. In other groups non-approved discussion might be labeled as "worldly" or lacking a spiritual or developmental purpose, depending on the ideological direction of the group. Of course people do continue to talk, and find protected areas in which to steal real conversation whether that be about mundane topics or, more seriously, about criticism of the group. But this is dangerous to the system and, if found out, can be grounds for punishment. This ideological control is used to prevent any and all kinds of potential conversations with others – conversations in which the reality of the situation might become clear.

And why would one need to engage in these conversations in any case? The Truth is already known, for now and all time, and all circumstances. Everything that can be said has been said, by the Master, the Chairman, Dad. All you need to do is study his or her great words or official interpretations thereof. The follower's only concern is to find out what that Truth is: and that is done by obeying, working, following the dictates of the leader, submitting to the group. This is how Truth will appear, not through any side investigations, considerations, conversations. These can only lead to dissent and becoming one whose "right to existence" can no longer be recognized.

This rigid limiting of communication impairs not only free communication with others, whether inside or outside of the group, but also impairs followers' own imaginations and ability to hold on to an independent identity. Jang Jin-sung, the North Korean poet, said, "I was restless with yearning to write realist poetry based on what I saw, and not loyalist poetry based on what we were all told to see."[37] (As doing so would lead to a death sentence, this yearning to describe reality eventually led to his defection.) In the O. a cadre burned over 400 of his poems written prior to joining – undoubtedly now understanding they represented his Bourgeois World Outlook. Thinking is constantly shepherded back into the appropriate channels, and followers are made to feel guilty should they let their minds wander. Masoud Banisadr was ordered to "obliterate" his past by burning all his "non-essential" papers. He duly burned his university Ph.D. thesis and Master's dissertation, all his notes, his research, his letters from family and friends and his own stories – all of his written and literary past.[38] He was also challenged by a fellow member of the Mojahedin: "When will you forget about those things you have read, forget your idealism and face reality? Please forget the reading, see the real Mojahedin." And indeed he did: "I lost my trust in the written word. I decided not to read any more books; for all the time I was with the Mojahedin, I rarely did."[39] He did, of course, continue to read Mojahedin literature. Only Mojahedin thought was allowed.

In the end-times, racist and right-wing cult the Covenant, Sword and Arm of the Lord, the group forced members to destroy anything to do with their pre-cult lives including photographs and high school yearbooks:

> They destroyed television and radios and other 'reminders of the outside world's propaganda.' They sold their wedding rings. They received little or no information from the outside world.[40]

As part of this restriction, the right to privacy – this space in which to engage in private conversations even within oneself – is denied in totalist groups, and reinforced by the ideology. All inner thoughts must be confessed and subject to critique, while no space for private personal contemplation is allowed. This is done by forcing followers to expose their private, innermost thoughts and feelings – a process Lifton refers to as the "Cult of Confession."[41] In the O., as in Maoist China, this was accomplished through the idea of self-criticism. One was to write up any bad thoughts – in the case of my group, on the Criticism/Self-Criticism form – and ascribe those bad thoughts to, for instance, having a bourgeois, or petit-bourgeois worldview. In other groups confession may be carried out in group settings where the follower must carefully ensure they have enough to confess to show humility and conform to the requirement to acknowledge their sin, worldliness or pride,[42] but not confess so much as to engender serious punishment. Again, followers may secretly try to protect parts of themselves from this process of self-exposure, but it is a difficult balance to maintain.

While no privacy is allowed, on the other hand no real non-cult communication is allowed either, as described above. The boundaries of the private and the public realm are collapsed together so that one has neither.[43] Jang writes: "In North Korea the institutional control of thought begins with the consolidation of language, a policy designed to unify the private and public spheres of thought."[44] Thus the restricted totalist language and the single Truth become the only valid means of communicating or even thinking.

Total ideology demands total transformation

In order to further subordinate followers to the leader, totalist ideologies insist on a "permanent revolution" of the self. Total transformation is needed. This achieves several things: to imply that the follower is flawed and must change; that the required change shall be directed by the group's ideological pronouncements and by following orders; that only the leader is truly transformed; that therefore everyone has to emulate the leader and yet – in a clever bit of trickery – while all shall aspire to be transformed like the leader, none, clearly, can ever attain this perfection.

In accepting that personal transformation is required, one's own person, one's *self* then becomes, by definition, unacceptable, wrong and without value. The old self must be shed and the new group-self continually monitored, improved, striven for. In the Newman Tendency this is expressed in Newman's ideas of "continuous growth and development" and in his statements that there is no goal, no point of "graduation," no "release date," no end to the process and thus, presumably, no reason to ever leave the group. It is perhaps not surprising, then, that many stay in social therapy for decades. Newman describes one couple who were "in individual therapy and in group therapy with me; at some point they were also in therapy as a couple."[45] "[T]hey've built the therapy into their life activity . . . I've been with them, and they've been with me, half their lives."[46] According to Newman this couple had been engaged in "continuous personal growth" for almost 20 years.

While in the O., I remember querying my comrade Jerri about the O.'s concept of the Internal Transformation Process. "Was anyone ever actually transformed?" I asked. She discreetly turned her eyes away from mine: "Well, there is one person . . ." Although she did not say the name – our leader kept a low profile – it was clear that she was referring to the revolutionary and fully proletarianized P.O.O. The same leader who, I was to later discover on finally leaving the group, was then in prison for murder. Transformed indeed.

Nonetheless all followers must strive for transformation. This demand puts the entire onus on the individual: anything that goes wrong must be your fault – lack of purity, prayer, work, struggle or commitment. Of course this feeds well into the cult of confession and gives the context for group members to criticize each other, since to be transformed one must expose one's failings. The push for transformation keeps the individual in constant motion in the service of attaining this unattainable goal, thus being another justification for the lack of free time, sleep and space to think.

The ideology of fear

In these ways the total ideology establishes the leader/group as the only safe haven while removing any other alternate safe havens: the outside world, other potential allies in the group, and one's own internal sense of "safety" and inner dialogue. The elements discussed above also contribute to the third step of creating a situation of fright without solution – that of creating an environment of fear, stress or threat. The wrath of god, the terror of being labeled "bourgeois" or an "agent of the state" (two of the preferred threats in the O.), or the evils of the outside world or whoever may be the enemy of the moment are examples of varying ideological means of conjuring up and keeping alive the fear stimulus required to ensure that followers turn to the group or leader as the only remaining source of "comfort." A former member describes this in the Twelve Tribes group led by Gene Spriggs:

> Filling their members with fear and dread, the community makes it difficult for devastated members to depart. As they are leaving, defectors may hear "Whoever has the Holy Spirit and leaves the body is turned over to death. You will not live long." In another teaching Spriggs says, "If a person even thinks about returning to Egypt, our Father will provide them an opportunity to return . . . If you go back, you will drown."[47]

Yogi Bhajan, a former customs inspector, moved to the US and formed a "Sikh" yoga cult, 3HO, "Healthy, Happy, Holy Organization." Their current website tells how the group will teach followers how to live:

> How to eat. How to dress. How to communicate. How to have relationships. How to raise children. How to do business. Yogi Bhajan infused every aspect of life with the beauty and grace of the Kundalini. When you raise your Kundalini and change your consciousness, every aspect of life gets transformed. The lifestyle teachings of 3HO are designed to support you through that transformation. In this way, you can live healthy, happy and holy; bountiful, blissful and beautiful; as a completely healed and sovereign human being.[48]

However, Yogi Bhajan was also known for the ferocity of his curses – curses which terrified followers and which he used to keep control. Bhajan told followers that if they left the group or in other ways broke group rules they would lose their souls, their spines would be crippled, they would develop red in their aura and get cancer, become prostitutes, die hungry and alone or as one former member reported: "would be murdered and my dead body would be thrown into an arroyo, my bones bleaching in the desert sun."[49]

Inducing fear is sometimes simple, direct and backed up by the force of the state as in North Korea's public executions, or the beatings and death threats that took place in Jonestown. ISIS/Daesh terrorizes those both inside and outside of the organization with brutal killings – most recently in the extreme form of the public execution of a mother by her son.[50] Or sometimes the threat is indirect as in the prophecies, curses and black-and-white thinking of apocalyptic cults that claim that "Either you are serving Jehovah God or Satan the Devil."[51]

The first function of the ideology, then, is to justify and reflect the absolute power of the leader while isolating and stressing followers. This supports the creation of a situation of fright without solution that bonds the follower to the leader or group, and causes the follower to dissociate in relation to that situation. The second function of the ideology is to reinforce this dissociation: as there is no relational escape neither is there a cognitive escape.

Total ideology as a dissociating barrier to critical thought

The task for the totalist group is to prevent members thinking about their feelings about their situation. The subversive orbitofrontal cortex that insists on reviewing feelings and sensory information from the right brain, thinking about it and evaluating, and then sending it over to the left brain in order to decide what, if any, actions to take about such feelings – well, it must be prevented from doing so at all costs. If not, a person under threat from a group would be able to understand that the group was, in fact, not the source of comfort at all, but actually the true source of the threat. With this clarity of thinking they may then be able to find a way out, a means of escape. So the group must disable this ability and to do that it must make sure followers remain dissociated in relation to any thinking about their condition.

The ideology directly supports dissociation in several ways. It does this by exhorting members either not to think, or not to feel, depending on the group. Followers must also be prevented from engaging in reality checking with others. Questions, doubts and dissent are disallowed. Leaders deliver the new fictional reality in either highly simplistic loaded language – Lifton's "thought-terminating clichés" – or, alternatively, by long, boring and complex screeds. Both these types of language are vague and notably absent of any concrete content.[52]

Disconnecting thinking from feeling

Looking at the ideologies of many cults and totalitarian systems it is almost startling to see the consistency with which they will prohibit either thinking or feeling, and certainly the integration of the two. In the O., the method of choice was to derogate feelings as bourgeois or petit bourgeois. One had to be objective. The worst criticism was to label someone subjective and individualistic. Everything was to be analyzed and thought about "objectively," using a variety of forms: the PS01, 02, 03 and 04. As with the MEK, there were no valid feelings – with the exception of being committed to "The Struggle."[53] On the other hand, in Cambodia the Khmer Rouge told the child soldiers and others "over and over, about a new disease in the mind: thinking too much. You must be like the ox, they say, no thoughts, only love for Angka."[54] Similarly, Nithyananda told followers to "Just become a flower. Make your heart and being available to the Master. Nothing more is needed." Especially not logic, or using your "head," "because the very nature of logic is cunning."[55] According to him, the intellectual mind is indeed an obstacle to enlightenment.

Fred Newman's ideology also proclaimed that there is no need to think – or talk – about one's feelings:

> In an important sense, then, social therapy is a way to help the group members to have their conversation be "about nothing." This is not in any way to deny the complex and painful feelings. It is rather to deny the correspondence between those feelings and what is said. Indeed, it is to deny that there must or should be such a correspondence.[56]

Instead, Newman said, "emotive conversation" should just be "performed" in order to "support the conversationalists (the group members) to abandon the realist assumption of truth (or object) referentiality in favor of the activity of performance."[57] In other words – don't think.

Whether in the O. or the MEK, where feelings were denied, or in the Newman Tendency, Angka or in Nithyananda's group, where thinking was denied, the result in all these cases is to sever the connection between thinking and feeling. A sort of virtual lobotomy is achieved with the group mandating a dissociative state in regard to the group and the disengagement of the orbitofrontal cortex, that part of the brain that thinks about what one is feeling. Either way, the effect is the same: to inhibit a person's ability to reflect upon their actual situation and sense perceptions, and to impede the use of their higher-level cognitive functions to make decisions about how to act on those perceptions.

In giving up that ability to think about one's feelings, the follower then hands over the power to interpret their reality to whoever places themselves as the holder of the correct interpretation, namely: the leader. As Nithyananda wrote, other than the Master, "Nothing more is needed." The leader, via the group, now provides interpretations of the follower's experience that do not, in fact, match or accurately describe the actual felt experience and aim to distort or replace the individual's own interpretation. This is not a neutral act, nor one without consequences. Social psychologist Solomon Asch said:

> one distinction of importance is between actions that aim to develop potentialities for thinking and feeling and those that aim to rob persons and groups of the possibility of seeing their situation and of acting according to their needs and insights.[58]

An example from the US right-wing Patriarchy Movement illustrates this:

> In 2014, politically powerful Bill Gothard resigned from his large and popular ministry, the Institute in Basic Life Principles (IBLP) – a $95 million non-profit organization – after more than 30 women made allegations of sexual abuse and failure to report child abuse cases.[59] His ministry was highly active in supporting major figures in the US Republican Party's religious right such as Rick Perry and Mike Huckabee. Gothard is a leader in the extensive Patriarchy Movement, and advocates conservative dress for women, that women should not attend college nor vote,[60] and should be totally submissive to their husbands, even when that involves spousal abuse. He leads a right-wing conservative homeschooling movement, opposes birth control and supports the "Purity Movement" where daughters submit to the authority of their fathers (and, weirdly, pledge their virginity to him) until marriage transfers that authority to their husbands.[61]

Under the label of the IBLP, Gothard publishes a piece on "counseling sexual abuse" that consists of multiple choice questions for the "counselor" to ask the abuse victim. One of these questions reads:

Why did God let it happen?
Result of defrauding by:

- Immodest dress
- Indecent exposure
- Being out from protection of our parents
- Being with evil friends

The document goes on to ask the abused person "Is there any guilt?" and suggests answers including:

- For disobedience?
- For not reporting it? (See Deutoronomy 22:22–24.) Failing to report it allows others to also be abused
- Clear guilt by confessing it to God (See I John 1:9.)[62]

Clearly here the intent is to blame the victim, turn the abuse back on them to prevent seeing the reality of the sexual abuse visited upon them, to "abandon the realist assumption of truth" and replace it with a "truth" more convenient for the leader. This is typical, perhaps, of abusers. What stands out here is that this is published in a document distributed by the IBLP for over a decade at their Advance Training Institute seminars.[63] This ideologically propagated view presents the victim as the guilty one.

This is merely one example of the way that, in this case, right-wing fundamentalist ideology twists reality and the followers' understanding of their abuse.

Disabling people's ability to think and talk about their feelings drastically impairs their ability to see their situation and to exert agency within it. When the leader gains the power to interpret a follower's feelings or thoughts, the right to agency –

to actions based on those feelings or thoughts – also passes to the leader. Power becomes utterly lopsided and unequal once the follower's ability to resist is disarmed in this way.

Enforcing a unanimous majority to prevent critical thought

Dissociation is also maintained by preventing reality checking with others. We know our worlds in discussion, conversation with others. It is by putting together with others our various thoughts and perceptions that we begin to understand the reality of our world. As human beings we are constantly verifying our sense perceptions in conversation with (or even merely by observing) those around us. As Asch's famous lines experiment showed, if others are unanimous in a clearly incorrect evaluation of even an obvious physically observable fact – such as comparing the length of lines on paper – we are likely to go along with that evaluation.[64] We are not as solidly independent as we would like to think. Classic experiments in social psychology have shown time and again how heavily we rely on the shared views of those around us – even when they are clearly immoral or wrong. This power of a unanimous majority in influencing our perceptions is well proven. On the other hand, when even a small minority dissent, then this "majority effect" is broken, and with just one other ally we are able to hold on to independent thought.[65]

But in a totalist system only the party line is allowed, and woe betide the person who tries to float another view. For example, recently within one month over 100 North Korean citizens were exiled to remote areas of the country after authorities found they had viewed or possessed South Korean videos and other types of recordings.[66] Prior to this, high-ranking officials of North Korea had been executed for the same lack of ideological purity. Dissent must be absolutely smothered to maintain the majority effect where the entire system is propagating a false view of reality that only benefits the leadership. Add to this the predictable restrictions on engaging with external sources of information such as non-group approved books, media and the vast world of ideas available through the internet, and the follower, surrounded by the single truth of the total ideology, soon becomes unable to hold on to an independent and factual view of reality.

As Gillian said, in looking back at her experience in the Newman Tendency:

> If you try to get clarification they say it's not something you can understand. You just stop asking. You just do. You end up by accepting that being confused is not a bad thing because there's really not anything to know, there's no truth. Anything you bring up from your own background is deconstructed. . . . After a while things that seemed preposterous seem normal.

Totalist ideologies disallow questions, doubts or dissent. Doubts can lead to questions, and questions can lead to critical thinking. Critical thinking can lead to dissent. So doubts and questions must be cut off at the pass, and total ideologies make sure to do this. Jonny Scaramanga described this in relation to his isolating fundamentalist Christian education:

> Creationists teach that either every word of the Bible is completely true or none of it is. If you have doubts, that is the devil trying to deceive you. I knew if I doubted, I risked losing my faith, and then I would go to hell. This provides a powerful disincentive against thinking critically. In that sense, the education militates against real learning.[67]

In the Newman Tendency questions were carefully managed, redirected and reframed. Bernice described interactions with her social therapist:

> I question a lot of things and I'm not shy about it. When I would question him about things – that I felt confused about – and this was just a consistent thing that went on the whole time I was involved over there, he would – he would address my questions in a manner in which – I felt like he answered the questions, but then it wasn't. A few minutes later, I was back again confused. So he was doing some kind of spin thing with me – some psychological thing where I wound up just – maybe even more confused than before I asked the question.

Often questions are turned back on the questioner. Louisa describes what happened to her:

> They always spin everything – they spin everything. They're always in control in this weird way, but you don't have conversations with them because they'll, they give you that look and then they start to spin it and they never . . . they answer a question with a question, constantly . . . I didn't realize this is what they were doing, and that's very intimidating because you do feel insane. I mean, do you know what I mean? I mean it's like, if you ask anything, they ask a question. I'm like, why the hell do they do that?

Any question, doubt or disagreement with the Newman Tendency was labeled as "conflict," which was described as being a problem internal to the group member, and thus something to be worked through in order to continue to "build" (another word in the Tendency's specialized lexicon) with, and "give" to, the group. In this way the Tendency labeled and provided an interpretation of the follower's discomfort, and thus neatly did away with it by deflecting it back onto the follower.

In the O. doubts and questions were deflected by followers being told: "Struggle with the practice." It was in doing the "practice" – that is, free labor for the group – that the answers would be found. It was too easy, so P.O.O. said, for us just to be *given* the answers: we must find them for ourselves through "struggle" – that is, working harder, sleeping less and criticizing ourselves more. Other groups require more prayer, chanting, labor or courses. Steve Hassan reported how as a Moonie – a member of the Unification Church – he was taught to constantly chant "Stamp out doubt, stamp out doubt" in order to do just that.[68] In Scientology doubts are managed by additional auditing (in itself a form of confession) and by paying to take more Scientology courses.

Dissent, of course, is never allowed. How can one disagree when everything has been covered already by the inspirational thinking of the great leader? In the New-man Tendency, when dissent has arisen, it has been duly disposed of by means of a power struggle where Newman insists on his control and then forces the dissenter out. Disagreement with his positions is not allowed and results in being labeled "hostile." Followers could withdraw and remain on the periphery (as long as they still gave money or other forms of support), but they could not disagree with Newman.

Although followers are not permitted to dissent or shift their thinking in any way, the leader is entirely within their rights to change their mind as new "insights" appear. Followers must ever be on the alert to jump to the leader's sudden ideo-logical shifts and reversals,[69] as when Orwell's pigs jettison the earlier revolutionary glorification of the four-legged and are obliged to rise up on their hind legs to chant the latest slogan, "*Two legs good, four legs bad.*"[70] Lyndon LaRouche made a sharp right-turn from a leftist ideology in the 1960s to an allegedly anti-Semitic conspiracy theory, an ideology that resulted in supporting a variety of dictatorships from apartheid South Africa[71] to Noriega's Panama.[72] From 1996 Fred Newman, too, allied with the Hitler-apologist, right-wing fundamentalist Pat Buchanan, claiming he represented a "populist" view. However the real motive was more pragmatic; as Newman said about the potential of the partnership, it "keeps the dollars coming in and it keeps us as America's major minor party."[73] Once the leader has set the new direction and no matter how oppressive life within the sys-tem may actually be, the new ideology cannot be challenged and woe betide the follower who fails to keep up with any abrupt twists and turns that it may take.

Preventing questions, doubts and dissent and prohibiting all but the leader's interpretation consolidates the follower's dissociation and obviously gives the leader undue power and control. Bowlby describes this in terms of the parent/child relationship:

> One of the more intractable forms [of dissociation] results from a parent implicitly or explicitly forbidding a child, perhaps under threat of sanctions, to consider any mode of construing either his parents or himself in ways other than those directed by the parent.... [T]he more persistent the disorder from which a person suffers the greater is the degree of disconnection present and the more complete is the ban he feels against reappraising his models.[74]

The secrets and lies of the fictitious ideology

The leader's interpretation – or construal – of the follower's reality is, by neces-sity, fiction. The ideology of totalism separates people from reality and erases "the distinction between fact and fiction (i.e. the reality of experience) and the distinction between true and false."[75] This makes it increasingly difficult for the follower to analyze their grim situation. If the leader is to seek to dissociate the minds of followers, to prevent them thinking about their feelings or about the situations in which they are super-exploited (and therefore, by definition feeling unhappy, stressed, fearful), then they must make up a story that says otherwise. To be factual rather than fictional would mean the ideology would have to represent the real world of the follower. But to do so would reflect the exploitation and misery of life in these oppressive systems and so would allow the follower to reintegrate their thinking brain with their feeling brain. That is, the words, the language, would reflect reality, validate the real experience of followers and thus reduce or break the dissociative state. A factual account would say to the follower:

> You are tired because you've only had four hours sleep a night for the last five years. You're unhappy and lonely because you're never allowed to see your family. You're exhausted because you work 20 hours a day. You are made to criticize those you once loved. And look: the leader has been sleeping with all the young women and girls in the group, lives off your hard labor, lies, cheats and steals, and has beaten or killed any who disagree with him.

Secrets and lies cover up the reality – if they did not do so, followers would have the information and knowledge to be able to think clearly about their condition, seek alternate, real safe havens and escape. The total ideology "establishes and safeguards the fictitious world through consistent lying."[76] And the further into the system one goes – into the innermost layers of the onion-like structure – the more the fictionalized ideology takes hold.

The secrecy within cults and totalist organizations is justified by the need to "protect" members from this evil or bourgeois or *haram* (religiously forbidden) outside world – at whatever layer of the onion one happens to be. Each layer may be privy to different levels of the belief system, as, for example, the previously discussed differences between propaganda and indoctrination. But within the organization itself are multiple layers with access to different layers of the ideology. A former member of the Iranian Mojahedin commented on the indoctrination efforts of the leadership circle and the ongoing emphasis on suicide operations – efforts that resulted in three rank and file members setting themselves on fire in Paris as a protest against the arrest of Maryam Rajavi:

> What was of the significance and vital for the organization was to keep rank and file in readiness and ripe for suicide operations through justifications that could be embedded in them from the top. I tell you for sure that if the subordinate members knew the truth and what they plotted at top layers, half of them would detach from the organization; their role was to materialize the chimeras of the leaders.[77]

The most fictionalized version of the ideology is restricted to the innermost circle. Here the leader truly *is* god, the next messiah, the next world leader just waiting to be recognized. Thus the closer to the center the layer, the more secrets are revealed, but then consequently the more distanced from reality, and thus the more controlled those close to the center must be.

Secrecy is enforced and supported by the norms of isolation and approved and non-approved topics of discussion. Nithyananda's "concubines" were not to tell anyone else about the sexual nature of their relationship with him, which was, according to him, a holy service they performed to help him come down into his physical body after his time spent in "Samadhi," a state of divine concentration.[78] In rural Minnesota, Victor Barnard told the underage "Maidens" who he sexually abused for years that they would "receive damnation from God" if they told anyone about the abuse.[79] He told their families that the 10 young girls he took to live with him were "virgins who were to be 'sacrificed to God' by being married to Christ." Christ, of course, being Barnard himself, who proceeded to systematically rape them. The girls were always to go about in pairs, when not with Barnard, to prevent them talking.

In my own experience in the O. secrecy ran through all levels of the organization. I was not to speak to my husband about any "organizational" issues, nor he to me about his activities in the group, past or present. Thus I was not to find out about how he was beaten for an unapproved relationship he had prior to our arranged marriage, nor did I hear of the physical and sexual abuses of others in the group. The rules of secrecy were justified ideologically in that we were supposedly an underground organization fighting for the people, under the radar of the bourgeois State. And the State would stop at nothing to infiltrate and destroy us and our work. In reality we were, by then, an organization of controlled and obedient followers protecting (granted unknowingly for most of us) a leader who was on the run from a murder charge.

It matters that total ideologies are made up of secrets and lies. Again, it is not neutral – not merely a question of freedom of religion, the freedom to believe whatever one wishes. This is the unhelpful argument that some scholars of religious movements throw up when cults are under the spotlight.[vi] But having strange, or unusual or different beliefs or holding strongly to a particular religious view is not what is in question. What is in question is whether the ideology is a totalist one: a veil that covers up behaviors of control, oppression and usually criminality. A totalist ideology denies the right to existence of any who do not adhere to it, and justifies, supports and hides actions by repressive leaders who seek to utterly crush and reject the independence and agency of followers. The one purpose of these belief systems is to

vi Some scholars refuse to take a position on the ethical problems in totalist systems, resting on a "value-free" assertion that converts are simply acting on their "free will." For example: Barker, E. (1984). *The Making of a Moonie: Choice or Brainwashing?* Oxford, New York: B. Blackwell. and Bromley, D. (1998). "Listing in black and white some observations on thought reform." *Nova Religio*(12):250–66. However these scholars tend to stay in the realm of the ideological rather than getting under the propaganda of these groups and looking at their actual practices.

control and keep followers subordinated to that control. In North Korea, for example, telling those living under the thumb of a totalist leader that they are living in the glory days while their children starve is a central element – along with isolation from reality-based perspectives – of keeping them from being able to fight back against the very system that is pressing them down. As the North Korean poet Jang Jin-sung said, "[P]eople in North Korea have no concept of basic human rights. They do not know what they should be entitled to. They have nothing to fight for."[80]

In Cambodia during Pol Pot's regime when children were forcefully taken from their parents and thus made into orphans, a counter-reality was sung in the propaganda song "We Children Love *Angkar* Boundlessly." In the song parents are referred to as "the enemy":

> Before the revolution, children were poor and lived lives of misery,
> Living like animals, suffering as orphans.
> The enemy abandoned all thought of us . . .
> Now the glorious revolution supports us all.[vii][81]

It matters, as Asch said, who we are dealing with:

> [W]e need to know when we are dealing with a person who is fleeing from fact and truth and when we are dealing with the opposite attitude, that of trying to reach a true understanding.[82]

It matters because if we know that we are being lied to we can begin to make out the shape of the wolf who is telling the lies. The biggest secret of all is that the ideology is a lie.

Loaded language

The way that these lies, these fictions, are told also matters. Loaded language is the language used to deliver the fictions of total ideology. This is made up of the thought-terminating clichés that Lifton discussed in his important work on thought reform within Chinese prisoner of war and reeducation camps. Loaded language consists of group jargon that acts as "verbal fetters"[83] preventing followers from articulating anything – any thought or feeling – outside the bounds of what the group determines is acceptable.

Loaded words in the Newman Tendency include "growth," "development," "build," "performing," "politics" and "giving," among many others, which they

---

vii For the full text see Kiernan, *The Pol Pot Regime*, p. 247. Kalyanee E. Mam concludes: "The policies implemented by the Khmer Rouge regime sought to destroy traditional family structure and substitute *Angkar* for it." Kalyanee E. Mam. *An Oral History of Family Life under the Khmer Rouge*. New Haven, Yale Genocide Studies Program Working Paper no. 10, 1999.

constantly reference in their written and spoken discourse, although the meaning of these terms is never spelled out. The word "politics," used as an overarching, total concept, is illustrated in a glossy Tendency publication from the East Side Institute, sent in a "cold" publicity/recruitment propaganda package to mental health practitioners. In a full-page testimonial from a "social therapy client" is the following:

> I rediscovered a word that I used to dislike intensely, but that I have learned to love. The word is *politics*. Put that word in front of those other words and suddenly their meaning is revealed. The *politics* of giving. The *politics* of never giving up on someone's capacity to grow. The *politics* of building community week after week. The *politics* of decency. Social therapy is the hand on my shoulder, an unusual guide, never giving answers. Social therapy has given me the world.[84]

Every cult or totalitarian system has its own loaded language. From the "energy," "heart," "commitment" and "humanity" vocabulary of Yogi Bhajan's kundalini yoga, to the terms "reactive mind," "suppressive person" and "case gain" of Scientology, loaded language is ubiquitous and yet specific to each group. A former member of the Lyndon LaRouche political cult has created an automatic "LaRouche internal memo generator" that uses this feature of the cultic language to humorous effect.[viii] The author of the generator states:

> For those exposed to LaRouche's rhetoric, they will eventually get to a feeling of "deja vu", something strangely repetitive, mechanical in LaRouche's mind. No matter how, where and in which order words, names, dates or sentences are placed, they always "make sense": LaRouche's "non-sense."[85]

Lifton describes the effects of this language:

> For an individual person, the effect of the language of ideological totalism can be summed up in one word: constriction. He is, so to speak, linguistically deprived; and since language is so central to all human experience, his capacities for thinking and feeling are immensely narrowed.[86]

In a totalist system loaded language funnels the individual's thought and experience into fewer and narrower channels until it is entirely inadequate for communicating a person's sensory perceptions and experience. Along with other dissociating techniques it is used to dominate, constrict thought, restrict conversation and communication. Language used in this function will be repetitive, canned and replete with jargon, as opposed to the "fresh"[87] language of open, imaginative and unfettered communication. Loaded language has a dreary, predictable and, often,

viii Try it yourself here: http://larocheplanet.info/pmwiki/pmwiki.php?n=LaRouche.Larouchememo

incoherent (especially to the outsider) quality. Orwell describes the function of the limited totalist vocabulary in *Nineteen Eighty-Four*'s appendix, "The Principles of Newspeak":

> Relative to our own, the Newspeak vocabulary was tiny, and new ways of reducing it were constantly being devised. Newspeak, indeed, differed from almost all other languages in that its vocabulary grew smaller instead of larger every year. Each reduction was a gain, since the smaller the area of choice, the smaller the temptation to take thought. Ultimately it was hoped to make articulate speech issue from the larynx without involving the higher brain centers at all.[ix88]

The dreary, repetitive and obfuscating quality of totalist language is an obvious result when an entire group or population must follow the language and interpretive rules dictated from on high. Loaded language frames, delivers and imposes the single Truth of the group. This Truth sits atop the actual experience of the individual, bearing no real resemblance to that experience and thus propping up the existing dissociation of followers.

Colin is not in the Newman Tendency, but his mother is and he is in touch with her and interacts with group members from time to time. He has this to say about the constriction that group members display when engaged in the "group mode":

> My mom said the exact same line to me [as others in the group]. You know, you can talk to them about Nader, and you can be in three different conversations at three different times and hear the exact same thing. . . . But if you only hear it from one person, or even two people, it's not weird. But I'm around them enough that I hear the same message . . . If you can't come up with your own individual thoughts, you can't make an intelligent argument on your own about something without spitting it out verbatim, and then it, it makes me question whether it's true or not, whether it's fact.
>
> . . . Most of the conversations are normal, yes. Most of the conversations are normal and like I said, it's only when the group comes up, and I kind of said this in the beginning, it's only when, in those periods when the group comes up, or when other people are involved talking about the group that it really gets, that I get a sense that it's not, that I'm no longer talking to my mom, I'm talking to somebody else. . . .
>
> Scripted. That's, I mean, that's the best way of saying it, it just, it feels scripted. You know, when somebody's being, you know, speaking their mind, speaking their emotion, you sense the honesty in it, I mean, which changes in their inflection, in their voice, there's changes in their facial reactions

ix *Nineteen Eighty-Four* by George Orwell (Copyright © George Orwell, 1948). Reprinted by permission of Bill Hamilton as the Literary Executor of the Estate of the Late Sonia Brownell Orwell.

or changes in their body language. Those things kind of stop, and you get, I mean – and those are probably part of some of the things that I key in on – the language changes. You know, I can stumble on words, saying, you know, reading my ABC's, but once you get to a scripted message, you tend to not stumble anymore. And so, those are the things that, that really kind of start up. And then, I mean, you're talking about an organization and a group that has *no negative aspects*.

The loaded language has a particular quality in its delivery as well as in its content. Rhythms of speech and gestures may also merge and become similarly constricted as group members mimic the leader's communication patterns. When Louisa observed a group of "lifer" Newman Tendency social therapists together she noted that:

> It's definitely a rhythm and dance that they're doing. Very specific – and they do this talk – that's how they talk – they talk ... like ... this ... [Slow, syllables separated] – it's a constant – I can hear the rhythm. They all sit the same like I'm sitting now, but you know, their legs crossed and they all do their arms a certain way and they do – they – Fred does his arm and he talks like this, and they all – it's a rhythm in their speech definitely – yeah, it's creepy. They talk like Fred – every one of them and, you know, it's obvious.

The dissociation of right and left brain, the block against thinking about feelings and therefore of making cognitive evaluations of the group is also achieved by the ideology lacking any concrete content. This too relates to Lifton's loaded language. Words stand in for things, without the things themselves actually being discussed in any detail. For example, a long-term Newman Tendency member approached me at a public political meeting I was observing of the Independence Party in Albany, New York. After some discussion I asked her about the organization she belonged to.

She told me, "We're a development community." I asked what she meant by "development."

"Human development," she said.

"But what do you mean? What kind of development is that?" I asked.

"Human development, people developing," she replied, and went on to repeat the term in a few more phrases without ever saying anything specific.[89]

The loaded language of overarching abstractions stands in for anything verifiable, any reality that might be thought about. If such-and-such a feeling, action or problem is labeled "subjective," "worldly," "sinful," or "an overt," for example, then it must not be thought about any further – it is, simply, bad. And therefore the individual must engage in more struggle, prayer, meditation, money, commitment, courses or development to overcome whatever the feeling or problem was. The label itself redirects thinking away from what is really happening to either vague notions that someone is bad – oneself or others – or to some yet-to-be-attained future in which good – Heaven, the Revolution, Enlightenment, the Master Race – will overcome.

These terms thus become vague abstractions that can stand for anything. They are repetitive, all-encompassing phrases – "thought-terminating clichés" – which serve as "interpretive shortcuts"[90] devoid of concrete content. Arendt states that:

> Total loyalty is possible only when fidelity is emptied of all concrete content, from which changes of mind might naturally arise. The totalitarian movements, each in its own way, have done their utmost to get rid of the party programs which specified concrete content . . . [E]very political program which deals with issues more specific than "ideological questions of importance for centuries" is an obstruction to totalitarianism.[91]

Pick any totalistic group and the emptiness of the language they use is apparent. The Shiva Trust is a small group in the UK headed by Rachel Ennis Cole (now known as Sri Ramana). Their web page states:

> Shiva Trust has been created for Sri Ramana, our satguru, to educate the world about the reality of God in an accessible and down to earth way. A satguru does not have an individual self in the way that we do. . . . Shiva Trust knows from experience that no matter who you are, where you're from, what you believe, sitting in the presence of Sri Ramana leads to enlightenment.[92]

The reality of belonging to the Shiva Trust, however, is that Sri Ramana tells followers what they are thinking or feeling, who they can date, how they raise their children, the kind of work they should do, where they must live, how much sleep they should have and so forth. Any questioning "is considered to be that person 'trying to be in control' or 'interrogating God'."[93]

Total ideology disengages central route thinking

These features of the ideology: its singular nature as the only Truth allowed, the lack of dissent, its fictional quality, the loaded language and lack of concrete content, all work together to support peripheral rather than central route thinking.[x] As discussed in Chapter 3, peripheral processing (automatic thinking) is a low-effort mode of thinking. We use it when we are tired, stressed, under time pressure and lack motivation to engage in its opposite: central route processing (systematic thinking).[94] When using central route processing we pay attention to the quality of the arguments being put forth and then evaluate these arguments using knowledge, logic

---

x This is also known as automatic versus systematic thinking or System 1 versus System 2 thinking: Kahneman, Daniel. 2011. *Thinking, Fast and Slow*. London: Allen Lane.

and careful consideration. People can be discouraged from central route processing and encouraged to peripherally process by creating distractions to prevent focal attention. Such distractions can include fear arousal, rapid delivery of the message (and lack of time to process it), quantity rather than quality of arguments, excessive repetition or complexity of language and delivery by an attractive or "expert" messenger. In the peripheral mode we are persuaded by the more obvious and easily accessible elements of a persuasion attempt, but do not engage in the more effortful work of thinking about the elements central to the question at hand. In fact, the main goal of dissociating a follower is to disengage their ability to use central route, or systematic and critical processing.

Peripheral modes of persuasion are used in both the propaganda and indoctrination phases. The dissociated (or soon-to-be dissociated) follower, also under attack by other stresses introduced by the group – sleep deprivation, overstimulation, distraction, fear, lack of privacy or time, possibly malnourishment, etc. – now is unable to engage in central route processing, which, as we have seen, requires the time, ability and motivation to think about a given object.

If the follower is unable to engage in the thoughtful evaluation required to gain a full knowledge of what the group actually is and does, new ideas can be introduced – ideas that normally would not stand up to careful scrutiny. The means of introducing these ideas rely on the methods of peripheral route communication: they are delivered rapidly; they are often confusing; they may "sound" good, using loaded language, but not actually make sense if they were to be taken apart carefully; they are delivered by an attractive or supposedly expert source (the leader or lieutenants).

The online videos of ISIS/Daesh exemplify the use of peripheral modes of persuasion. A study of one month's production of ISIS/Daesh propaganda videos illustrates these methods:

> By creating so much content that it is literally impossible to keep a mental track of, IS's media men try to prevent us from understanding what they are doing.
>
> They flood the internet with information to a point that it becomes impossible to decode the brand they are building.
>
> They overawe and overwhelm their adversaries while at the same time luring the curious and vulnerable.[95]

The content of this daily flood of material is comprised of a mix of brutal punishments and horrific images of stonings and beheadings alternating with bucolic scenes of agricultural and economic prosperity and paradisical beauty. Of course, interestingly these also represent the twin poles of terror and "love" germane to the creation of fright without solution.

Fred Newman and the Newman Tendency provide a good example of how a totalist group employs these elements of peripheral route communication. Newman – granted not physically attractive! – nonetheless presented himself as an expert with his Ph.D. and his (choppy) background as a university lecturer. His charisma added to his attractiveness as a source of knowledge and expertise. He kept followers extremely busy and exhausted so that they would not have the time or ability needed for central route processing.

In the Newman Tendency there are many features of communication that lead to peripheral processing. Members are constantly discouraged (i.e. de-motivated) from putting focal attention to the central content of the messages. This is set up early on in encounters with the group. Here is an example from my field work:

> I attended a play, *Mommsen's Future*, written and directed by him at the Tendency's off-off Broadway Castillo Theater. The previous day I'd bought my ticket at the theater, which – oddly – involved a sit-down interview with a theatre administrator (at her initiative, not mine). In discussing the play (about a German playwright) she told me: "The director [Newman] said that when you watch it, 'Don't try to understand the language,' just watch and take in the visuals." I asked, "Is it in German?" "No, it's in English, but it's very dense." When I attended the performance, I saw, in the program, and then in a video on stage prior to the live performance, a similar message was repeated: *PRETEND YOU UNDERSTAND THE WORDS; LISTEN TO THE MUSIC; WATCH THE PERFORMERS DANCE.*[96]
>
> This set up in theatergoers the expectation that the language would not be understandable (which indeed it wasn't), and directed them to attend to the secondary (non-linguistic) elements: the music, and the dance. Thus the audience was guided to switch off central route processing of the play's spoken language. As I wrote in my field notes: "It was endless stuff that was impossible to concentrate on. Various bits about the Berlin wall, Marx, Jews, existential musings, much stuff that was simply not understandable at all." While the speeches were rapid, dense and impossible to understand, distraction was provided by the female cast members (who were, incidentally, "lifer" members of the Tendency). One was dressed in tight silver pants, and the other in a diaphanous summer dress with gold tights. They danced in a highly sexually charged way throughout the speeches. The effect was dulling and confusing, but, perhaps, in a naïve viewer, might have seemed very clever and "post-modern."

Thus distraction from the language used was a key aspect of the performance. As an isolated incident this may not be noteworthy – after all, theater is an arena in which the way language is processed is routinely manipulated and explored. But in the overall context of Newman's group it adds another piece to the puzzle of how language is used as part of their delivery of the total ideology. Newman's written language is another area in which peripheral route processing results. Not only is his work full of abstractions, repetition, circular references and a kind of pseudo logic, but he makes frequent use of highly distracting parenthetical statements. For example, one sentence, picked more or less randomly, from his earlier *A Manifesto on Method*, contains four parenthetical statements, lodged in his Marxist phraseology of the period:

> Bourgeois thinking (cognition) is the alienated though productive employ-ment of mental processes (using alienated though productive mental means of production) to produce interpretive beliefs (or more accurately systems of beliefs) which correspond to (a bourgeoisified conception of) reality.[97]

The effect of these, often multiple parenthetical statements in one sentence is not to clarify, but to interrupt and further obscure meaning. Each set of parentheses requires breaking off from the flow of the sentence. One ceases to focus on the meaning of the sentence – it simply becomes too confusing. It is also utterly dull. The result is one either gives up, or takes Newman's expertise on faith.

This type of language, by using distraction and extreme complexity, edges the reader away from a careful reading of the central elements of a persuasion attempt into the less stressful right-brain peripheral route processing. This is not to say we must always be in our logical left brains. Indeed, listening to a stirring piece of music, losing oneself in the "oceanic sense"[98] of a beautiful landscape – these are marvelous parts of life. But when committing or submitting oneself to something as all-encompassing as a totalist system, the ability to hang on to the logical, critical part of one's mind can be a literally life-saving act. When such commitments are at stake it truly matters whether peripheral or central routes of processing are engaged. It matters for our ability to carefully evaluate what is happening in a group, and what is happening to ourselves in relation to that. It also matters in regard to memory and to later trauma effects.

When we are being persuaded by the superficial attributes of peripheral route persuasion we get a "sense" that it looks okay and may agree. We do not elabo-rate our thinking and carefully consider the arguments. This lack of elaboration means that it is our implicit, unconscious attitudes that are changed, rather than explicit attitudes that we can defend and support with thoughtful arguments. Similarly these implicit attitudes are not then stored effectively in cognitively based, left-brain, explicit memory, but in the more emotion-based, implicit mem-ory associated with the right, non-verbal, feeling side of the brain. This is the area of memory in which feelings are stored, rather than the left-brain where language resides.[99]

Peripheral route processing has been shown to result in only unstable, short-term persuasion, while central route processing results in long-term stable changes of attitudes and beliefs.[100] Thus, when the persuasion messages stop – when the fol-lower leaves the totalist environment – the ideology is generally given up, more or less entirely, and often quite rapidly. The former Tendency members I interviewed discarded the belief system on exit. For many ex-members leaving required a fun-damental reevaluation of the all-encompassing web of beliefs, and sorting through that tight, tangled web is one of the most difficult tasks facing former members. Unfortunately, many may leave and fail to successfully untangle that web and are left – though perhaps disenchanted with the group and its beliefs – confused and disoriented, sometimes for decades.

For persons who are in the dissociated state caused by disorganized attachment, memories to do with the traumas experienced within that relationship are encoded into implicit (right-brain) rather than explicit (left-brain) memory. So there is a double effect – encoding into implicit memory through peripheral route persuasion, *and* through dissociation. On top of this the sleep-deprivation found in totalist systems obstructs the REM sleep cycles necessary for the storage of memory in explicit memory.[101] So we can see that many of the methods used by totalist groups combine to disable the follower's ability to access their higher-level cognitive functioning – especially in terms of thinking about the group itself. This has follow-on effects in terms of how those experiences are stored, namely in implicit memory regions where they are yet further from being subject to careful thought and analysis.

Thus, cognitive processing about the group, its ideology and the follower's relationship with the group is disabled overall and never truly makes it into the higher-order brain regions where thinking about feeling takes place. This dissociation and the taking on of the leader's interpretation in certain realms does not, however, entirely eradicate the person's self. They may retain elements of the self that can correctly interpret certain parts of the reality they are operating in, particularly if those parts are not directly subject to the trauma response. Followers may well be able to engage in other tasks perfectly well: in my case working in the computer industry, or, as an extreme case, the Nazi doctors who Lifton[102] studied being able to regularly and routinely switch between organizing death camps to a more or less normal family life in their homes.

Doubling: The creation of a segregated self

Though thinking about the group is disabled, other thinking does not entirely disappear, but it is segregated and exists under a kind of shadow. The real, thinking self is still there, but it is shoved away. This dual persona is what Lifton[103] refers to as "doubling" – where the totalist self sits "on top of" the self that is still able to engage, or at least has the potential to reengage with reality, and with the ability to think about their situation and the inputs from their senses. As a former "comrade" of mine said after getting out of the O., "It was like my mind was under a tarpaulin" as she gestured with her hand as if the tarpaulin was pressing down her head.

Arendt said of Adolf Eichmann who organized the transport of millions of Jews and others to the death camps:

> the only specific characteristic one could detect in his past as well as in his behavior during the trial and the preceding police examination was something entirely negative: it was not stupidity but a curious, quite *authentic inability to think*.[104]

This, perhaps, is the banality of evil – it rests upon the follower's inability to think directly about the group or their relationship to it while on the other hand being able to think clearly and intelligently about specific tasks disconnected from the context in which these tasks are taking place. That context is explained away by the justifying and dissociating total ideology.

The total ideology does not stand on its own but serves the isolating structure and dissociating goals of the leader. Total ideologies and their particular methods of delivery are not the same as any deviant, odd, extreme, magical or other types of beliefs that may, perhaps, be distasteful to the mainstream, but do not present the same level of threat. The dissociating rejection of the individual's own inter-pretation of their individual experience, the insistence on one and only one abso-lute Truth, the use of loaded language, secrets, lies, lack of concrete content and peripheral route processing in espousing that Truth are useful warning signs that can alert observers to dig beneath the ideology and investigate the source. These signs indicate that the source of such ideology is a totalist system: one that is closed and isolating in structure, headed by a charismatic and authoritarian all-controlling leader, and seeking absolute control over followers.

Dennis Tourish wrote about the four young British men who perpetrated the 7/7 London transport bombings:

> It is likely, I think, that the London bombers spent their last moments in a final silent scream, designed to obliterate in their minds the pending screams of their soon-to-be victims. It is a sound we all must now attempt to deal with.[105]

These four young men had undoubtedly been successfully put through an intense and dissociating social process bolstered by and injected with a total ideology. The image of the obliterating "silent scream" describes well the extreme effects of dis-sociation – of the *inability to think* – that the total ideology supports. That inabil-ity results from followers becoming utterly trapped, so trapped that they can be deployed in the service of destruction.

Notes

1 Belcher, Erin. 2003. *Summer Camp, Larouche-Style* (http://blogcritics.org/where-would-we-be-without-pc/).
2 Arendt, Hannah. 1948/1979. *The Origins of Totalitarianism.* Orlando: Harcourt Brace, p. 349.
3 Ibid., p. 470.
4 Arendt, *The Origins of Totalitarianism*, p. 325.
5 Schein, Edgar H. 1961. *Coercive Persuasion: A Socio-Psychological Analysis of the "Brainwash-ing" of American Civilian Prisoners by the Chinese Communists.* New York: W.W. Norton.
6 Mannheim, Karl. 1936. *Ideology and Utopia: An Introduction to the Sociology of Knowledge.* San Diego: Harcourt Brace Jovanovich.
7 Arendt, *The Origins of Totalitarianism*.
8 Kent, Stephen A. 1994. "Lustful Prophet: A Psychosexual Historical Study of the Chil-dren of God's Leader, David Berg." *Cultic Studies Journal* 11(1):135–88.

9 Lofland, John. 1977. *Doomsday Cult: A Study of Conversion, Proselytization, and Maintenance of Faith*. New York: Irvington Publishers; distributed by Halsted Press, p. 14.

10 Arendt, *The Origins of Totalitarianism*.

11 Hassan, Steven. 1988. *Combatting Cult Mind Control*. Rochester, VT: Park Street Press.

12 McArdle, Matthew. 2006. "Alleged Cult Sows Seeds Via Campus Event," in *UCSD Guardian*. San Diego: University of California, San Diego.

13 Personal communication.

14 Administrator. 2006, "Providence Songs" *Heaven's Rapist: The Cult of Jyeong Myeong-Seok, JMS cult forums*. Retrieved May 29, 2014 (http://jmscult.com/forum/index.php?PHPS ESSID=74ef5782f8210a0ba7c8216400abc97e&topic=111.0).

15 Administrator. 2008, "JMS Bible Study: The 30 Lessons" *Heaven's rapist: The Cult of Jyeong Myeong-Seok, JMS cult Forums*. Retrieved May 29, 2014 (http://jmscult.com/forum/index.php?PHPSESSID=74ef5782f8210a0ba7c8216400abc97e&topic=346.0).

16 Straits Times. 2009, "Cult Leader Jeong Myeong-Seok Gets 10 Year Sentence after Appeal" *Religion News Blog*: Retrieved June 1, 2014 (http://www.religionnewsblog.com/23254/jeong-myeong-seok).

17 McArdle, Matthew. 2006. "Alleged Cult Sows Seeds Via Campus Event," in *UCSD Guardian*. San Diego.

18 Finn, Jack. 1977. "Proof: Therapy Cultists Lied to Community," in *Heights and Valley News*. New York City.

19 Schein, *Coercive Persuasion: A Socio-Psychological Analysis of the "Brainwashing" of American Civilian Prisoners by the Chinese Communists*. New York: W.W. Norton.

20 Newman, Fred and Phyllis Goldberg. 1994. *Let's Develop!* New York: Castillo International, Inc, p. 22.

21 McCormick, Patricia. 2013. *Never Fall Down*. London: Random House, p. 43.

22 Newman, Fred and Lois Holzman. 1997. *The End of Knowing*. New York: Routledge.

23 Singleton, Anne. 2003. *Saddam's Private Army: How Rajavi Changed Iran's Mojahedin from Armed Revolutionaries to an Armed Cult*: Iran-Interlink UK.

24 Ibid.

25 Ibid.

26 Lifton, Robert Jay. 1961. *Thought Reform and the Psychology of Totalism*. New York: The Norton Library, p. 433.

27 Husain, Ed. 2007. *The Islamist: Why I Joined Radical Islam in Britain, What I Saw Inside and Why I Left*. London: Penguin.

28 Jones, Celeste, Kristina Jones and Juliana Buhring. 2007a. *Not without My Sister*. London: Harper Element.

29 Scaramanga, Jonny. 2014. "Creationism and the 'Conspiracy' of Evolution: Inside the UK's Evangelical Schools." *New Statesman*, 5 February.

30 Ortiz, Marina. 2003, *Slave to a Dream: Inside the International Workers Party*: Ex-iwp.org. Retrieved March 15, 2007 (http://69.93.222.170/~marinajo/docs/Ortiz-Others/Slave%20to%20a%20Dream.htm).

31 Ibid.

32 2012. "Sexual Assault Case: 'Missing' Nithyananda Surrenders," in *The Indian Express*. Bangalore.

33 Personal communication.

34 Banisadr, Masoud. 2004. *Masoud: Memoirs of an Iranian Rebel*. London: Saqi, p. 452.

35 Kester, Dannetta. "Survivor Statement" *Survivor statements from Former Hephzibah girls*. Retrieved June 1, 2014 (http://survivorstatements.webs.com/testimoniesdg.htm).

36 Jang, Jin-sung. 2014. *Dear Leader*. London: Random House, p. 56.

37 Ibid., p. xi.

38 Banisadr, *Masoud: Memoirs of an Iranian Rebel*.

39 Ibid., p. 179.

40 Stern, Jessica. 2003. *Terror in the Name of God: Why Religious Militants Kill*. New York: Ecco, p. 16.

41 Lifton, *Thought Reform and the Psychology of Totalism*.

42 Stern, *Terror in the Name of God: Why Religious Militants Kill.*
43 Arendt, *The Origins of Totalitarianism.*
44 Jang, *Dear Leader*, p. 33.
45 Newman, *Let's Develop!* New York: Castillo International, Inc, p. 80.
46 Ibid., p. 87.
47 Anonymous. *Reasons for Leaving.* (http://www.twelvetribes-ex.org/whyileft.html).
48 Healthy Happy Holy Organization. *3ho Lifestyle.* Retrieved June 2, 2014 (http://www.3ho.org/).
49 Photon. 2014, *Forum: The Wacko World of Yogi Bhajan.* Retrieved June 2, 2014 (http://m.delphiforums.com/kamallarose/messages/2534).
50 Hall, John. 2016. "Isis Is Brainwashing Children to Murder Their Own Parents, Child Soldier Who Escaped from Raqqa Reveals," in *The Independent*, January 18, 2016. London.
51 Watchtower Books. 1982. *You Can Live Forever in Paradise on Earth.* New York: Watchtower Books, p. 208.
52 Arendt, *The Origins of Totalitarianism.*
53 Banisadr, Masoud. 2004. *Masoud: Memoirs of an Iranian Rebel.* London: Saqi.
54 McCormick, *Never Fall Down*, p. 44.
55 Nithyananda, Paramahamsa. 2011. *Rising in Love with the Master: The Greatest Love Affair.* Bangalore: eNPublishers pp. 37, 38, 77.
56 Newman, *The End of Knowing*, p. 116.
57 Ibid.
58 Asch, Solomon E. 1952. *Social Psychology.* New York: Prentice-Hall, p. 620.
59 Bailey, Sarah Pulliam. 2014. "Conservative Leader Bill Gothard Resigns Following Abuse Allegations," in *The Washington Post.* Washington DC.
60 Personal communication.
61 Posner, Sarah. 2011. "'Taliban Dan's' Teacher: Inside Bill Gothard's Authoritarian Subculture." *Religion Dispatches*, 6 February; Knowles, Francine. 2014. "Ex-Head of Suburban Religious Organization Denies Sex Harassment," in *Chicago Sun-Times.* Chicago.
62 Institute in Basic Life Principles. *Counseling Sexual Abuse.* A.T. Institute: Institute in Basic Life Principles.
63 Recovering Grace. 2013, *How "Counseling Sexual Abuse" Blames and Shames Survivors.* Retrieved June 2, 2014 (http://www.recoveringgrace.org/2013/04/how-counseling-sexual-abuse-blames-and-shames-survivors/).
64 Asch, Solomon E. 1951. "Effects of Group Pressure Upon the Modification and Distortion of Judgements," in *Groups, Leadership, and Men*, edited by H. Gvetzkow. Pittsburgh: Carnegie Press, pp. 177–90.
65 Ibid.
66 Yong, Lee Sang. 2014. "More Than 100 North Koreans 'Banished to Remote Areas for Watching Foreign Video Footage'," in *The Guardian.* London.
67 Scaramanga, Jonny. 2014. "Creationism and the 'Conspiracy' of Evolution: Inside the UK's Evangelical Schools." *New Statesman*, 5 February.
68 Hassan, *Combatting Cult Mind Control.*
69 Arendt, *The Origins of Totalitarianism.*
70 Orwell, George. 1946. *Animal Farm.* New York: Signet Classic.
71 See LaRouche group publication: Hammer, David. n.d., *British Steer Plan for Bloody War on Kwazulu.* Retrieved June 2, 2014 (http://lyndonlarouche.org/larouche-southafrica5.pdf).
72 Chitwood, Bryan R. 2008. "Ex-Panamanian Official Links Larouche to Noriega," in *Loudoun Times-Mirror.* Loudoun.
73 Tourish, Dennis and Tim Wohlforth. 2000. *On the Edge: Political Cults Right and Left.* Armonk: M.E. Sharpe, p. 121.
74 Bowlby, John. 1980. *Attachment and Loss, Loss*, Vol. 3. New York: Basic Books, p. 249.
75 Arendt, *The Origins of Totalitarianism*, p. 321.

76 Ibid., p. 383.
77 Sahar Family Foundation. 2009, *Hierarchical Administration of Information within Mko: An Interview with Batool Soltani on Mko Self-Immolations*. Retrieved June 2, 2014 (http://www.nejatngo.org/en/post.aspx?id=2778#.U4x0B_ldWSo).
78 Personal communication.
79 Kahler, Karl. 2014. "Minnesota Cult Leader Called the Girls 'Brides of Christ' – and He Was 'Christ'," in *Pioneer Press*. St. Paul.
80 Liston, Enjoli. 2014. "Jang Jin-sung: 'If Anyone Thinks North Korea Is Opening up, They Are Mistaken'," in *The Guardian*. London.
81 Kiernan, Ben. 2006. "External and Indigenous Sources of Khmer Rouge Ideology," in *The Third Indochina War: Conflict between China, Vietnam and Cambodia, 1972–79*, edited by Odd Arne Westad and Sophie Quinn-Judge. London, Routledge, pp. 187–206.
82 Asch, Solomon E. 1952. *Social Psychology*. New York: Prentice-Hall, p. 20.
83 Lifton, *Thought Reform and the Psychology of Totalism*, p. 430.
84 East Side Institute for Short Term Psychotherapy. n.d., *An International Center for New Approaches to Human Development and Community Building*.
85 *The Larouche Internal Memo Generator* (n.d.). Retrieved June 3, 2014 (http://larouche-planet.info/pmwiki/pmwiki.php?n=LaRouche.Larouchememo).
86 Lifton, *Thought Reform and the Psychology of Totalism*.
87 Main, M. and R. Goldwyn. 1998. *Adult Attachment Scoring and Classification Systems*. Berkeley: University of California.
88 Orwell, George. 1949. *1984*. New American Library: New York, p. 254.
89 Field notes, Albany, NY, February 3, 2006.
90 Lifton, *Thought Reform and the Psychology of Totalism*, p. 429.
91 Arendt, *The Origins of Totalitarianism*, p. 324.
92 Shiva Trust. 2014, *Shiva Trust Satguru Sri Ramana*. Retrieved May 11, 2014 (http://www.shivatrust.org.uk/).
93 Personal communication.
94 Petty, R.E. and J.T. Cacioppo. 1986. *Communication and Persuasion: Central and Peripheral Routes to Attitude Change*. New York: Springer/Verlag; Kahneman, Daniel. 2011. *Thinking, Fast and Slow*. London: Allen Lane.
95 Winter, Charlie. 2015. "Fishing and Ultraviolence." *BBC News*, 6 October.
96 Field Notes, Castillo Theater, May 18, 2004.
97 Newman, Fred and Hazel Daren. 1974. *A Manifesto on Method: A Study of the Transformation from the Capitalist Mind to the Fascist Mind*. New York City: International Workers Party.
98 Koestler, Arthur. 1968. *Darkness at Noon*. London: Longmans.
99 Siegel, Daniel J. 1999. *The Developing Mind: Toward a Neurobiology of Interpersonal Experience*. New York: Guilford Press.
100 Petty, R.E. and J.T. Cacioppo. 1986. *Communication and Persuasion: Central and Peripheral Routes to Attitude Change*. New York: Springer/Verlag.
101 Siegel, *The Developing Mind*.
102 Lifton, Robert Jay. 1986. *The Nazi Doctors: Medical Killing and the Psychology of Genocide*. New York: Basic Books.
103 Ibid.
104 Arendt, Hannah. 2003. "Thinking and Moral Considerations," in *Responsibility and Judgment*. New York: Random House LLC, p. 159.
105 Tourish, Dennis. 2005. "How Cults Can Produce Killers," in *The Irish Times*.

8

FROM THE INSIDE OUT

There was a mentality, you know, while you were in it, that, that, that you would more or less die if you actually ever became outside of it. So there was a lot of confusion about that, you know, sort of, how am I, how am I no longer in it anymore? I didn't even think that was a possibility.

Excerpt from *Newman Tendency Group Attachment Interview*

In the previous chapters I have explained the elements of a totalist system, from the leader to the isolating structure that is supported by the total ideology and which together enable fear-driven processes of brainwashing. This relational trauma results in the paradoxical and entrapping response of an individual seeking protection and comfort from the source of fear. The dissociation caused by this situation of fright without solution splits apart the normally more-or-less integrated processes of thinking about feeling.

But followers, while brainwashed, are not robots. The self that takes in and feels the real world through their sense perceptions remains, even though deeply buried. This is the self that reemerges (or emerges, in the case of people born or raised in these systems) given the right conditions, and can resist and perhaps make an escape. As the ways into these systems varies (as described in Chapter 3), so there is variation in how people resist and – when possible – come out.

The grey zone

Totalist leaders – charismatic authoritarian persons with a likely disorganized attachment status and a psychopathic personality – engage suitable victims using methods of coercive persuasion or brainwashing within closed and isolating totalist systems. But, while it is the leader who drives the system, we must also be aware of what Primo Levi describes as "the grey zone," "the space that separates" the victim from the perpetrator:

> It is naive, absurd, and historically false to believe that an infernal system such as National Socialism sanctifies its victims: on the contrary, it degrades them, it makes them resemble itself, and this all the more when they are available, blank, and lacking a political or moral armature. From many signs it would seem the time has come to explore the space which separates . . . the victims from the persecutors . . . Only a schematic rhetoric can claim that that space is empty: it never is, it is studded with obscene or pathetic figures . . . whom it is indispensable to know if we want to know the human species, if we want to know how to defend our souls when a similar test should once more loom before us.[1]

Levi cautions us to resist simplistic answers to the complex questions that arise out of the world's experience of totalism. He is also suggesting that we do not so easily separate ourselves from either the totalist lieutenants, collaborators or their victims. To do so is to assume our immunity. And to falsely assume immunity is to make ourselves vulnerable; we may then fail to gain the real knowledge necessary to strengthen our ability to resist. But despite research indicating that victims of totalism do not have special, 'cult-seeking' or self-victimizing tendencies or weaknesses prior to becoming trapped in totalist environments,[2] people continue to say, "It could never happen to me."

This separation between "resister" and victim (us versus them) also results in a tendency to blame and shame victims. A particularly disturbing form of this is discussed by Levi where he describes the intense shame experienced by survivors of Hitler's concentration camps for not having resisted 'enough': "You too could have, you certainly should have [resisted] . . . Consciously or not, [the Holocaust survivor] feels accused and judged, compelled to justify and defend himself."[3] This is a similar shame experienced by battered women and former cult members ("Why didn't you leave?"), or victims of child sexual abuse ("Why didn't you tell?"). This shaming only serves to give a false sense of security to those on the outside. It does not help them to understand the actual dynamics at work so that they may protect themselves in the future.

Security of attachment isn't foolproof

Although I – and others – emphasize time and again that security of attachment or other personality factors are not a protection against recruitment and conversion to totalist systems, nonetheless differing preexisting attachment statuses may influence a follower's pathway through such a system. It may be, for example, that the preoccupied are somewhat more susceptible to the wolf-in-sheep's-clothing charms of the charismatic authoritarian leader, and the dismissing may be drawn to the rigidity of a totalizing ideology and a totalist system. And, as we have seen, situational factors also affect even the securely attached, those who might otherwise be considered resistant to such dynamics. None of us, therefore, can consider ourselves immune, and the discussion of resistance and resilience must proceed from this understanding.

Secure attachment can be related to Lifton's concept of the protean self, which he describes as a flexible and open approach to life that allows fluid rather than totalist all-or-nothing relationships to both beliefs and people. Proteanism involves an adaptable shape-shifting, the ability to tolerate uncertainty and to cope with the changing nature of the world without needing to resort to the absolutism of fundamentalism. Proteanism both requires, and would tend to reproduce, secure attachments, which are defined as flexible, open, communicative and responsive.[4] Fundamentalism or authoritarianism, on the other hand, which exerts control by laying claim to an absolute Truth and an "unalterable moral certainty,"[5] tends to be produced by rigid, closed and frightening attachments and would similarly reproduce such attachments.

On the one hand, one might expect securely attached, resilient people to be resistant to the seductions of charismatic authoritarian leaders. However, in certain totalist situations, some of the very features of resilience also predispose people to recruitment, namely: faith, activism, openness,[i] putting one's goals into action, joining a social formation to enact one's goals and so forth: "resilient survivors champion the underdog, dedicate themselves to causes and benefit [by] being *attached to something that matters* (my emphasis)."[6] When combined with other, quite general factors such as normal life transitions, or being between affiliations,[7] this moral sense, idealism and desire to contribute can become predisposing factors for recruitment to an ideologically based totalist system.

Resiliency is "the ability to use internal and external resources successfully to resolve stage-salient developmental issues" and features the capacity to adapt and function well despite stressful circumstances or following traumatic events.[8] But importantly, researchers also define resiliency as the ability to function within the "environment of adaptedness." The situation of fright without solution is, by definition, *outside* this environment of adaptedness and therefore the resiliency of secure attachment does not necessarily offer complete protection when faced with this type of strong situation.

Pathways through totalism: An attachment approach

While secure attachment is not, therefore, a foolproof protection against totalism, nonetheless prior attachment status can be an interesting way to look at the variations in how people move through these oppressive and dangerous systems. This is a difficult area to research, but here I present some tentative ideas.

---

i As my colleague Doug Agustin says, "It's important to have an open mind, just not so open that your brains fall out."

In an earlier study of mothers in cults I described a pattern of resistance where,

> the mother may continue to consciously disagree with the cult practices, but will give in externally to resolve the pressure being applied on her . . . she may live in a constant state of resentment and be characterized as a bad group member.[9]

Such mothers attempt to be counterassertive, at least internally, to the bullying of the cult. This is similar to how secure children prevent the bullying dynamic when paired with dismissing (avoidant) children by maintaining distance or by standing up to the victimizer.[10] Others may even question openly, voice doubts and objections, and try to protect others. I suggest that this type of counterassertive behavior reflects that of the securely attached and may lead some of those persons to more frequent early withdrawal or expulsion from totalist groups. This counterassertive behavior will certainly risk punishment. However, other previously securely attached individuals may simply comply and be conscientious yet perhaps less vindictive followers than others.

An originally preoccupied attachment status may correspond to the cult member taking on the status of victim with less resistance and perhaps with more of a desire for attachment to the charismatic authoritarian leader. As regards the mothers in my study, I concluded that: "Some mothers may repress their sense of right, fully embracing the group's ideology, yet maintain an unconscious feeling about what is right . . . these may be the 'good' cult members."[11] These members would be more likely to accept the "bullying" of the cult leader and internalize humiliation by the leader. Lalich's description of Miriam suggests this possibility in a political cult member:

> Soon enough Miriam herself was being blamed by Baxter for having allowed a renegade [Helene] to worm into their group . . . Miriam was never able to outlive this derogatory image. Despite having been Baxter's original connection to the group, a founder, well read, and a hardworking activist, Miriam was never again given a position of responsibility in the organization. This negative stereotyping of Miriam was the beginning of many moves by Baxter over the years to discredit, denounce, humiliate, demote, and in some cases, expel the 12 other founders. In fact, eight were expelled. Three others were relegated to low-level, nonleadership positions; their images were that of the *incompetent but loyal follower* (my emphasis).[12]

Similarly, several studies of victims of domestic violence have found a correlation between preoccupied attachment and susceptibility to abuse.[ii]

---

ii See for example: O'Hearn & Davis, 1997, and studies cited in Hesse, Erik. 1999. "The Adult Attachment Interview, Historical and Current Perspectives," in *Handbook of Attachment: Theory, Research and Clinical Applications*, edited by Jude Cassidy and Phillip Shaver. New York: Guilford Press, pp. 395–433.

Initially dismissing (avoidant) victims are also likely to be "good" followers, taking on the ideology and perhaps becoming both competent and loyal. Perhaps it is some of these people, as well as the initially disorganized, who rise to become lieutenants. In my own group, the lieutenant "Debbie" had a predictably harsh and cold manner of implementing directives from the leader, and mirrored well the authoritarian personality described by Adorno: submissive to those above one in status and authoritarian to those below.[13] In Sroufe et al.'s studies of children the dismissing (avoidant) children tended to bully the preoccupied (ambivalent) children,[14] while the secure tried to protect the bullied.

The key to resistance is the ability to maintain or develop trusting relationships in order to preserve an integration of thinking and feeling, along with the ability to find ways to act independently and avoid, as much as possible, enmeshment and identification with the oppressive system.

In studying former prisoners of Chinese Communist prison camps, Lifton described three categories of response to that totalist situation and the program of thought reform that was imposed: the Obviously Confused, Apparent Converts, and Apparent Resisters.[15] These groupings also suggest a correlation to preexisting attachment styles. Lifton gathered narrative accounts from his subjects, and extrapolated his three categories from those narratives.

The Obviously Confused (the most frequently found response), on being interviewed after release, "could recognize that he had been affected by some of the Communist message and each felt a need to reconsider the problems of who he was and what he believed."[16] Although they had gone along with group norms in the camps, and changed some of their beliefs, the Obviously Confused group's subsequent attempts to untangle their experience were consciously, flexibly and openly dealt with – a process parallel to the development of a *coherent narrative*[iii] by the securely attached. Being in a prison camp and under physical, as well as psychological, coercion limited their ability to actively resist (unlike the securely attached children who were able to resist bullies). But what distinguishes this group is their open and conscious effort to deal with the subsequent effects of the thought reform process to which they were subjected, and it is this that suggests their possible preexisting security of attachment.

The Apparent Converts "were those who made newspaper headlines, who emerged from prison in a state loudly proclaimed as 'brainwashed'"[17] and enthusiastically mouthed the ideology on leaving. However their doubts did surface after a period of time following release and their reactions then became similar to those of the Obviously Confused. This appears to correspond with preoccupied attachment: a submission, though temporary, to the "bullying" process. Eventually these individuals regained their original identity and beliefs, but without the conscious rebuilding of a coherent narrative.

---

iii The coherent narrative is an important concept in attachment theory and refers to the ability to tell one's story to another in a coherent and collaborative manner. It is an indicator of secure attachment. This is discussed more fully in the next chapter.

The Apparent Resisters emerged "denouncing the cruelties of prison thought reform"[18] and, to a large extent, denied the actual impact of the process on themselves. However this supposed "resistance" was not entirely what it appeared. Lifton discusses how their resistance was based on a rigid and inflexible certainty, which their captors were, in fact, often able to subvert and "to a certain degree penetrate this . . . framework and [begin] replacing it with their own."[19] In one of Lifton's examples, the individual, Dr. Bauer, was an adherent of Nazi ideology, and his rigid belief in this other totalist ideology was indeed part of what allowed him to "resist." Lifton describes, however, how the penetration of the new extremist ideology would sometimes show itself at quite unexpected moments much after the fact with slippages into the new totalist thinking. The fundamental feature of Apparent Resisters was their attempt to battle one totalist thought system by hanging on to another. In addition, Dr. Bauer and another prisoner characterized as an Apparent Resister both (at different times) took on the role of authoritarian group leader and each was feared and disliked by the other prisoners. This seems to correspond with the enforcing lieutenant or bully role of dismissing individuals.

This "false" method of resistance is one that Lifton classifies as a *pseudo-strength* – a potential psychological danger:

> I am referring to his inability to come to conscious terms with thought reform influences, and his need instead to make use of the psychological mechanisms of denial and repression in order to keep from himself the recognition of undue 'weakness'.[20]

The thought reform (brainwashing) influences become new demons that the apparent resister now must reject in a totalist manner.

In another example of resistance, Lifton, in *The Nazi Doctors*, discusses Dr. Ernst B. and what allowed him to be perhaps the lone Auschwitz doctor to retain a level of humanity. He refused to perform selections, saved many lives and treated inmates as human beings. Lifton points out, however, that while Dr. B. obviously resisted the totalist system within Auschwitz, he nonetheless had a divided response – doubling, or developing a shadow self – which seems to be almost a universal response to immersion in a totalist environment. Dr. B. retained a Nazi affiliation, and justified certain of National Socialism's actions and ideologies even after the war. But still he,

> could resist the kind of doubling necessary for that task [of performing selections] . . . more fluid than fixed in his style of connection, he was probably less bound than others to the kind of absolute loyalty and obedience that would have carried him over the threshold of doubling into the selections. At the same time an aspect of integrity (modeled on his father originally perhaps, but now his own), having to do not only with nondissembling but also with decency, help, and healing, had become part of his self-process.[21]

Lifton stresses, however, that the extreme nature of Auschwitz's totalist environment generally broke down other doctors' resistance, which though frequently present initially, collapsed, usually within hours and generally within not more than two or three weeks of their arrival.

Methods of resistance

While acknowledging that resistance is not absolute or sure, Lifton details the former prisoners' methods of resistance as follows:

"The acquisition of a sense of understanding, a theory about what is going on, an awareness of being manipulated."[22] While understanding the process of manipulation did not offer complete immunity it did help to "dispel the terrifying fear of the unknown and the sense of complete helplessness – two great stimulators of human anxiety on which thought reform depends."[23] This fear and helplessness are the feelings of fright without solution experienced within a relationship of disorganized attachment. Perhaps Lifton's key point is that this dispelling of fright without solution – finding a solution in knowledge and comprehension of the situation – then allows the subject to avoid dissociation and consciously mobilize other methods of resistance. This points to the importance of preventive education based on an understanding of these dynamics of manipulation.

Avoidance of emotional participation. This method entailed avoiding emotional connection to the captors or to the "group structure of the cell" that would further integrate the subject into the prison world, and enmesh them in the disorganized bond. The resisting prisoners kept as much distance as possible from the thought reform process. Jacobo Timerman, a political prisoner during Argentina's "Dirty War," describes how,

> I tried to maintain some [imaginary] professional activity, disconnected from the events around or that I imagined to be going on around me. . . . At times, something in the mechanism would fail, and I had to devote several hours to reconstructing it: some lingering physical pain following an interrogation, hunger, the need for a human voice, for contact, for a memory. Yet I always managed to reconstruct the mechanism of withdrawal, and thus was able to avoid lapsing into that other mechanism of tortured solitary prisoners which leads them to establish a bond with their jailer or torturer.[24]

Sroufe's[25] description of how the securely attached avoid bullies by distancing themselves fits with this method of resistance.

Because complete avoidance would be impossible, *a neutralizing attitude* helped resistance. Rather than hostile confrontation, which would yield more pressure, neutralizing techniques deflated the pressure. Humor, which broke the levels of tension, anxiety and guilt required for thought reform, was a common way to neutralize the pressure. A good joke is a fine way to resist.[iv] As a result most totalist

---

iv Lessing, 1987 and Hunter, 1956, also discuss the use of humor as resistance.

systems are notably intolerant of real humor. Humane stoicism, a kind of passive resistance, also had a neutralizing effect.[26]

Lifton characterizes *identity reinforcement*, a belief in oneself or in one's preexisting beliefs (of whatever variety), as the most important resistance technique. This could take the form of keeping a sketch diary, to writing poems and memorizing them, to asserting a religious belief.[27] Likewise, Primo Levi in *The Drowned and The Saved* notes that "the believers in any belief whatsoever, better resisted the seduction of power."[28] This identity reinforcement could be seen as closely related to secure attachment, in that the securely attached individual has a strongly defined, yet flexible sense of self such as Dr. Ernst B. above – yet this should not be confused with the rigid belief system of the dismissing. Identity reinforcement could also involve maintaining internalized attachments: Arn Chorn Pond relates how he was ordered to have no thoughts other than "love for Angka. But inside my head I keep a door, always lock, where I hide my family."[29] But this is far from foolproof: under the unrelenting terror he suffers he eventually:

> can't see them anymore, I can't make the faces come back.
> All this time I work so hard to hide them; now I can't find them. All this Khmer Rouge talk of forgetting, always I think I can disobey, always I keep my family alive in my mind. But now the Khmer Rouge, they win. They kill the family in my mind.[30]

An additional factor is the development of *Dissident Group Feelings.*[31] An important aspect of resistance occurs when a 'dissident' group can form (generally secretly) within, but separate from, the totalist group structure and provide support to its members in their efforts to resist. In such a dissident group – what I call an island of resistance – its members create a "safe space" in which they preserve a level of "non-isolation," where they can, in small ways, remain themselves.

Lifton discusses the need for character balance between flexibility and totalism. The presumed dismissing Apparent Resisters did possess strength of identity in contrast to the converts, but this was with the cost of inflexibility that prevented an open review of their experience later. The Obviously Confused were able to be more flexible in accepting or rejecting parts of the new influence. Lifton emphasized, however, that "None [of the three responses] held a monopoly on human limitation, strength, or courage."[32]

Getting out of totalist systems

Given the strength of the disorganized attachment bond formed by the follower to the group, leaving a totalist group presents extraordinary challenges. It is not merely whether people weigh the emotional and material costs and benefits of involvement versus exit,[v] but whether *they are even able to think about such choices.*

---

v See this discussion of exit costs: Zablocki, Benjamin D. 1998b. "Exit Cost Analysis: A New Approach to the Scientific Study of Brainwashing." *Nova Religio* 12:216–49.

An attachment, or trauma, view of this proposes that such rational and evaluative thinking is hijacked by the means of splitting apart emotional and cognitive processes.[33] As Grace, a former member of the Newman Tendency said: "You actually thought that not being a member would be death itself, you couldn't even conceive of it really."

So, in understanding the exit process, it is important to ascertain how people resolve this block to thinking about their feelings in relationship to the group: how do they reintegrate their thought processes enough in order to be able to arrive at the point of making a choice? (Some, however, do not resolve this block – or do so much later – but may leave a group for other reasons, as discussed later in this chapter.) The emotional obstacle to this reintegration is the isolation from trusting relationships and the follower's unterminated state of fear arousal. In this way the group, or the idea of the group, remains the only available safe haven. The cognitive obstacle is the fear-based dissociation of the thinking part of the feeling brain – the inability to even begin to think about the problem. This goes along with cognitive isolation: isolation from alternate sources of information.

Three types of fear

The fear arousal aspect of disorganized attachment is the essence of totalist deployability. Three different types of fear operate to retain people in totalist environments. First is the fear of leaving a total world: leaving all the people, and often the job, housing and other sustaining elements of life, all of which have been within or controlled by the group. The leaver faces the overwhelming tasks of then having to reestablish all these basics of life and the development or redevelopment of family, friendship and affiliative ties.

Second is the fear of retribution by the group: will the group retaliate against the individual's defection? All too often they do – either chasing down the former member, threatening them and/or silencing them in various ways. And if they don't directly do these things then nonetheless the group member lives in fear that this will happen. Totalist groups warn the potential leaver in no uncertain terms of the risk they are placing themselves at. These first two types of fear are real and present, but they have potential practical solutions for which plans can be drawn up. In other words, one could plan how to meet new people, look for a job, even how to hide from the group should that be necessary.

However there is a third, and in my view, more critical, element of fear that the group member who is considering leaving must struggle with: this is a type of existential fear, or "speechless terror.[34] This third fear is the element that is specific to a trauma/disorganized attachment bond, and reflects the state of fright without solution. It is a generalized terror that cannot be clearly thought about or articulated given the dissociation between emotional and cognitive processing that characterizes the disorganized relationship. Emotionally, the leaver experiences intense separation anxiety and a terror of the aloneness that seems to be the only option. And cognitively there is a fear of total loss of meaning. This is a paralyzing fear of both relational and cognitive "nothingness," a feeling of being cast into a void. In leaving the group the individual faces both the loss of their only known and available safe haven, and a potentially terrifying absence of identity until a new identity can be established within a new social context, a process that can take years. The group member cannot draw up plans to deal with this third type of fear, precisely because the emotional-cognitive links have been disrupted by the situation of fright without solution. This is the glue that, up until leaving, has bound the group member to the group. Lifton describes this in his eighth criterion for totalism, the "dispensing of existence":

> For the individual, the polar emotional conflict is the ultimate existential one of "being versus nothingness." . . . The totalist environment – even when it does not resort to physical abuse – thus stimulates in everyone a fear of extinction or annihilation.[35]

In my own case, as I left the O., I remember the feeling of leaving as being as if I were stepping off the edge of the planet, off the edge of the known world into an infinite black abyss. It was absolutely terrifying. Even though I was slowly starting to develop a supportive relationship with two other members who were leaving with me (and that was key in my ability to leave) I still felt deep inside myself as if I had no one to turn to, no place of safety at all and that the outside world was a life-threatening vacuum. When I finally did start breaking off from the group it was as if I had to leap across this bottomless chasm to an entirely unknown destination on the other side.

This element of existential fear cannot be reduced to a simple cost/benefit analysis as some have suggested.[36] The follower who is trying to leave must instead find a way to disrupt the disorganized attachment bond that is preventing even thinking about the relationship with the group, and that is responsible for this primary and paralyzing form of fear.

So how do members break this terror-based bond? These systems are not foolproof. They are human systems with a variety of potential weak spots – in particular the ability to control all relationships all the time. Attachment theory leads us to two major pathways out of the totalist trap. First are other, mitigating attachment relationships that both provide escape hatch safe havens that can moderate the condition of fright without solution, and allow thinking, and possibly even discussion, of doubts in order to reintegrate thinking with feeling. We would thus expect to see that developing an alternate attachment bond goes hand in hand with at least some reorganization of thought processes. Second, we might look for a reduction in other aspects of the disorganized bond – that is, a failure of the group to maintain the situation of fright without solution by a weakening in the function of the group as either a safe haven and/or as a threat, and as the sole source of information. Sometimes, too, the group itself rejects or kicks out followers thus also ending, or at least weakening, the disorganized bond.

The power of alternate safe haven attachments

To take the first point – mitigating attachment relationships: several avenues may exist where escape hatch safe havens are, or become, available. Sometimes islands of resistance are able to be formed even within the group, where a small set of followers find a way to ally with and trust each other. In my own case, at a time when discipline was slightly lessened in the O. (later, I discovered, because the leader was in prison), another comrade, Kris, and I began meeting together – ostensibly to get exercise at the gym (itself a sign of the temporary weakness of discipline) – and slowly began feeling each other out. She was, she had told me, ready to talk about "problems in the leadership." Kris had already begun establishing a level of trust with her cult-arranged husband, as I wrote in my memoir, *Inside Out*:

> "Bill and I have already started talking," she said.
> And I knew immediately what she meant: they were breaking security, they were talking about what they really felt about the O., in the way I had tried to with Ted. I couldn't stop myself then. Tears started rolling down my face. I'd waited almost ten years for this, for someone to lift up the belljar, to say, "I'm in here too, and I think there's still life outside." I turned to her and hugged her . . . The relief was a completely tangible thing.[37]

Eventually, as we continued to talk and to build trust, the three of us were able to plan our way out together. Sometimes couples are able to get close enough to support each other to first think, and then leave the group. This is the key reason the leader must keep such attachments from becoming truly close and trusting.

More commonly, perhaps, people external to the group reach in to the group to help the follower escape. Often former members represent an alternate safe haven. They may contact the group member and assist them to come out through a combination of emotional and cognitive support: sharing experiences, knowledge and feelings (perhaps particularly an understanding of the "panic or terror" that accompanies leaving). Both Juliet and Myrna had former members help them in this way to get out of the Newman Tendency. Similarly several of my former comrades from the O. got out in the year following my departure – we managed to keep a chain of communication open and feed in information and support, which allowed seven others to exit later that year.

Alternatively the group may not have effectively eliminated contact with prior attachment figures and these persons remain available as safe havens at the point of a crisis in the group, or for the individual. Sidney's continuing connection to an old friend and to his family illustrate this pathway. He had resisted attempts by the Newman Tendency to sever those connections and both his family and old friend had kept up a steady critique of the group's practices. When he eventually left he was able to fairly readily pick up those relationships again.

Here also we can place the many instances of the planned interventions known as exit counseling, which usually include both prior attachment figures – close family and friends – as well as former members of the group. Steven Hassan experienced an early form of this when his family organized an intervention that enabled him to leave the Unification Church. He went on to become an exit counselor himself developing a method he calls the Strategic Interaction Approach.[38] A type of "soft," informal – though professionally advised – version of this is what enabled Ted, my cult-arranged husband, to finally exit the O.

Another possible mitigating attachment involves the arousal of the caregiving system. The caregiving behavioral system is the reciprocal of the attachment system where parents are motivated to keep their children close for the purpose of protecting them. The attachment of the follower to his or her children can then sometimes trump that to the group. Where the group is directly threatening the member's relationship to their child, the emotional and cognitive split may (it doesn't always) resolve itself in favor of maintaining proximity to, and safety for, the child. A conflict is set up: continued integration of thought processes in relationship to the child and their well-being versus the dissociation of thought processes in relationship to the group that is threatening the child's well-being. The arousal of the caregiving system can then sometimes help the parent overcome the group-induced dissociation, at least enough to enable them to leave. As I described in Chapter 5, Helen left her bible-based cult after the accumulation of violence and threats to her children overcame her fears of leaving. Celeste Jones, born into the Children of God, finally broke away when she had a child:

> When she was just a few weeks old I began to be horrified at the debauchery that was still raging around me. I constantly suffered flashbacks to the abuse I'd suffered and I knew I could never allow my own daughter to suffer the same fate.[39]

But even this can fail if the situation is strong enough – clearly the mothers who died with their children at Jim Jones's Jonestown were physically unable to protect their children by escaping – their passports had been taken, they were deep in the jungles of Guyana and surrounded by armed guards. In other groups, if the parent feels totally helpless and unable to protect the child then the caregiving system may not represent a way out but can instead become another disorienting aspect of the situation of fright without solution.

A different version of the potentially liberating effect of the caregiving system is the case of Masoud Banisadr discussed earlier. While ill in hospital for several weeks he cared for an immobilized fellow patient and this human connection – something not allowed in the cult – reestablished his feelings of attachment.[40]

A change in the group member's situation can have the same effect, especially when it involves removing them from the sphere of influence of the group. Maajid Nawaz left the extremist Hizb Ut-Tahrir group after he was imprisoned in Egypt for several years as a result of this affiliation. In prison he slowly established new trusting relationships with a mentor and other prisoners – former jihadis who had renounced extremism. With the encouragement (but not coercion) of his fellow prisoners he began to read widely and think for himself about his beliefs. In addition, he writes:

> My desire to question my own assumptions was greatly encouraged by my being adopted by Amnesty International as a Prisoner of Conscience. Amnesty's efforts taught me that even those who knew that I considered them my "enemies" had the capacity to stand for justice in my case. It was their outreach that enabled me to be emotionally prepared to question my deeply-held prejudices.[41]

In this situation he became educated as to the solely political goals of Islamism and finally rejected it as an ideology, later becoming a vocal counterextremist activist.

Cults rarely wish to use resources on cult members who are not fully productive, so illness too, and particularly hospitalization, may provide a useful respite, which, given access to other attachments and/or information, can be a pathway out.

The leader's failure to maintain control

The second, often interrelated, point is the failure of the group to maintain the safe haven/threat elements. In other words, the group, for a variety of reasons, may not be able to fully uphold the situation of fright without solution. Once again it is important to remember that these are human systems with human fallibilities. Any weakness in the group's control can create small openings in the environment in which the renewal of organized attachments and reintegrated thought can take place, as listed previously.

This loosening of the grip of the leader can occur when the leader is absent – through death, illness, or imprisonment. Unless there is another charismatic and authoritarian leader in the wings,[vi] who can take over their role, (as for example Karen Zerby, who took over the leadership of the Children of God after David Berg's death) often this presages the end of the group. Heaven's Gate, Peoples Temple and David Koresh's Branch Davidians all came to an end with the deaths of their leaders – deaths that also were forced upon their followers in tragic and violent ways.

In some cases the group may not come to an end, but the absence or change of leader may at least create space for some members to begin to reestablish trusting relationships and/or be able to have time to regain some cognitive evaluation

---

vi Another exit pathway may exist for individuals who are themselves charismatic and authoritarian. In this case, there is likely to be a struggle for dominance in the group. The charismatic authoritarian follower is less likely to be susceptible to the threats of the group and more likely to themselves respond in a threatening manner, thus avoiding forming an attachment bond to the group, and often eventually splitting off and forming their own group. This would explain, for example, Newman's rapid exit from the LaRouche group, or Werner Erhard's exit from Scientology, which he left in order to start est, later to become Landmark Education.

of their experience in the group. This was another element in my own case, when Theo Smith, the leader of the O. served a year in prison for manslaughter. The easing up of pressure that occurred in that year meant I had more time and less oversight. In that space, Kris, Rob and I each began to think, and then talk and then plan our way out. This cross-communication – in addition to the critical emotional support – also added the cognitive element: each of us had information that, once pooled, gave a fuller picture of Smith's power and control, and our own lack of it.

The cognitive element can become important in the reintegration of thoughts with feelings under these conditions where control slips or has not yet been consolidated for one reason or another. Access to outside information or discussion, even the repetition over many years of certain dynamics and failed promises can lead to reintegration and to restored critical thinking. Many Jehovah's Witnesses finally leave after discovering the multiple failed predictions of the "The End"[vii] or when they stumble across too many inconsistencies and unexplained changes in doctrine in the study materials.[42] Others may leave their groups when the demands placed upon them are too extreme for the level of brainwashing thus far achieved. This gap between demands and level of indoctrination can sometimes be enough to help a person find a way through the suffocating and engulfing ideological justifications and thought-stopping of the system.

For example, in the Newman Tendency, Fred Newman initiated a "Want Fred" meeting in which followers were essentially ordered to proclaim their sexual desire for Newman and his latest wife. Two members left after the "Want Fred" meeting, feeling that this bizarre loyalty ritual went too far. As Ruiz said wryly, "I really didn't want Fred. I mean, I wanted [female leader] once in a while, you know, but I didn't really want Fred." It was after this meeting that control really tightened up. The cognitive aspect can help members out if they discover revelations about abuse, and have the time and ability in which to think about them, or about the contradictions and deception of the group.

In the case of the imprisonment of the leader, this does not necessarily terminate their control. If the leader still has the means to continue communicating with their followers, their influence can also continue. This has been the case with Warren Jeffs who continues to preach to and direct the lives of his followers in the Fundamentalist Church of Latterday Saints from his prison cell[43] – a cell he occupies due to his conviction for multiple counts of child sexual abuse and assault. If the sentence is short then the leader, as in the case of Theo Smith, the leader of the O., can delegate to their lieutenants while imprisoned and resume control on their release. Lyndon LaRouche's right-wing organization survived his five-year absence in prison for fraud and conspiracy,[44] and he returned unopposed to his leadership

---

vii It may take many such failed predictions for this to have a clarifying effect. In his classic book *When Prophecy Fails*, Leon Festinger famously documented the increased commitment of many cult members following such a missed prediction. It was out of this work that he developed the important concept of cognitive dissonance. See: Festinger, Leon, Henry W. Riecken and Stanley Schachter. 1956. *When Prophecy Fails*. Minneapolis: University of Minnesota Press.

position, continuing his perennial runs for US president, along with his total control and abuse of followers.

Some groups fall apart entirely due to the inability of the leader, for whatever reason, to maintain control and the group is closed down from the inside by followers. The California-based Democratic Workers Party is an example of this. A rank and file rebellion took place while the leader, Marlene Dixon, was away on a trip to Eastern Europe. Her alcoholism, paranoia and increasing instability, combined with her absence and thus temporary loss of control, prompted party lieutenants to begin talking to each other. They called a vote and the membership voted to expel her and to dissolve the party.[45]

In other instances external intervention brings about the demise of the group. Clearly this is the case in terms of national conflicts such as the military defeat of Pol Pot's regime by the Vietnamese army. As a current example it is very interesting to watch the holes develop in the isolating wall that North Korea has relied on for so long – with mobile phones, films and videos, the internet and other types of media providing means of communication through the blockade. Yeon-mi Park fled North Korea for the South. Despite the threat of imprisonment or even execution for watching foreign films, she and her friends viewed pirated copies of Hollywood films like *Titanic*. Park said these films gave them "a window for us to see the outside world":

> In North Korean culture, love is a shameful thing and nobody talked about it in public ... The regime was not interested in human desires and love stories were banned. That's when I knew something was wrong. All people, it didn't matter their color, culture or language, seemed to care about love apart from us – why did the regime not allow us to express it?[46]

Even the current autocratic young leader Kim Jong-Un has brought in outside influences such as Mickey Mouse and basketball, encountered during his education in Switzerland. The outside world is seeping in and the totalist regime seems unable to stop it entirely.

Other endings

A non-compliant or non-productive group follower may unwittingly and unwillingly find themselves at the exit door by being expelled from the group. In the cultic studies literature they are known as "kick-outs" or "cast-aways." This can be a particularly traumatic way out as the follower can find it difficult to later find a recovery pathway – the group may have succeeded in making that person feel guilty and inadequate, unable to rise to the standards required. Sometimes these persons, while not allowed in the inner core, may be encouraged to remain in the "periphery," providing various types of support to the group while not requiring much effort or resources from the group itself. Thus they may be officially out of the group, and living largely independent lives, but still providing a degree of support and being shut off from recovery.

If a group implodes, or is shut down by external forces, then followers are out by default. This leaves followers to rebuild their lives outside of that structure, again, sometimes facing some of the same problems as kick-outs, possibly internalizing a sense of failure and having limited or no access to recovery resources and information.

Many followers are never able to leave due to the strength of the situational forces and the lack of resources and pathways out. Too many end their lives with the cult as in the numerous cultic and extremist tragedies that splash regularly across the headlines. "Lifers" may die of old age still "in harness," having lived limited lives within these oppressive regimes. As of this writing thousands are being recruited into a variety of Islamist totalitarian movements, and dying for a cause that has the hallmarks of what Arendt termed an absolute ideology: claiming truths that stand for all of history, the present and the future, and the collapsing of private and public life together under Sharia law. These groups are exemplars of totalitarian movements, movements where there is no discernible final goal other than a boundaryless caliphate supposedly uniting all Muslims under one leader.[17] How to create pathways out for these followers is a question currently under intense debate.[48]

Retribution and shunning

As with entering a group, exiting is a process rather than a single act. There may be many steps and many false starts. Since leaders do not wish to be left they rarely make it easy for the member to depart – unless they are in charge of the departure. The more dangerous and militaristic cults such as the Kony's Lord's Resistance Army, simply threaten death to keep child soldiers from escaping.[49] Cults on the "peace and love" end of the spectrum may have much milder sanctions, but with the same effect. A young woman trying to exit a Kundalini Yoga cult said to me: "I want to leave nicely." But no matter how nicely she wished to leave in order to be able to feel good about her exit and to have "good closure," the leader was unlikely to allow this to happen. A follower who leaves is breaking the controlling bond that is the psychological lifeline for the disorganized leader. As with the case of femicide in relationships of controlling domestic abuse, leaving is often the most dangerous time for the follower.[50] Retribution – one of the three things the leaver fears – is a very real possibility. Defectors, as in my own case, must often plan their way out carefully in order to protect themselves or their children.

As a rule those who leave totalist groups are shunned on exit. This is well known in the case with large groups such as the Jehovah's Witnesses where family members who remain loyal must never again have contact with their mother, father, siblings or children who have left or been "disfellowshipped" for some infraction. Haredi communities of extreme Orthodox Jews similarly shun leavers including parents shunning adult children who leave.[51] Scientology has a policy of "disconnection" from those who leave. The prospect of being shunned is another immense barrier for those considering leaving. But some cultic groups manage to keep former members in some kind of contact as long as they don't directly oppose the group and its dogma. Given the wish of the leader to maintain attachment and access to the resources of his followers, it is perhaps not surprising that many leaders find ways to keep followers involved at some level even when they reject fulltime involvement. Fred Newman showed considerable skill in keeping people on the periphery of the Newman Tendency as long as they left without becoming hostile and continued to provide material support of some kind. In this way the group achieves a "cultural victory"[52] over fellow travelers in the periphery, some of whom, along with "lifers," may never truly move away from the group's sphere of influence. In short, shunning is reserved for the "unsupportive," while those who remain "friendly" can stay on the periphery helping in various ways.

But generally speaking, those who leave totalist systems face losing all the contacts they had within the group. Lofland stated, in relation to joining a totalistic group, that: "in a manner of speaking, final conversion was coming to accept the opinions of one's friends."[53] The condition for becoming a "total" convert, as he put it, was being surrounded by cult-affective ties, and having intensive interactions with other total converts. The opposite happens on exit: leaving the group and questioning its beliefs and methods means coming to accept, not only the loss of all one's friends, but also the loss of one's opinions, meaning and belief structure. The loss of one's friends and family – even those "replaceable others" discussed in Chapter 5 – is one of the most painful losses for former members. In fact, most of the interviewees in my study focused primarily on their loss of relationships when asked about leaving the group, rather than the loss of their belief system.

Recovery and residual effects

In whatever way that the follower leaves, there is a prolonged period of recovery and adaptation back into the external world. The list of negative emotions experienced on leaving a cult is long. Though many leavers also experience great joy, relief and the beauty of freedom, sadly it is their feelings of fear, pain, grief, shame, anger, loneliness and guilt that tend to be more universal. Former members need time, non-judgmental support from trusted others and knowledge of the mechanisms of totalism to be able to work through these feelings and to discover, or rediscover, an autonomous sense of self and identity. Practical support is also needed for people to reintegrate into the outside world and take up an independent life.

Much more could be written about life after the cult and how people do or don't adjust. Some of this is addressed in the next chapter, and helpful recovery books exist.[viii] But for the purposes of this book, the focus is on looking at the mechanisms of totalist control and what Zablocki termed the resulting "psychological traces" of the brainwashing effect.[54] Along with Zablocki, I believe that, even once out of the group, psychological traces remain, which can help us understand

---

viii I refer the interested reader to the excellent recovery book: *Take Back Your Life*. Lalich, Janja and Madeleine Tobias. 2006. *Take Back Your Life: Recovering from Cults and Abusive Relationships*. Berkeley: Bay Tree Publishing.

that something really did happen to drastically affect the individual's brain during their time within the totalist system. These traces certainly may not last forever, and a full recovery and reintegration can sometimes eliminate them entirely. But unfortunately most former members do not have access to the types of help that can accomplish this. Even with such help some of these traumas are so severe that there are significant long-term consequences.

In this chapter we have looked at endings – how people leave totalist systems, or end their lives still within these systems, and how the groups themselves come to an end. Even after leaving, however, the effects of life in a system that uses brainwashing as a control mechanism can be seen in how the experience is retained in the mind. It is these effects and their significance that I discuss next.

Notes

1   Levi, Primo. 1986. *The Drowned and the Saved*. New York: Vintage Books, p. 40.
2   Briggs, Rachel and Ross Frenett. 2014. *Policy Report: Foreign Fighters, the Challenge of Counter-Narratives*. London: Institute for Strategic Dialogue; Crenshaw, Martha. 2011. *Radicalization and Recruitment into Terrorism*. Paper presented at the Processes of Radicalization and De-Radicalization, April, Bielefeld, Germany; Singer, M.T. and J. Lalich. 1995. *Cults in Our Midst: The Hidden Menace in Our Everyday Lives*. San Francisco: Jossey Bass.
3   Levi, *The Drowned and the Saved*, p. 70.
4   Bowlby, John. 1988. *A Secure Base*. New York: Basic Books.
5   Lifton, Robert Jay. 1993. *The Protean Self: Human Resilience in an Age of Fragmentation*. New York: Basic Books, p. 11.
6   Davis, N. 1999, *Resilience: Status of the Research and Research-Based Programs*: Center for Mental Health Services. Retrieved November 15, 1999 (http://www.mentalhealth.org/specials/schoolviolence/5–28Resilience.htm), p. 193.
7   Singer and Lalich, *Cults in Our Midst: The Hidden Menace in Our Everyday Lives*.
8   Egeland, B., E. Carlson and L.A. Sroufe. 1993. "Resilience as Process." *Development and Psychopathology* (5): 517–28, 518.
9   Stein, Alexandra. 1997. "Mothers in Cults: The Influence of Cults on the Relationship of Mothers to Their Children." *Cultic Studies Journal* 14(1): 40–57, 50.
10 Sroufe, L.A. 1988. "The Coherence of Family Relationships," in *Relationships within Families*, edited by R.A. Hinde and J. Stevenson-Hinde. Oxford: Clarendon Press, pp. 27–47.
11 Stein, "Mothers in Cults."
12 Lalich, Janja. 1993. "A Little Carrot and a Lot of Stick: A Case Example," in *Recovery from Cults*, edited by M. Langone. New York: Norton, p. 60.
13 Adorno, Theodor W. 1944. *The Authoritarian Personality*. New York: Norton.
14 Sroufe, L.A. 2005. *The Development of the Person: The Minnesota Study of Risk and Adaptation from Birth to Adulthood*. New York: Guilford Press.
15 Lifton, Robert Jay. 1961. *Thought Reform and the Psychology of Totalism*. New York: The Norton Library.
16 Ibid., p. 87.
17 Ibid., p. 117.
18 Ibid., p. 132.
19 Ibid., p. 132.
20 Ibid., p. 148.
21 Lifton, Robert Jay. 1986. *The Nazi Doctors: Medical Killing and the Psychology of Genocide*. New York: Basic Books, p. 335.
22 Lifton, *Thought Reform and the Psychology of Totalism*, p. 146.
23 Ibid., p. 146.

24 Timerman, Jacobo. 1981. *Prisoner without a Name, Cell without a Number*. New York: Knopf: distributed by Random House, p. 37.
25 Sroufe, L.A. 1988. "The Coherence of Family Relationships," in *Relationships within Families*, edited by R.A. Hinde and J. Stevenson-Hinde. Oxford: Clarendon Press, pp. 27–47.
26 Hunter, Edward. 1956. *Brainwashing*. New York: Farrar, Straus and Cudahy.
27 Ibid.
28 Levi, *The Drowned and the Saved*.
29 McCormick, Patricia. 2013. *Never Fall Down*. London: Random House, p. 44.
30 Ibid., p. 69.
31 Hunter, *Brainwashing*.
32 Lifton, *Thought Reform and the Psychology of Totalism*, p. 151.
33 Main, Mary. 1991. "Metacognitive Knowledge, Metacognitive Monitoring, and Singular Coherent Vs. Multiple Incoherent Model of Attachment," in *Attachment across the Life Cycle*, edited by C.M. Parkes, P. Marris and J. S. Hinde. London and New York: Tavistock/Routledge, pp. 127–159; Herman, Judith. 1992. *Trauma and Recovery*. New York: Basic Books.
34 van der Kolk, Bessel A. 1996a. "The Body Keeps the Score: Approaches to the Psychobiology of Posttraumatic Stress Disorder," in *Traumatic Stress: The Effects of Overwhelming Experience on Mind, Body, and Society*, edited by B.A. van der Kolk, A.C. McFarlane and L. Weisaeth. New York: Guilford Press, pp. 214–241.
35 Lifton, *Thought Reform and the Psychology of Totalism*, p. 434.
36 Zablocki, Benjamin D. 1998b. "Exit Cost Analysis: A New Approach to the Scientific Study of Brainwashing." *Nova Religio* 12:216–49
37 Stein, Alexandra. 2002. *Inside Out: A Memoir of Entering and Breaking out of a Minneapolis Political Cult*. St. Cloud: North Star Press of St. Cloud.
38 Hassan, Steven. 2000. *Releasing the Bonds: Empowering People to Think for Themselves*. Somerville, MA: Freedom of Mind Press.
39 Jones, Celeste. 2007. "Enslaved by the Cult of Sex . . . for 25 Years." *Mail Online*. (http://www.dailymail.co.uk/femail/article-468046/Enslaved-cult-sex–25-years.html#ixzz3KCThMRGl).
40 Banisadr, Masoud. 2004. *Masoud: Memoirs of an Iranian Rebel*. London: Saqi Books.
41 Nawaz, Maajid. 2012, *Maajid Nawaz Speaks About Journey from 'Extremism to Democratic Awakening'*, London: Quilliam Foundation. Retrieved November 26, 2014 (http://www.quilliamfoundation.org/in-the-media/maajid-nawaz-speaks-about-journey-from-extremism-to-democratic-awakening/).
42 See for example: Kelly, R. E. 2008. *Growing up in Mama's Club: A Childhood Perspective of Jehovah's Witnesses*. Tucson, AZ: Parker Ridge Publishing.
43 Hannaford, Alex. 2014. "The Evil Preacher Who Runs His Cult from Prison," in *Telegraph*. London.
44 Associated Press. 1994. "Larouche Exits Prison after Fraud Sentence," in *LA Times*. Los Angeles.
45 Lalich, Janja. 2004. *Bounded Choice: True Believers and Charismatic Cults*. Berkeley: University of California Press.
46 Thompson, Nathan. 2014. "'Watching Titanic Made Me Realise Something Was Wrong in My Country,' Says North Korean Defector," in *The Guardian*. London.
47 Nawaz, Maajid. 2014, "Why Islamists Beat Liberals in the Middle East" *War on the Rocks*. Retrieved December, 2014 (http://warontherocks.com/2014/08/what-the-middle-east-needs/).
48 See for example: Saltman, Erin Marie and Jonathan Russell. 2014. *The Role of Prevent in Countering Online Extremism*, edited by Quilliam. London: Quilliam Foundation.
49 Watch/Africa, Human Rights and Human Rights Watch Children's Rights Project. 1997. *The Scars of Death: Children Abducted by the Lord's Resistance Army in Uganda*, Vol. 3169: Human Rights Watch.
50 Campbell, Jacquelyn C., Daniel Webster, Jane Koziol-McLain, Carolyn Block, Doris Campbell, Mary Ann Curry, Faye Gary, Nancy Glass, Judith McFarlane and Carolyn

Sachs. 2003. "Risk Factors for Femicide in Abusive Relationships: Results from a Multi-site Case Control Study." *American Journal of Public Health* 93(7):1089–97.

51 Personal communication from a mother of five who left a North London Haredi community.

52 Goffman, Erving. 1962. *Asylums: Essays on the Social Situation of Mental Patients and Other Inmates.* Chicago: Aldine Pub. Co., p. 13.

53 Lofland, John. 1977. *Doomsday Cult: A Study of Conversion, Proselytization, and Maintenance of Faith.* New York: Irvington Publishers; distributed by Halsted Press, p. 52.

54 Zablocki, Benjamin D. 1999. "Hyper Compliance in Charismatic Groups," in *Social Perspectives on Emotion,* Vol. 5, edited by D. Frank. Greenwich, CT: Jai Press.

9

DEPLOYABLE, BUT NOT MANCHURIAN

It's a human thing

[D]uring activation of a traumatic memory, the brain is "having" its experience: The person may feel, see, or hear the sensory elements of the traumatic experience but he or she may also be physiologically prevented from translating this experience into communicable language. . . .

Chronic physiological arousal and the resulting failure to regulate autonomic reactions to internal or external stimuli, affect people's capacity to utilize emotions as signals.

Bessel A. van der Kolk, *The Body Keeps the Score: Approaches to the Psychobiology of Posttraumatic Stress Disorder*[i] [1]

There are real and observable effects on the mind from the ongoing traumatic experiences of the totalist relationship, and in this chapter I discuss my exploratory study using the Group Attachment Interview that sought to discern and classify those effects. I also connect Lifton's concept of "doubling"[2] – a phenomenon he saw in doctors who had served the Nazi regime – to that of disorganized attachment.

The Group Attachment Interview

The disorganized attachment bond is, in essence, a chronic (it occurs not just once, but over a period of time) relational trauma. As with other experiences of trauma there are ongoing effects even after the trauma has ceased. One of the purposes of my own research has been to attempt to observe these effects of relational trauma

---

i van der Kolk, Bessel A. 1996. "The Body Keeps the Score: Approaches to the Psychobiology of Post-traumatic Stress Disorder," in *Traumatic Stress: The Effects of Overwhelming Experience on Mind, Body, and Society*, edited by B.A. van der Kolk, A.C. McFarlane and L. Weisaeth. New York: Copyright Guilford Press. Reprinted with permission of Guilford Press (pp. 218, 234).

by creating an instrument based on the Adult Attachment Interview (AAI),[3] a well-validated research tool already in use. The AAI was developed in order to assess and classify patterns of attachment in adults to their early attachment figures (usually their parents). Among these patterns of attachment statuses is that of disorganized attachment. This is demonstrated by responses in the interview regarding discussion of prior abuse or loss where the interviewee's behavioral and attentional strategies collapse.[4] This is seen in a variety of lapses that: "often occur in a high-functioning individual and are normally not representative of the speaker's overall conversational style."[5] In other words, the interviewee's discussion of these difficult, traumatic events becomes disorganized and disoriented.

My goal was to investigate whether the same markers of trauma and dissociation would be observable in former members of a totalist group. I modified the AAI to create the new Group Attachment Interview[ii] (GAI),[6] which looks at the individual's relationship, not to their early caregivers, but instead, to their group. The GAI is a method to determine whether a person's relationship to a group can be classified as one of disorganized attachment.

To develop and test the new GAI I conducted a study in which I compared the totalist Newman Tendency with the non-totalist, democratically run US-based Green Party. Like many closed groups, the Newman Tendency was not easy to study. First, one cannot easily talk to current members – I tried. I called an old friend who I knew had become a Newman follower to see if she would talk to me. She was polite and friendly but when I asked if I could talk to her about her life in Newman's group she said, "Let me get back to you on that." She never replied. During my field work attending public events I asked several other members if I could talk to them about their experiences. In the friendliest of ways they would repeat the phrase: "Let me get back to you." None ever did. This was as I expected – in their shoes (which I had indeed been in) I would have done the same. That is, I would have contacted "leadership," forwarding as much information as possible, and waited for permission. Apparently Fred Newman didn't permit. This did not affect my study, however, as, like the AAI, the GAI relies on retrospective accounts and is geared to looking at the effects and memories of *past* relationships and so former members were suitable interview subjects. I therefore recruited 12 former Newman Tendency members and 11 former Green Party members. I also went to public events (some of which I was disinvited from in the case of the Newman Tendency once they learned my identity), researched group history and activities, and conducted the GAI, along with a semi-structured interview and two surveys, with former members from the two parties.

As expected, the Newman Tendency met all five criteria of a totalist organization, while the Green Party matched none.[7] Fred Newman[iii] was the charismatic and authoritarian leader of the Newman Tendency: a "benevolent despot" according

---

ii This was done with the oversight of Alan and June Sroufe, and with the knowledge and approval of Mary Main, co-author of the Adult Attachment Interview.

iii Fred Newman died in 2011, after my study was completed.

to his own publication. The Green Party, in contrast, has no single leader and it consciously promotes a policy and structure of "weak leadership" to combat the emergence of such "cults of personality." The structure of the Tendency is hierarchical and closed. It was hard to leave the group, or, in some cases, even to imagine life outside. The Green Party, on the other hand, has a flat, decentralized and open structure and demands only a partial commitment from its members.

Newman alone dictated the total ideology of The Tendency. He responded to dissent by purging and expelling those who disagreed with him. The Green Party has a unifying set of Ten Key Values, ranging from "Grassroots Democracy" to "Ecological Wisdom," but the group encourages discussion, disagreement and voicing of a variety of opinions. Newman created Social Therapy as the process that implements coercive persuasion or brainwashing by isolating members from their prior sources of social support, presenting the group as the only remaining support, and bringing to bear a new totalistic belief system through intense group pressure and psychological attacks. There is no evidence of the practice of coercive persuasion seen in the Green Party. The result of these totalist features in the Newman Tendency was exploitation and deployability of followers: labor and sexual favors flowed up the chain of command, while orders, control and the total ideology were passed down from Newman to the membership. The Newman Tendency maintained an arms cache and engaged in weapons training to protect Newman and the assets he controlled. Greens did not report exploitation. Participation was strictly voluntary and based on what each individual wished to contribute at a given time. Greens' personal lives and relationships were largely unaffected by their membership.

The first question I looked at in my study was whether the relationship the former members had had with the Newman Tendency was indeed an attachment one. An attachment bond has two key markers: it is to a *specific other*, and the individual experiences *great distress on separation*.[8] Had the former members of the cultic group formed an attachment bond to the group? And was that a different form of tie than that of the Green Party members to the Green Party?

While in the Newman Tendency, followers clearly felt there was no other group that could take its place. The quote from a former member that she could not "even conceive of being out of it" shows this specific nature of the attachment. Newman Tendency members did not consider other alternatives while in the group. Even after leaving, former members took many years before they (if ever) engaged again in a formal group setting. Green Party members, however, found little difficulty in joining other political or environmental efforts to continue to pursue their goals once they left the group – the Green Party represented just one avenue for them. And in fact, during their tenure they had also belonged to a variety of other groups, including political ones.

Those followers who left the Newman Tendency – like other cult leavers – certainly experienced great distress on separation from the group. Those I interviewed described the leaving process as exceptionally difficult, with many expressing ongoing trauma about it. Several expressed a feeling that there was "nothing to live for now" while others felt "terrible," "devastated," "zonked," or that life was "flat." Former members were deeply confused. Some described having suicidal feelings. These statements illustrate the "existential" fear described earlier.[iv] Others described severe depression and/or anxiety. Gillian described how she felt after leaving. She said it was:

> unbelievably bad. I can't even begin to explain. It was just, I, I, I honestly don't know how I did it, how I didn't end up in a hospital or something. I mean I really performed well. I mean, I kept up with all my kids, and my responsibilities but . . . oh my god, I would just, I couldn't stop crying. I could not. I mean, just . . . I can't even, I just felt like screaming, I, it was horrible for the first few months, just horrible.

Their responses indicate that former members of the Newman Tendency had formed an attachment bond with the group: one that was intense, specific to that group and difficult to break.

On the other hand, former Green Party members generally didn't see leaving as a dramatic event, but as either a hiatus or a quiet retreat. As Lynn said:

> I wasn't really too active but I wasn't like, I didn't, like, say, I'm not a member of the Green Party, I'm not going to pay my money. It wasn't until the . . . election that I finally said, I've had enough. I mean I'm just on sabbatical, I'm not, I didn't, like, leave and say, I don't like the Green Party, I just, like, said, well I'll just step away and see what it looks like [laughs].

Green Party followers had a looser and more generalized affiliative bond. Though some experienced anger or annoyance at the group they did not have extreme distress on leaving. This type of affiliative tie is one that is much more likely to be found between an individual and a group, unless that group is totalist.

It is important to note here that usually relationships to groups are not attachment ones, but are affiliative. It is relationships to close other *persons* that are generally seen to be attachments. And it is precisely this elevation of the relationship with the group to one of attachment that concerns me. This atypical and exclusive group attachment bond – as opposed to a more moderate affiliative tie – utterly dominates the follower and prevents them from having any other freely chosen attachments *or* affiliations.

---

iv Given this distress on leaving it is perhaps not surprising that often people who leave cults without sufficient support on the outside find themselves returning, legs between their tails. This was the case in my own experience when I left after a year, but found myself utterly isolated. I returned to the cult for another nine years before I was able to finally extricate myself with the support of other leavers. Others who leave a cult without then understanding their experience may jump into another totalist group – this is known as cult-hopping, and highlights the need for adequate recovery counseling and education.

In the Newman Tendency the attachment bond was put in place in a number of ways:

- through establishing the group as a presumed safe haven.
- through creating fear or threat to arouse the attachment behaviors of members.
- through eliminating or weakening alternate attachments, which might provide other safe havens able to terminate attachment behaviors caused by fear arousal.
- through the structural creation of material dependency on the group, which also prevented seeking of alternate safe havens capable of terminating attachment behaviors.
- through cognitive isolation, preventing alternate sources of information.

I then wanted to know if this bond was a disorganized one – in other words whether the follower exhibited dissociation, an inability to think about one's feelings (Bowlby's "segregated systems")[9] – in relationship to the group. The Group Attachment Interviews are a small start at gathering empirical evidence for the presence (or absence) of a disorganized attachment bond to a group.[v] Because of how memory is stored in cases of trauma we are able to observe this evidence after the fact – sometimes even decades later if the trauma is not resolved.

The GAI explores the use of language as a marker of how memory has been stored in the brain, and what the individual's *current* state of mind is in relation to the group. People who have experienced trauma tend to have trouble recounting these difficult past experiences in a coherent way – rather they show lapses of various kinds in their discussion of this past. These lapses indicate unresolved trauma or loss. So, even if the incident took place a long time ago, the ability to recount the experience in a coherent narrative may be affected.

As with the AAI, the GAI attempts to "surprise the unconscious"[10] by asking the former member first for five adjectives that describe their relationship with the group:

> Now I'd like to ask you to choose five adjectives or words that reflect your relationship, as you remember it, with [group x], starting from when you first became involved? [if participant is an ex-member add: and up to when you ceased to be involved with the group . . .]. [11]

The interviewee is later asked a series of follow-up questions, including asking for examples of memories or incidents that illustrate why they chose to describe the relationship using each of the adjectives. Special attention is paid to discussion of trauma, loss or abuse.

v For the complete study see: Stein, "Attachment, Networks and Discourse in Extremist Political Organizations."

Responses to these and other questions are coded to identify three distinct types of change in the speaker's conversational style that are markers of disorganized attachment. They indicate that the memories have not been "metabolized" or processed and stored in an ordered, coherent narrative, but remain unprocessed and intrusive: still "alive" and present as if the incident had occurred in the present day. These trauma memories carry with them a potency and immediacy that continues to be overwhelming, troubling and intrusive. Unresolved trauma memories are stored in implicit memory, which involves the central nervous system and the "older" areas of the brain associated with the brain stem and limbic region. "Metabolized" memories, on the other hand, are processed through the use of language to become stored in explicit memory where there is a conscious and subjective experience of remembering. Explicit memory is associated with the frontal lobe, neocortex and hippocampus (later developing areas of the brain).

In disorganized attachment, encoding of experiences of the frightening relationship into explicit memory is impaired. The victim of this chronic traumatic stress may focus on a non-traumatic aspect of the environment or on their imagination during the trauma as a means of "escape." This focus away from the trauma is believed to be what leads to encoding of the experience in implicit but not explicit memory. That is, the traumatic experience remains at the level of the "older," more primitive areas of the brain and is not processed, through use of language, to become stored in the "higher-level" neocortical regions of the brain. Also, the release of stress hormones in trauma and excessive discharge of amygdala activity in response to threat,

> may impair hippocampal functioning. The outcome for a victim who dissociates explicit from implicit processing is an impairment in autobiographical memory for at least certain aspects of the trauma . . . [I]mplicit memory . . . is intact and includes intrusive elements such as behavioral impulses to flee, emotional reactions, bodily sensations, and intrusive images related to the trauma.[12]

This dissociative process results in the narrative about trauma or loss becoming incoherent in a particular way, namely: cognitive lapses, loss of sense of time or place, vivid sensory images as if the experience is currently still happening, long pauses and loss of thread of the narrative.[13] In the same way as occurs in post-traumatic stress disorder (PTSD), the experience has not been processed linguistically and this results in an incoherent narrative where the individual being interviewed is attempting, but failing, to put language to the experience of the relationship of "fright without solution."

In contrast, a speaker who has either not experienced trauma, or who has had an opportunity to resolve traumatic experiences, shows a consistent ability to maintain a coherent narrative throughout the Group Attachment Interview. That is, the speaker is able to recount the experiences to the interviewer in a coherent and collaborative manner as their experiences have been stored in explicit memory which they are able to consciously retrieve. The memories do not overwhelm their ability to discuss them.

The three elements indicating a disorganized narrative are: lapses in reasoning, lapses in discourse and extreme behavioral response in regard to the loss, abuse or trauma related to the group. These "lapses and discrepancies between feeling and thinking"[14] indicate a continued dissociation regarding that frightening relationship and the intrusion of implicit memories into the interview. Here are examples of each from my Group Attachment Interviews with former members of the Newman Tendency.

Lapses in reasoning

<u>*Unsuccessful denial of the occurrence, nature or intensity of the abuse.*</u>[vi] Speech patterns surrounding these denials often become confused and irregular. This former member uses the loaded language of the group, in particular the term "performing":

> *Well, I think I'm just learning those – if there were, I think that it's just now – and like I'm struggling, like I told you with that – that I feel – I still have that mindset of – that – you know, I can't see the setbacks. I keep thinking I'm a failure because of what, you know, I'm not performing. I still am stuck in that. I can't – I haven't gotten beyond it yet, you know, so I'm sure there are, but I keep thinking it's my fault. They really do a number on you there and I can't let go of it. I'm still not beyond it yet. That's gonna take some – a lot of deprogramming and I just don't know if I'll be able to get rid of that thought, you know, if only I had pushed harder, harder, harder, you know – I still can't quite – you know, it's getting the best of you, you know, that's what I was thinking in the group, I was performing better and I was doing more and I did do the play readings and now when I think – hell, I couldn't do that again, you know, and so I think, well maybe I really was doing better. I'm still real confused about that, you know, maybe I sh – you know, I really was doing better. I didn't have as much anxiety. I was doing things that I did enjoy. It was like they did have a good point about performance, you know, that there's validity in what they're saying. I don't know who they're screwing this to, but yeah, I'm totally still very confused with that.*

This speaker veers back and forth between the benefits she felt she got from social therapy and stating "they really do a number on you there." She also has a <u>*sense of being causal in the abuse and deserving of it in a personal sense*</u> (another lapse in reasoning) shown in the references to "it's my fault" and "I'm a failure." The "failure to deny" is in contrast to her reports in other parts of the interview that the Newman Tendency

---

vi In this section, all *underlined and italicized* phrases and sentences are taken from the Adult Attachment Interview coding manual: Main and Goldwyn, *Adult Attachment Scoring and Classification Systems*, as descriptions of the various markers.

therapists were:"*scary as hell . . . they scare me to death . . . it just scares me – I wouldn't go up there in that center. I'd be scared to death of those people.*" She later also says:

> *I would really like to give myself a break, but I just can't seem to do it. You know I can still hear them beating me with the whip, you know, "Get out there and make your mark on the world. We're revolutionaries!"*

<u>*Reports effort to dissociate memories of the experience:*</u> In relationship to boundary violations by her Newman Tendency therapist, and general feelings about what was going on, Bernice stated:

> *I even, I mean, I consciously thought, uh, this is so strange, but I would like just tuck it away.*

<u>*Disorientation with respect to time:*</u> Former Newman Tendency members showed many of these markers, frequently slipping into the present tense when describing therapy, their leaving or other difficult times during their tenure. This speaker left the group 25 years ago. He describes how he was ordered not to take time off to see his parents, with whom he had previously been close. He then says:

> *But that was the culminating – that was the straw that – you know, five years ago I might actually gone along with them if they asked me 'cause I was still in my enthusiastic and believing stage, but at this point . . . it had been building over the past year and a half or so and that was it.*

He is actually discussing a time 30 years ago when he says "five years ago." He wants to say, "five years before that," but he's had a subtle shift to the present – he is in the moment of the conflict that led to him leaving, and says "five years ago" and the "past year and a half" and "this point," not "that point."

Celia, who left over a decade before, shows another example of a shift to present tense:

> *But I felt that anger when I left, of people towards me that I had been, I'm a betrayer, I sold out, you know, I hurt Fred, you know, I'm a revolutionary traitor. I'm the worst.*

Louisa also frequently slips into the present tense. For example, when describing therapy several years after she left, she says:

> *I still have a hard time with it, but that's how they were intimidating because no matter what you said, what you did, they could spin it and they would make a question out of it and they would push you back. It's like they're always shoving you, like you can't just say something and then it's just okay – never did that happen – and really,*

it makes you crack up. You feel like your brain is gonna explode out of your ears. It was horrible, and I thought I was – it was horrible because I couldn't get it.

Disoriented speech – lapse in the monitoring of discourse

In this marker of disorganization, the interviewee is unable to keep track of the interview, of the fact he or she is engaged in communicating with another person – they become lost or absorbed in the traumatic memory.

The following speaker left the Newman Tendency over ten years ago and is discussing her tenure on the security team. Towards the end she is <u>suddenly unable to finish the sentence</u> as she gets absorbed and disoriented by the memory:

And just the idea that I might have to shoot somebody – or that we might get broken into, get shot, you know. I mean I, I felt confident that, I also, before, when I was living in [City 1] I took self defense courses and then I taught self defense, so I knew I could handle myself physically – um, but I didn't know about running across people with guns, you know. So there was always, there, at the back of your mind you're always, when you're on the security shifts, worried about you know, you know, if something would happen to like one of your, you know, "I wish I was home," you know

Her words also have an ominous sense where <u>*"Words or phrases that seem to stand for the abuse are used in an odd way as though the person is unable to name it."*</u> She can't state what she is afraid will happen: "if something would happen." She has also shifted the pronoun from "I" to "You."

The references to death, being dead or dying, in referring to the Newman Tendency, are also notably frequent in these interviews (and are absent in Green Party interviews), further reflecting this *ominous speech*. Another example of ominous speech is the kind of vague fear spoken of by several Newman Tendency members. For example:

I had a fear of the void of not being involved – that something bad was going to happen to me – it was just really, it really all, it was just, all con, all consuming – and I don't mean that positively.

There is a sense of a hidden threat in these comments, which even the speaker cannot fully grasp. When discussing his entry into the group (in which he earlier has stated that he was "*frightened all the time*"), the next speaker says:

I mean, it's – it's hard to – I went in so young it's hard to judge, you know, what I would be like if I didn't go in um – go in, it sounds like prison.

He goes on to state that:

I'm one of the few people that I know that are ex-members that think of it as a positive um – but you know, you take the negative with the positive. I think it was – overall, it – it was an improvement on my personality.

This appears to also be a form of *denial of occurrence of abuse*. He is trying to look at the experience positively but he also realizes that "it sounds like prison." Further examples of *ominous speech* are demonstrated by the next speaker who had left the group about 16 years previously. I had asked her to expand on the word "exhausting" she had used to describe her experience. In the middle of a long, incoherent passage about being on the road almost 20 years before, petitioning to get Newman's presidential candidate Lenora Fulani on the ballot, she says:

> I was down in State 5 um, I had uh – no I think it may have been City 3. In State 5, well, in City 3 – I can't remember to be honest with you, I think I was in State 5 second 'cause in State 5 is where my body physically just stopped. I got, and I was so afraid – um – of not being able, of what, what they might do to me. I was just, like, so – you know that, that story about the elephant and he's hooked up with a, a chain on the pole, and he's trying to, you know, little elephant and he's trying to get, break free – then there's, as, ele – eventually you can hook the elephant up with a rope because in their mind, in that animal's mind it, like, believes that it can't break free, and that's what it was like for me, looking back.

She finds it very difficult to tell this story. She is *suddenly unable to finish sentences*. She uses *words that stand for the abuse*: "What they might do to me." And she shifts from the topic and generally speaks in a disoriented manner. Later in the same passage she uses another marker of disoriented speech: the intrusion of vivid visual sensory images with unusual attention to detail:

> It was just so hard – just getting out there in the sun and – pounding on your, pounding on you. Um . . . [5 secs] ask, stopping people, you know, in the summertime and you know, they were like, I have ice cream in my bag.

After 20 years, this experience has still not been metabolized and she is unable to tell the story in a coherent manner. She finishes the passage by stating:

> I, it was just so exhausting. I hated that . . . I really did. [laughs] I can't believe I did it. But you know I was so young and I just felt – [sighs] –

She again gets absorbed back into the memory and cannot finish the sentence. She is unable to put language to what she felt.

Prolonged silences are another indicator of a lapse in the monitoring of discourse. They again indicate absorption in thinking back to the past, and a failure to keep track in the current conversation. In response to whether there were any aspects to her involvement that she feels were a setback to her development, this speaker says:

> I always wanted to produce or whatever. I wasn't really sure but something . . . [4 secs] and I um – the, I was – told that a political career is what I was – my life, you know, I signed on the line to join this thing and I signed my life over . . . [3 sec]. I signed my life over . . . [18 sec]

Losing track of the question happened frequently as interviewees became absorbed in their memories and thus lost track of the interview context. For example, when asked about how he felt after leaving the group, this speaker ended his response in the following way:

> It wasn't like I didn't like Fred and didn't know him. I knew Fred and I didn't like him. Um – and what was the question?

Three other speakers showed evidence of "flooding" of memories during the GAI interview, with comments like: "Oh gosh, so many memories . . ." This flooding indicates a sense of being overwhelmed and thus presenting an obstacle to maintaining a coherent discourse about their experience – they seem then, as Solomon and George put it in relation to disorganized children, "helpless to control their own narratives."[15] Bowlby[16] discusses this flooding in terms of a "deactivated" and segregated system that breaks through into consciousness from its generally "excluded" state.

Extreme behavioral responses

These responses also indicate ongoing trauma and a failure to fully process the initial trauma at a conscious level.

Almost half of the Newman Tendency participants spoke of having suicidal feelings after they left. Celia described her feelings thus:

> I also even felt suicidal at some points after leaving them because um – you know, there is a sense of – there was a sense of incredible loss and hopelessness and emptiness, loneliness, you know.

The following speaker describes a range of extreme behavioral responses in the period immediately after he left:

> I became like, very reckless, you know, almost suicidal . . . It made me drink, you know, which I've come out of. I still drink but I don't like, get crazy. You know I don't go out binging, I used to go out binging and pass out in the bathroom, you know . . . that kind of stuff. I guess it did, it did for a while, it made me, like, really reckless, I just did really crazy stuff, you know, um just basically trying to get killed, you know.

Another former Newman Tendency member reports continuing efforts to try to organize herself and her understanding of her experience. When asked about her wishes for her future (a concluding question in the GAI), her first wish is that:

> I would love to get rid of that voice that goes, "You're not performing" you know, I hear it all the time and I would give anything to get that – you know, it's ok to have weaknesses. It's okay not to push yourself until you want to die to try to have growth,

development. Maybe I've got as much as I'm gonna get, but see, they always tell you that you never stop growing and developing. You have to keep pushing to keep continuing and I can't get that out of my head. I would love for that to go away. I'd give – I'd go into a booth and put electrodes in my head if I thought it would get rid of that.

Although the discourse examples shown above are generally incoherent, this does not mean that these speakers were *globally* incoherent. The following speaker, for example, has clear, coherent speech when discussing his recent Democratic Party involvement, in contradistinction to several incoherent passages related to his Newman Tendency membership in the same interview:

Yes, I'm very involved with the Democratic party. I'm on the executive committee of the independent neighborhood Democrats, which is a [Place 3] neighborhood Democratic club. I am a past president of the [Place 2] Independent Democrats for two and a half years. Still support them, by the way. In fact, I went to their dinner two weeks ago, and I have a lot of contacts – a lot of people I still see in that group, so yes, I'm very involved in Democratic party politics. The Democratic party is my political home right now.

Former Greens, on the other hand, related their experiences easily, with neither stories of abuse, nor with the kind of disoriented language reflecting a memory of trauma. They certainly had disagreements, and some even anger on leaving but leaving the group was not a traumatic split. For example, Kelly describes her post-Green life in a fresh, balanced, humorous and coherent way:

Hmm, yeah, I just think it's like, it would be like we're neighbors but we, and we don't even need a big fence between our yards [laughs], you know, we're just, we're just coexisting, we're not, we don't really have a relationship.

Former Newman Tendency members said that they felt a great relief in telling me their stories – even years after the fact they still were absorbed and tangled in their memories; they were glad of the opportunity to try to piece their stories together in the presence of a sympathetic and interested listener. The Greens were friendly and helpful, but there wasn't a sense that telling the story itself was important to them.

Eleven of the twelve former members of the Newman Tendency who participated in this study still, often many years after the fact, demonstrated linguistic and cognitive markers of a disorganized attachment status to the group. None of the eleven former Green Party members showed markers of a disorganized attachment to the Green Party.[vii]

No evidence exists to suggest that these former Newman Tendency members were disorganized in relation to other attachment figures, or that they were predisposed to this type of attachment. Such a study remains to be done. I am often

---

vii See Appendix A for full results of the GAI.

asked if the securely attached are protected from recruitment to cults or other totalist systems. However, as mentioned earlier, even the securely attached may also become disorganized given the right conditions and a strong enough situation.[17] Like others, the securely attached will seek protection when under threat, and so are vulnerable to the forces of terror and "love," of authoritarianism and charisma, that are put into place in an isolating totalist system. On the other hand security of attachment may provide a certain element of resilience to the process and result in a quicker recovery from trauma.[18] But it is vital to remember that security of attachment alone does not guarantee resistance to coercive persuasion. Arn Chorn Pond, for example, could not simply leave the Khmer Rouge, or for that matter recover his cognitive abilities. He was physically and cognitively trapped. However, after his rescue from the refugee camp, he worked to recover from the trauma and his ability to do so likely reflected both his new secure environment and his early secure attachment to his family of origin.[19]

Complex post-traumatic stress disorder

An intense, exhausting, chronically traumatizing relationship with the Newman group, with no one outside the group from whom to get feedback, resulted in followers experiencing a dissociative split between the cognitive and emotional parts of the brain. The GAI is a means of observing this split after the fact by analyzing language markers demonstrating "leaks" or slips in the monitoring of reasoning or discourse. The "unmetabolized" experience remains as vivid and immediate as when it happened and continues to absorb the speaker in its emotional impact. However this is not all that happens. If it were, we would be merely observing a dissociation of the cognitive and emotional parts of the brain as in "simple" PTSD. What differentiates this phenomena from PTSD is that it is chronic and *relational* in essence. Judith Herman has proposed a new classification of Complex PTSD to clarify this important difference.[20] The GAI is a means to observe this relational impact, which is that a disorganized and hard-to-break attachment bond is formed.

In my study the majority – 7 out of 12 – of former Newman Tendency members also showed elements of preoccupied attachment to the group (subsidiary to the disorganized bond).[viii] This is significant because this attachment status results when an attachment figure is unreliably available (sometimes there, sometimes not) and so the individual becomes "preoccupied" with gaining what little care might be forthcoming. The preoccupied person becomes clingy, with separation anxiety leading to becoming enmeshed and dependent. Those with preoccupied attachment fail to have their attachment needs fully met or "terminated" by their

---

viii In this research method, based on the AAI protocol, subcategories are also applied when coding interviews. A person with a disorganized attachment status is also assigned a best-fitting second category – whether secure, dismissing, preoccupied or cannot classify: Main, and Goldwyn, *Adult Attachment Scoring and Classification Systems.*

attachment figure. In the absence of reliable care their cortisol levels remain high, and so they continue to seek proximity to the attachment figure in the hope of gaining what available care might come their way. This need to stay close means the preoccupied are unable to use the carer as a secure base from which to autonomously explore their environment. This seems to fit well with the dynamic set up by cults or totalist groups – it clearly benefits the leader to have enmeshed and dependent followers. Leaders therefore set up the conditions for preoccupation and clinginess (as the particular subtype of induced disorganization) by their alternation of assault and leniency, of terror and "love" through, for example, "the capricious granting of small indulgences,"[21] in order to fuel this dependency.

Disorganization and doubling

In disorganized attachment the disjoint between implicit and explicit memory – the failure to process implicit memory through language into stored, explicit memory – is restricted to the traumatic relationship in question.[ix] Thus, persons with disorganized attachment might be able to discuss (and behave in) other areas of life in a coherent manner, but be flooded with implicit, unmetabolized, intrusive memories when triggered, or when attempting to discuss the trauma or frightening relationship. In this way the Group Attachment Interview captures the process in the mind that Lifton referred to as "doubling." Bowlby's concept of internal working models – internalized representational models of attachment relationships – is important here.[22] For example, an organized secure, open, flexible and responsive relationship with an attachment figure translates to a single and coherent internal working model of openness, flexibility and responsiveness within a person's mental state. However, in disorganized attachment, the fear-arousing attachment relationship is internalized as multiple and self-contradictory models – that is, contradictory models of the same aspect of reality.[23] There is no longer an integrated and coherent state of mind. The group member experiences fear caused by the group, but at the same time is told by the group (and believes) that everything in the relationship is fine: thus the member must try and hold two different and contradictory views of reality at the same time.

This new internalized but unintegrated working model does not erase prior working models (say, of a previous secure relationship). It does, however, exist in a segregated area of consciousness, as suggested by Bowlby. This idea closely parallels Lifton's observations of persons who had been subject to coercive persuasion in totalist systems: the former "self" coexists with the brainwashed "totalist self." This is the "doubling" effect,[24] which he defines as "The division of the self into two functioning wholes, so that a part-self acts as an entire self." For example, Nazi

---

ix When the incoherence is seen globally throughout the AAI transcript, then a different classification is given: Cannot Classify. Adults with this classification are, like the disorganized, disproportionately represented in clinical and offender populations. Hesse, Erik. 1999. "The Adult Attachment Interview, Historical and Current Perspectives," in *Handbook of Attachment: Theory, Research and Clinical Applications*, edited by Jude Cassidy and Phillip Shaver. New York: Guilford Press, pp. 395–433.

doctors in Auschwitz performed the most brutal acts, and yet were able to return at night to love and care for their families.

That the coercive relationship is internalized is seen in some former Newman Tendency followers' discourse in the GAI such as in expressions of feeling causal in the abuse, of the failure to deny that the abuse occurred, and in other disorganized markers, as well as in ongoing, yet unconscious, use of Newman Tendency language. Unless resolved, such self-talk (or the internal working model of the totalist relationship) remains internalized in the follower, sometimes, as seen in the speakers in this study, for decades.

This two-fold functioning, this existence of a totalist self alongside (or "on top of" and suppressing) the non-totalist self created by the induced dissociation of the totalist system, goes both ways. It allows the most terrible evil to be perpetrated by people who would be unlikely to engage in such acts outside the strong situation of totalism. But at the same time it also means an autonomous self remains as a part-self, and it is this part-self that may – given the right conditions – be able to resist the system. Doubling is a terrible acrobatics that the human mind performs while in the totalist situation of isolation and fear – the creation of a totalist self as a means of surviving. But at the same time the autonomous self, which experiences and senses (though perhaps doesn't comprehend at the time) these real conditions, also exists. This gives some grounds for hope within the terror.

I have introduced the Group Attachment Interview as a way to look at the psychological traces that remain after these dissociating and frightening relationships. The ability to observe these effects can help us understand the mechanisms of brainwashing within totalist systems and can provide evidence after the fact of the traumatizing relationship that drives these systems. But although the scars of the totalist relationship are long-lasting, they are not absolute and survivors can reclaim independence – and eventually – coherence of thought.

Notes

1 van der Kolk, Bessel A. 1996. "The Body Keeps the Score: Approaches to the Psychobiology of Posttraumatic Stress Disorder" in *Traumatic Stress: The Effects of Overwhelming Experience on Mind, Body, and Society*, edited by B.A. van der Kolk, A.C. McFarlane and L. Weisaeth. New York: Guilford Press, pp. 218, 234.

2 Lifton, Robert Jay. 1986. *The Nazi Doctors: Medical Killing and the Psychology of Genocide*. New York: Basic Books.

3 George, C., N. Kaplan and M. Main. 1996. *Adult Attachment Interview Protocol 3rd Ed.* Berkeley, CA: University of California.

4 Main, M. and R. Goldwyn. 1998. *Adult Attachment Scoring and Classification Systems*. Berkeley, CA: University of California.

5 Hesse, Erik. 1999. "The Adult Attachment Interview, Historical and Current Perspectives," in *Handbook of Attachment: Theory, Research and Clinical Applications*, edited by J. Cassidy and P. Shaver. New York: Guilford Press, p. 405.

6 Stein, Alexandra. 2007. *Attachment, Networks and Discourse in Extremist Political Organizations: A Comparative Case Study*. Doctoral Dissertation, Sociology, University of Minnesota, Minneapolis.

7 Ibid.

8 Bowlby, John. 1982b. *Attachment and Loss, Attachment*, Vol. 1. New York: Basic Books; Hazan, C., N. Gur-Yaish and M. Campa. 2004. "What Does It Mean to Be Attached?" in *Adult Attachment: Theory, Research and Clinical Implications*, edited by W.S. Rholes and J.A. Simpson. New York: Guilford Press, pp. 55–85.

9 Bowlby, John. 1980. *Attachment and Loss, Loss*, Vol. 3. New York: Basic Books.

10 George, C., N. Kaplan and M. Main. 1996. *Adult Attachment Interview Protocol*. 3rd Ed. Berkeley: University of California.

11 Stein, Alexandra. 2004. *Group Attachment Interview*. University of Minnesota.

12 Siegel, Daniel J. 1999. *The Developing Mind: Toward a Neurobiology of Interpersonal Experience*. New York: Guilford Press, p. 51.

13 George, Kaplan and Main, *Adult Attachment Interview Protocol*.

14 Liotti, G. 2004. "Trauma, Dissociation, and Disorganized Attachment: Three Strands of a Single Braid." *Psychotherapy: Theory, Research, Practice, Training* 41(4):472–86.

15 Solomon, J. and C. George. 1999. "The Place of Disorganization in Attachment Theory: Linking Classic Observations with Contemporary Findings," in *Attachment Disorganization*, edited by J. Solomon and C. George. New York: Guilford, p. 18.

16 Bowlby, *Attachment and Loss, Loss*.

17 George, Kaplan and Main, *Adult Attachment Interview Protocol*.

18 Siegel, *The Developing Mind: Toward a Neurobiology of Interpersonal Experience*; Sroufe, L.A. 2005. *The Development of the Person: The Minnesota Study of Risk and Adaptation from Birth to Adulthood*. New York: Guilford Press.

19 Glatzer, Jocelyn. 2003. *The Flute Player*. POV PBS.

20 Herman, Judith. 1992. *Trauma and Recovery*. New York: Basic Books.

21 Ibid.

22 Bowlby, *Attachment and Loss, Loss*.

23 Main, Mary. 1991b. "Metacognitive Knowledge, Metacognitive Monitoring, and Singular Coherent Vs. Multiple Incoherent Model of Attachment," in *Attachment across the Life Cycle.*, edited by C.M. Parkes, S. Hinde, and P. Marris. London and New York: Tavistock/Routledge, pp. 127–159.

24 Lifton, *The Nazi Doctors: Medical Killing and the Psychology of Genocide*, p. 418.

10

THE FLUTE PLAYER

What should an open society do?

The greater man's ignorance of the principles of his social surroundings, the more subject is he to their control; and the greater his knowledge of their operations and of their necessary consequences, the freer he can become with regard to them.

Solomon Asch[1]

The coherent narratives of survivors

Arn Chorn-Pond escaped death at the hands of the Khmer Rouge by becoming one of their musicians. Playing the flute saved him. Almost all of his family had been killed during Pol Pot's regime. In 1979 he reached a refugee camp in Thailand where an American minister and aid worker adopted him, and brought him to the US. He attended university and, starting as a student, became a human rights activist telling his story around the world. Chorn-Pond now educates young people about the genocidal history of Cambodia. He does this by working to bring back the classical music that Pol Pot attempted to destroy by ordering the killing of musicians, including Chorn-Pond's own family of opera performers. Chorn-Pond brings the few surviving musicians from that era together with young Cambodians so they can learn the traditional instruments, along with Cambodia's history, and heal the rift created by Pol Pot's totalist regime. Though still traumatized – but not controlled – by his own memories, he works to heal Cambodia and to educate young people through culture and remembrance of the past. Playing the flute saved his life – music also held his memory of his past and became his means of healing and reconciliation.[2]

At the age of 14 Emmanuel Jal escaped with 400 other child soldiers from the Sudanese Peoples Liberation Army and found his way to a refugee camp. Like

Chorn-Pond he was then rescued by an aid worker. Supported by her and others he started a journey that led him to speak out about his experiences – both in song and by writing a book, *Warchild*.[3] Now an internationally known singer, Jal is active in charity work in Africa, and relates his experiences as part of his human rights activism. As he wrote in his song *Warchild*: "I believe I've survived for a reason, to tell my story, to touch lives."[4]

Juliana Buhring, Celeste Jones and Kristina Jones are three sisters who reunited after each separately escaped the bible-based Children of God/The Family. Together they wrote *Not Without My Sister*,[5] the story of the abuse and suffering they endured as children in this sexually, physically and emotionally abusive cult. They were separated from each other and their family as children and brought up in a variety of "missions" around the world, environments that encouraged and sanctioned the sexual abuse of children as young as 2 or 3 years old. Among the losses they have suffered are the dozens of suicides of their contemporaries also born into the cult. The three sisters have now each rebuilt their lives and started a charity to help other young people leaving the cults they were born into. As they say in their book:

> Thousands of the Family's second generation have had to deal with the devastating consequences of their parents' blind faith in a leader who claimed he was the voice of God on earth. Those who have bravely spoken out about their suffering have been vilified and slandered by their former abusers. Our hope is that in telling our story, you will hear the voices of the children they tried to silence.[6]

Marina Ortiz emerged from Fred Newman's cult and became active in exposing it, and in helping others who left put their experience in perspective. She too spoke out, telling her own story and curating a website that sheds light on the complex and secretive web of organizations that front the Newman Tendency.[7] She is now a journalist involved in cultural preservation efforts in East Harlem and in documenting the Puerto Rican community there.

Masoud Banisadr has written two books – *Masoud: Memoirs of an Iranian Rebel* and *Destructive and Terrorist Cults: A New Kind of Slavery*. This is how he has shared the lessons from his experience in a totalist organization in order to contribute to healing and prevention efforts.

These are just a few of the survivors who have been trapped in totalist systems but lived to tell the tale. Autobiographical narratives of the trauma of totalism range from those of Primo Levi's testimony of Auschwitz,[8] to Deborah Layton's account of surviving the murderous cult of Jim Jones's Peoples Temple.[9] Others have participated in media interviews and found other avenues for telling their stories. These survivors feel both a sense of responsibility to those they leave behind as well as a need to warn others of the dangers of these organizations. Telling the story of their experience is a way to reassert agency and to reclaim their own ability to interpret that experience.

In this reclaiming of their own narratives survivors also move towards resolution of the dissociation between their felt experience and the official narrative that the group imposed. These reclaimed narratives link the writer's implicit memories of trauma with an explicit cognitive understanding and analysis. Telling the story from their own perspective, rooted in their own experience, allows the individual to process that experience vividly, centrally, with focal attention, and, in putting language to their experience, it is stored in explicit memory, thus integrating and "defusing" the traumatic memories previously segregated in implicit memory. This helps to prevent unintegrated traumatic memories from continuing to intrude and disturb daily life years after the fact.[10] Telling the story is an imperative for resolving complex post-traumatic stress disorder.[11] These are coherent narratives, or "organized" accounts – where the survivor, as part of mastering the trauma, and once outside of the conditions of fright without solution, retrospectively interprets and organizes their experience. In putting creative (what attachment researchers call "fresh"[12]) language to the experience, these speakers produce both some resolution and integration for themselves as they also bring news to the outside world from the totalist land of the silenced about the actual nature of these environments.

Rejecting denial

Those who deny the validity and value of these accounts – from Holocaust deniers on a grand scale, to the minor pitched battles within sociology[13] – serve only to slow the development of knowledge and understanding about these systems. This denial stigmatizes victims and impedes the important process of resolving the dissociation suffered by these individuals. Primo Levi spoke of returning "from the camp with an absolute, pathological narrative charge."[14] His greatest fear was that he would not be believed, and, indeed, he encountered great resistance to his testimony from various quarters at different stages in his life. He described his task of relating a coherent narrative in this way:

> When describing the tragic world of Auschwitz, I have deliberately assumed the calm, sober language of the witness, neither the lamenting tones of the victim nor the irate voice of someone who seeks revenge. I thought that my account would be all the more credible and useful the more it appeared objective and the less it sounded overly emotional; only in this way does a witness in matters of justice perform his task, which is that of preparing the ground for the judge. The judges are my readers. All the same, I would not want my abstaining from explicit judgment to be confused with an indiscriminate pardon. No, I have not forgiven any of the culprits, nor am I willing to forgive a single one of them, unless he has shown (with deeds, not words, and not too long afterwards) that he has become conscious of the crimes . . . and is determined to condemn them.[15]

Instead of denying these accounts we must raise up these narrators as heroes, a few already recognized with awards and exposure, others more quietly bringing these stories to light. Far more suffer in silence, or never leave, and lacking material, emotional and social resources are never able to tell their stories. So it remains for those who have had access to this support to bear witness, to tell the reality of life within these isolating, secretive, dangerous and unbearable situations, to speak both for themselves and for those who are unable. As survivors these narrators have a drive to hold to account the perpetrators, to prevent others experiencing the same thing. These are the heroes of totalism. Their voices tell us about these closed and silenced worlds. Who else can? We must listen.

If we do not listen the effect is to shore up the absolutist, exclusive ideologies that shroud these top-heavy totalist structures, structures that suffocate those within them. Where a unitary Truth is demanded, as in totalism, thus "destroying all space between men and pressing men against each other"[16] then each person's individual experience is denied and the lessons available to the rest of us are lost.

Sharing stories in the public realm

Hannah Arendt describes how storytelling between people in the public realm – such as in the examples above – is a revealing of each to the other. This reflection of one in the other, or this listening to and seeing one another, gives each person an existence, allows them to "be seen." In isolation one cannot be seen. These stories can be about each person, or about the things and events in the world, but they are marked by revealing the particular, unique viewpoint of the teller. "The presence of others who see what we see and hear what we hear assures us of the reality of the world and ourselves."[17] The African-American poet, June Jordan, puts it this way in *Poem for a Young Poet*:[i]

> Most people search all
> of their lives
> for someplace to belong to
> as you said
> but I look instead
> into the eyes of anyone
> who talks to me . . .
> Okay!
> I did not say male
> or female
> I did not say Serbian

---

i "Poem for a Young Poet" by June Jordan from *Directed by Desire. The Collected Poems of June Jordan.* Reprinted with the permission of the June M. Jordan Literary Estate Trust, and Copper Canyon Press. www.Junejordan.com

or Tutsi
I said
what tilts my head
into the opposite of fear
or dread
is anyone
who talks to me[18]

In Anthony Sampson's biography of Nelson Mandela, he describes another way of looking at this – how as people we need the reciprocal understanding of others:

> Mandela was brought up with the African notion of human brotherhood, or *ubuntu*, which described a quality of mutual responsibility and compassion. He often quoted the proverb *"Umuntu ngumuntu ngabantu,"* which he would translate as "A person is a person because of other people," or "You can do nothing if you don't get the support of other people." This was a concept common to other rural communities around the world, but Africans would define it more sharply as a contrast to the individualism and restlessness of whites, and over the following decades *ubuntu* would loom large in black politics. As Archbishop Tutu defined it in 1986: "It refers to gentleness, to compassion, to hospitality, to openness to others, to vulnerability, to be available to others and to know that you are bound up with them in the bundle of life."[19]

Similarly, P.C. Chang, one of the drafters of the UN Declaration of Human Rights, described the meaning of the Chinese word *ren* in discussions about that document. *Ren* "in literal translation meant 'two-man mindedness,' but which might be expressed in English as 'sympathy,' or 'consciousness of one's fellow men'"[20] or "the ability to see things from another's standpoint as well as from one's own particular point of view."[21] Whether in the family, community, nation or world, a person is a person because of other people. And we know each other through sharing our experiences and listening to each other.

Arendt states that this sharing of stories and experiences supposes a multitude of truths, of ways of seeing, of points of view: it involves conversation between people with different views in order to understand the world. However, this is not relativist – the points of view are about something that exists – it is not all social construction. She uses the fable of blind men describing an elephant to explain. Each blind man needs the others to get beyond their limited perception: one feels the elephant's trunk, another touches its sharp tusk, or its soft, flat ear, yet another, a large and solid foot, or the leathery, supple tail. Only by talking together and sharing their experience and perceptions can they hope to approximate a view of the whole magnificent creature (who exists in its own right, regardless of their perceptions). It is this talking and acting together in the world that is at the heart of this idea. And the gathering place in which they talk is the public realm. "[T]he reality of the public realm," she says, "relies on the simultaneous presence of innumerable perspectives and aspects in which the common world presents itself."[22] Civil society is where we can keep alive, or revive, the public realm by gathering people together – out of their isolation – to talk and work together in active participation in a pluralist society.

Pluralism, Arendt continues, grants each individual a unique view of reality. Through this variety of unique views something approximating a shared understanding of reality can be arrived at:

> Human plurality, the basic condition of both action and speech, has the two-fold character of equality and distinction. If men were not equal, they could neither understand each other and those who came before them nor plan for the future and foresee the needs of those who will come after them. If men were not distinct, each human being distinguished from any other who is, was, or will ever be, they would need neither speech nor action to make themselves understood.[23]

It is only by speaking and listening to each other that we create and hear the varieties of stories and thus begin to grasp a collective sense of the fabled elephant. This is what Arendt would call "common sense":

> The only character of the world by which to gauge its reality is its being common to us all, and common sense occupies such a high rank in the hierarchy of political qualities because it is the one sense that fits into reality as a whole our five strictly individual senses and the strictly particular data they perceive. It is by virtue of common sense that the other sense perceptions are known to disclose reality and are not merely felt as irritations of our nerves or resistance sensations of our bodies. A noticeable decrease in common sense in any given community and a noticeable increase in superstition and gullibility are therefore almost infallible signs of alienation from the world.[24]

The telling of our stories, plurality and common sense are, in a way, the public forms of communication that parallel that which occurs within relationships of secure attachment – they represent open, flexible and responsive communication as opposed to coercive communication, or coercive persuasion.

In a complex society, the active participation required by the exchange of stories can be a way of reclaiming the spaces in-between people, and equally, in-between diverse cultures and identities. This is part of building the open "web of relationships" that is central to reducing isolation in an atomized society and preventing totalism.[25] The "web of relationships" in the public realm can connect people in an open, flexible, yet supportive and mutually recognizing manner – opposite to being pressed together in a totalizing single truth where there is no space in-between across which to talk. Conversation, in fact, *requires* this space, this difference between people. Without difference there is nothing to talk about.

Defining identity as being *different from* (as in fundamentalist, nationalist or identity politics) can lead to closed, isolated systems, with accompanying absolutist values, resulting in the absurd phenomenon of each of these different systems laying claim to the one and only Truth. This is a fear-driven response. But defining identity as being a particular part of a complex and changing whole, where one's difference is an integral part of this diverse whole – *different with* – can allow a reaching over the divides that prevent us sitting together at a common table.

Telling stories, through literature, historical accounts, or other means, is a time-honored method of human learning.[26] From the stories of victims of torture, to the accounts of war veterans, prisoners of war, survivors of concentration camps, abusive relationships, slavery, prostitution or refugees – the telling of the stories of those affected, in conjunction with activism and academic study, has led to de-privatization of the abuses and the effects of abuse;[27] to legitimization of the associated recovery and awareness movements; and, in some cases, to a change in social norms.

Universal human rights

Human beings have certain basic needs for food, shelter, sex and attachment that must be met to ensure their survival. These human needs form the basis for people from various cultures to recognize the bonds among them; they are the "common world" – the elephant – about which we need to talk and act in the public realm. Fundamental human needs form the basic commonality of human experience – they are the content of our "sameness." *Culture*, on the other hand, is the particular expression of how these needs are met, evolving out of particular geographies, times and histories. Culture expresses the different ways that people have adapted the meeting of these fundamental needs within a given environment and set of conditions; it moves with the development of society to pass on the stock of knowledge from the past and adapt it to the present.[28]

In the contemporary world, with rapid, global change, isolation and atomization, along with the intermixing of cultures, the usefulness of fixed, static cultures is diminished. Fundamentalist and totalist responses to the modern condition of rapid transitions are Canute-like attempts to stop the waves of change by denying them and instead looking backwards to archaic forms of closed cultures proclaiming absolute and unitary truths. We have seen only too often how maladaptive these responses are. They are led by powerful, charismatic and authoritarian figures who have "unusual insight into societal attachment behavior"[29] and can therefore manipulate, coalesce and coerce atomized individuals to create deployable followers. These leaders hold out a fraudulent promise of safety, certainty and community, but instead deliver totalist social structures that only allow for one Truth and therefore only one story – at least, only one "good" or "right" story. All other stories or interpretations are evil and therefore have no legitimate right to existence.

The discussion of universal human rights emerged as a result of World War II and out of the world's experience of totalitarianism. The ongoing efforts to create expressions of universal human rights are an attempt to recognize the commonalities of human beings and to describe this in a universal language in order to protect our survival. The articulation of universal human rights becomes more and more important as this process of globalization and the rise of totalitarian movements and groups continues.

The expression of human rights specific to fundamental human needs seems relatively clear and easy to agree with: people need to be free from pain, hunger, cold and loneliness. But where the discussion of human rights enters into the realm of culture then difficulties begin. The conversation about shared values must proceed together with: openness, inclusivity and open discussion; a refusal to use fear and coercion as organizing principles; mutual respect; negotiation; a rejection of fundamentalism and exclusivity; a commitment to addressing obstacles to participation; and conscious monitoring and balancing of this participation. Attempts at developing such open, flexible and responsive action are taking place at different levels in society: internationally and globally it is taking place at the level of ongoing work to develop, articulate and implement these international human rights instruments; and locally at the level of participatory grassroots organizing and engagement – cultural, political and social.

The universal need to belong

While I have suggested that individuals' different pathways through totalist groups may have some relation to their attachment style, an overarching issue is the *general* tendency, or desire for people to affiliate and to form attachments. As there is an individual need for attachment to another particular individual, so there is the need of an individual to belong to a group, to have a place in a social context. Individual attachment provides security while belonging to or participating in communities provides the means to access resources and realize goals.[30] People have a "universal need for human connectedness."[31] It is clearly a normal and (potentially) adaptive response to the atomization of society to make attempts to affiliate with others.

But the transient, fragmented state of contemporary society makes this difficult. The world is opening up, becoming global, restructuring itself towards an unknown future. This global sense of *anomie* engenders a basic existential crisis and fear. In isolation the fear response triggers attachment behavior regardless of the adaptive nature of such behavior in a given situation. Without open, flexible and responsive social supports, there is, therefore, a vast pool of atomized individuals vulnerable to charismatic authoritarian personalities.[ii] We see this in any number of ways: in the Western countries, particularly those with intensifying isolation and atomization

---

ii Arendt refers to people feeling uprooted and superfluous: "To be uprooted means to have no place in the world, recognized and guaranteed by others; to be superfluous means not to belong to the world at all"; this leads to vulnerability to the appeal of fundamentalism. Arendt, Hannah. 1953. "Ideology and Terror: A Novel Form of Government." *Review of Politics* 15(3):303–27. p. 323. Also see, for example, Fromm, E. 1941. *Escape from Freedom.* New York: Henry Holt. and Arendt, *The Origins of Totalitarianism.*

such as the US, we see fundamentalist totalizing ideologies, cults, religious and political movements and gang activity on the rise. The incidence of cults and extremism is also growing in Africa, Eastern Europe, the Middle East, China – all societies in rapid transition – some trying to transition from totalitarianism, yet encountering mini-totalitarian leaders in ample supply to step into the vacuum.

We need to belong, but how do we find healthy ways to do so? Learning the difference between healthy and unhealthy forms of belonging is one place to start.

Prevention – a public health approach

There is now an accumulation of both data and resulting theories that support a scientific view of brainwashing (or thought reform, extreme undue influence, coercive persuasion or whatever other term one wishes to use) within totalist systems. It is not an "incomprehensible" mystery that is out there and happens to other strange, weak and needy people. We now have the basis to understand what it is and how it works. There exists a rich seam of scholarly work from Lifton, Schein and Singer's early case studies of brainwashing in China and Korea to Arendt's brilliant analyses of totalitarianism, and from the theoretical contributions of Solomon Asch and Stanley Milgram to those of Lofland, Cialdini, Zablocki, Lalich and Herman. As for data there is a growing library of personal accounts of the survivors of totalist coercion who have come out the other side to tell their stories. We have data and we have theories that explain that data.

In this volume I have added my own insights based in attachment theory. With this evolutionary-based theory, along with newly emerging understanding of the underlying neuroscience of trauma, dissociation and memory, we can put yet more pieces of the puzzle together. It's a human thing. If a charismatic authoritarian psychopath succeeds in putting people in conditions of social and emotional isolation, then engulfs them in a fictional world that distorts their perception of reality and, finally, creates an environment of chronic fear arousal, they can, in most cases, disable the follower's "thinking part of the emotional brain." And once that's gone, they can do their thinking for them, resulting in a deployable and exploitable follower.

We know how this is done. The task at hand now is to both continue deepening the research, but, perhaps more importantly, to tackle the problem of disseminating this knowledge in order to strengthen society's defenses against the threatening forces of totalism. So how can we develop methods of prevention to "immunize" people and societies against the violation of totalist systems?

While we have many studies stating that we cannot predict who will be recruited,[32] on the other hand we *can* predict the situational factors and the recruitment techniques and the organizational structures and methods behind recruitment attempts. Many scholars and researchers agree that knowledge of the methods of totalist recruitment and indoctrination is central to prevention.[33] This means we need prevention education across the board on a) understanding these organizations and how they work, and b) understanding the personal and social risks of involvement with such groups so people may protect themselves, their families and their communities.

What is far less developed are educational methods to disseminate this knowledge in an experiential and broad way. I would argue that a public health education approach, building on the lessons learned from other contemporary public health efforts such as safe sex education, anti-tobacco education, child abuse and domestic violence prevention would be a starting point. The public health profession has much to offer about how to effectively, and strategically, disseminate usable information on these complex issues.

To prevent totalism we need strong social supports and secure attachments, predisposing situational factors must be addressed, and we must be able to identify and have methods to recognize and avoid charismatic authoritarian leaders, totalist groups and brainwashing attempts when we are faced with them. We must learn to distinguish between the flexibility and safety of secure relationships as opposed to the disorienting and disempowering dynamics of the disorganized.

Secure attachment

Prevention of the development of charismatic authoritarian, totalist leaders is based on a general improvement in securely attached relationships both in early childhood and in communities. In particular, it is critical to minimize the development of disorganized attachment through interventions and support to protect children who live in frightening, isolated environments. Prevention of other forms of insecure attachment similarly requires improved secure attachment in childhood. Studies show that isolation and lack of connectedness to community impacts a family's ability to provide secure attachment, while socio-economic stress also impacts attachment in cases of poor "goodness of fit" within families. These are large questions that must be addressed at a societal level by improving the social, economic and community supports available to families, and improving education on the importance of secure attachment. These are, I hope, obvious issues, and issues that many people with a variety of concerns are already trying to work on. This is simply to state that these basic questions of societal well-being also impact secure attachment, atomization and the dynamics of the charismatic and authoritarian relationships of totalist groups.

Recognizing and teaching about totalism

Individuals and society as a whole must learn to identify the features and methods of totalism and brainwashing, and have the means to both call attention to them and hold totalist leaders and groups accountable for their abusive activities. Despite some mystification of this issue, people can learn to recognize and identify these features and methods. As discussed earlier, these features overlap with many different kinds of social relationships. Since the inception of the battered women's movement, much work has been done to educate people in how to identify abusive intimate relationships. Similarly, some schools help children learn how to identify and resist bullying.[34] Others are concerned with extremist political groups and hate crimes – such as efforts by the Southern Poverty Law Center in their Teaching Tolerance program.[35] More recently there are attempts around the world to address and prevent recruitment to extremist terrorist groups. The cult awareness movement has worked for many decades to disseminate the warning signs of cultic organizations. Work is also being done on gang prevention and prevention of prostitution. Common identifying characteristics link these different forms of isolating social structures and coercive control. The work to teach children about child sexual abuse and sexual consent is also closely related. In this work children are taught about their physical and emotional boundaries and about not keeping secrets. Bringing these efforts under a common rubric – particularly in understanding the dynamic of assault and leniency, of "love" and terror, and the disorganized, disorienting fear/attachment response – and piggy-backing the efforts in one area onto another would strengthen and support the work in each area.

There are many former victims of totalism (in its many guises) speaking about their experiences and using them to teach others in an effort to 'inoculate' the general population. It is they (that is, those who have 'processed' their experience through reflection afterwards and have developed a coherent narrative) who have lived through this and understand the internal processes at work. Support and expansion of their efforts would be beneficial to prevention activities.

A public health approach would suggest disseminating this knowledge at a variety of levels. As discussed above, the key is to train the trainers – to teach teachers, university, health, legal and social work professionals. Students should be learning about influence techniques, bullying, dangerous relational dynamics and the features and methods of totalist groups from primary through to tertiary education. This goes beyond the idea that simply teaching "critical thinking skills" is enough. While that is, of course, important, we also should be teaching about the specific kinds of mechanisms that *interrupt* the ability to think critically.

In Germany education about totalitarianism was required after the defeat of Hitler. Following the occupation by the Western Allies, education in Germany was reorganized to support democratic principles and later, in 1962, this was:

> supplemented by the "Guidelines on the treatment of totalitarianism in teaching", in which confronting the issue of totalitarianism was declared to be an important part of civic education. Teachers working in all the different kinds of schools were urged " … to familiarize pupils with the characteristics of totalitarianism and the main features of Bolshevism and Nazism as the two most important totalitarian systems of the twentieth century."[36]

We would do well, I think, in the current period where totalitarian movements show no signs of abating, to expand this brief far beyond the boundaries of Germany.

Monitoring and accountability

When we recognize the dynamics of totalism and brainwashing processes at work, we must then pay particularly close attention to the possibility of abuse and violence occurring in such situations. Given that the very nature of these systems is to be closed, self-sealing[37] and secretive, the problem of how we can observe such abuses comes to the fore. Some headway has been made with this in the cases of child sexual abuse and domestic violence through public health efforts and educational efforts in supporting victims, in naming the abuse and in attempting to break through the levels of shame associated with it. Doctors, social workers, police and teachers have been drawn into these efforts. In Minneapolis, for example, the police are obliged to make an arrest where probable cause exists in a domestic violence case – the victim is not required to make the charge. This has been shown to be far more effective in curtailing repeat offenses of spousal abuse than did either advice or separation by police officers at the time of the incident.[38] The effectiveness of this method is likely due to the fact that it precludes the victim from having to press charges, which, due to the dynamics of the battering relationship, is often impossible. Similar methods (and awareness) could be expanded to situations of cultic abuse.

More progressive laws are now coming into effect in the UK that criminalize psychological domestic abuse (called coercive control) as well as strictly physical abuse.[39] However, this is still limited to "intimate or family relationships." Hopefully this too will be able to be extended to the psychological abuse that occurs in groups such as cults, as has already happened in France with the About-Picard Law against "mental manipulation."

In cases of group abuse the very fact of complaints and identification of the group as a closed and secretive system should raise a red flag for authorities, and extra efforts must then be made to be alert for and to investigate abuses. An example is the institutionalized beating of children by the leader of an Atlanta cult, the House of Prayer. One child was beaten for talking to his mother while she was being shunned by the group. Parents whose children were taken away by the social services refused to have the children returned if it meant they could not allow the leader to continue to beat their children with sticks, belts or switches.[40] To those who understand the dynamics of totalism this does not come as a surprise, but rather is a fully predictable result of the closed, isolated and totalist nature of such systems. When we see the signs and symptoms of totalist systems, we must, then, actively look for such abuses, and act decisively when they are found, based on protecting the human rights of those involved (rather than demonizing a specific set of beliefs no matter how absurd they may seem). It is the process of how a set of beliefs work in a *totalizing manner* with the presence of charismatic authoritarianism that clues us in to be alert for abuses, and further, that those abuses are likely to be conducted in secret, and with the victims' ability to name, resist and escape the abuse greatly impaired. There must, therefore, be legal mechanisms that enable outsiders to step in to both monitor and stop these abuses.

As of this writing there is a controversy in British university campuses regarding whether to vet invited speakers to university events. On one side academics resist this in the name of academic freedom and freedom of speech. On the other side, government officials and others seek to curtail the unfettered access of extremist recruiters to campus facilities and therefore to students.[41] These students continue to be exposed to recruiters with neither protection nor warning and campuses globally have indeed proved to be a fertile recruiting ground for recruitment to violent extremism. I would propose that instead of setting up an opposition between free speech and repression of speech on campus, we reframe the argument to oppose free speech to coercive and coerced speech – in other words to that speech that is emanating from organizations that use coercive techniques to recruit and retain members. This type of speech cannot be called "free."

It will only be when institutions can agree on a means to identify totalist organizations and are willing to engage in the background work to do so (to get under the secretive skin of these groups) that this distinction between free speech and coercive speech can be made. In fact, we *do* know, and have the basis to identify these groups – but this knowledge is not disseminated. As discussed, this knowledge has been contested by a small but vocal group of academics studying "new religious movements" from a cultural relativist viewpoint, and holds back the work needed in this area. Others do not yet have adequate background in the field and so "training the trainers" is a primary requirement. But recognizing and then holding totalist groups to account and, indeed, monitoring their activities and behavior to both those inside and outside of the group is an important step in protecting all of us. And, critically, we must educate students to recognize and challenge coercive and coerced speech.

Social organization and community life

Healthy community can mitigate against the encroachment of totalist groups in two ways: by recognizing and limiting the influence of pathological individuals, and by addressing the "everyday experience of loneliness"[42] and building social connectedness in a healthy non-totalist manner. Healthy community will likely produce fewer potential totalist leaders and fewer potential victims, and in strengthening positive connections between people at the individual level (secure attachment) and the community level (the public realm), provide fewer situational factors for the development of totalism.

On an individual level people can learn how to identify healthy versus unhealthy social networks, and be encouraged to work actively to build and maintain positive networks. A healthy social (personal) network is open, not closed, with a variety of strengths of relational ties ranging from close "irreplaceable" attachment ties, to "loose" affiliative ties. Strong, close ties are critical for feelings of emotional security. Loose ties are important as links to other networks, to resources and to the possibility of becoming close ties should additional attachments be needed (providing redundancy in the network). Loose ties also help keep personal networks open rather than closed. A healthy personal network has overlapping but not concentric and all-inclusive social circles. In other words, persons in one's social circle may also know persons in another of one's social circles. In a healthy social network one should not have totally separate connections to a variety of other social circles with no overlap between any of them. This presupposes a discontinuous social network lacking community integration. On the other hand, complete community integration without any ties leading outside the community suggests a closed, totalist network. A healthy network changes and is flexible. Part of the changing nature of a healthy network in contemporary life means that the individual is obliged to engage in ongoing maintenance of their network to prevent isolation should the network become too sparse. Relationships within a healthy social network aim to be "eye-level" and egalitarian, rather than authoritarian and abusive.[iii]

An unhealthy social network is closed, is made up of "replaceable others" and is shaped as a series of concentric circles, the members of whom are controlled by the leader who sits at the center. The only truly sanctioned emotional attachment is to the network/group rather than to specific individuals.

Positive community in an "age of fragmentation"[43] must include within it the very qualities that disarm totalism:

* *A baseline of accepted human rights,* such as the UN Declaration of Human Rights (and related Declarations concerning women and children) has attempted to provide. This baseline can be a yardstick by which to measure 'crimes against humanity,' or other unethical behaviors and processes and provides a minimum set of standards and principles by which to contain pathological behavior. Recent moves to hold North Korea to account for human rights abuses are long overdue, but nonetheless welcome.[44] These universal standards of human rights can be used in the process of monitoring and holding accountable the actions of totalist leaders. Totalist groups – both large and small – do, in fact, abrogate almost every one of these rights. Thus the UN Declaration of Human Rights can be one of the useful measures by which to evaluate whether a group is totalistic or not. But we must go beyond the obvious culprits, such as Joseph Kony of the Lord's Resistance Army, currently wanted by the International Criminal Court. When we see signs of totalism we must be assertive about investigating and prosecuting for abrogations of human rights despite the deception, legitimizing fronts and propaganda that these systems use to try to distract and deflect.

iii See Appendix B.

- *Supporting the social norm of speaking up against prejudice, refusing to participate in prejudicial actions*. Social-psychologists such as Lewin[45] and Asch[46] have found that the corollary of the power of social pressure to conform within a group is that when just one person refuses to go along and presents another view (such as, for example, speaking up in public against a racist or otherwise abusive comment) others then are able to move away from the initial group pressure. Certain social norms, such as politeness, reciprocity and so forth, are routinely manipulated to their advantage by totalist leaders and are a powerful component in building totalism.[47] Therefore teaching people the power of standing up and speaking out can contribute to positive community.

- *An appreciation and encouragement of diversity* in its broadest sense. This includes allowing a variety of cultures to flourish, acknowledging the interrelation between different cultures and building bridges between diverse cultures via an acknowledgment of our common human rights and a sharing of our stories. This also implies a connectedness between different communities and developing some shared understanding and empathy across cultures. It is important for communities to develop a sense of "different *with*" rather than "different *from*."

- *Adaptability and fluidity of community*. Today's rapid change necessitates flexible community structures. This adaptability and fluidity must extend to individuals also.[48] This is a unique challenge for our times. Healthy community needs many diverse legs or supports – if one part of the community falls away, another can be strengthened to take its place. For instance, if a child only has a single parent and no extended family (or relationships with neighbors, etc.) then the weakness of that atomized family makes the child highly vulnerable, should the single caregiver be unable to provide sufficient support. And as we know, that adult caregiver also needs social support so that they feel secure and able to provide security for their child. A child's chances of success and resilience are greatly enhanced if even *one* adult in their lives provides a secure attachment, therefore attention to the maintenance of healthy social networks, as described above, is critical.

- *The public realm*. Channels are needed for people to directly participate in both the decision-making and the active daily life of their community. People must have a way to participate actively in the public realm in order to build connections and lessen atomization. The necessity for *active participation* implies that this take place at all levels of society, but particularly at the local level where everyone can have the opportunity to directly participate, whether politically, culturally or in other ways.

- *Use of conflict resolution/mediation models*. These models provide an alternative to either/or, black/white, polarizing models of dealing with differences. They can promote mutually respectful 'eye-level' relationships in opposition to authoritarian relationships. Such models are already in place in many schools, communities and in international diplomacy, but there is a long way to go in further disseminating and implementing these methods, especially at the grassroots.

We need small steps and many different solutions, all based on an agreement on fundamental and universal human rights and a willingness to negotiate. The process of finding these solutions and taking these small steps takes place in the public realm. This is part of creating a public realm that works in our fragmented society, one that does not yearn for an idealized past and a closed vision of community, but looks forward to an open, welcoming, safe and diverse, pluralist view of community life where children are valued, universal human rights are valued and varied cultural expressions that respect these rights are valued.

Marina Ortiz, Masoud Banisadr and myself were young and intelligent when we were recruited. All three of us wanted to help build a more equal and fair world. Others like us were simply on our way to a variety of goals: to get help through therapy, to grow spiritually, to get involved in theater, to take fitness classes or to be involved in a positive way in politics or religion. We did not set about looking for an unhappy, powerless tenure in dangerous organizations where later our children came to be at risk. And these children did not join these organizations but grew up in them – they certainly had no choice. But it is not a choice for anyone when totalist groups obscure their actual methods and goals beneath layers of deception and coercion. Had we known . . . had we known that we would become isolated, engulfed in a secretive world and subjected to an unpredictable seesaw of terror and "love" . . . Well, that knowledge would have saved us from wasted, frightening and dangerous years, from being recruited "by accident"[49] on our way to other aims, much as the young terrorist recruits of today are psychologically coerced into lives that they do not understand. Indeed we were young and intelligent and with preventive education we could have recognized and resisted these dangerous relationships.

It is time to educate children and young people to protect themselves and the societies in which they live by teaching them the "distinctness and inseparability of group and individual [and] how group conditions penetrate to the very center of individuals and transform their character."[50] Taking on this task is a choice that we, as a society, can still make.

Notes

1 Asch, Solomon E. 1952. *Social Psychology*. New York: Prentice-Hall, p. 268.
2 Glatzer, Jocelyn. 2003. *The Flute Player*. POV PBS.
3 Jal, Emmanuel. 2009. *War Child: A Boy Soldier's Story*. London: Abacus.
4 Jal, Emmanuel. 2015, "Emmanueljal.Com." Retrieved February 13, 2015 (http://emmanueljal.com/bio/).
5 Jones, Kristina, Celeste Jones and Juliana Buhring. 2007b. *Not without My Sister: The True Story of Three Girls Violated and Betrayed*. London: Harper Element.
6 Ibid., p. x.
7 See: http://www.ex-iwp.org
8 Levi, Primo. 1986. *The Drowned and the Saved*. New York: Vintage Books; Levi, Primo. 1987. *Survival in Auschwitz*. New York: Macmillan.
9 Layton, Deborah. 1998. *Seductive Poison: A Jonestown Survivor's Story of Life and Death in the Peoples Temple*. New York: Anchor Books.
10 Herman, Judith. 1992. *Trauma and Recovery*. New York: Basic Books.

11 Ibid.; van der Kolk, Bessel A., Alexander C. McFarlane and Lars Weisaeth, eds. 1996. *Traumatic Stress: The Effects of Overwhelming Experience on Mind, Body, and Society*. New York: Guilford Press.

12 Main, Mary and June Sroufe. 2002. *Adult Attachment Interview Training Session*. Institute of Child Development, University of Minnesota.

13 Bromley, David. 1998a. "Listing in Black and White Some Observations on Thought Reform." *Nova Religio* (12):250–66; Lalich, Janja. 2004. *Bounded Choice: True Believers and Charismatic Cults*. Berkeley: University of California Press; Zablocki, Benjamin D. 1997. "The Blacklisting of a Concept: The Strange History of the Brainwashing Conjecture in the Sociology of Religion." *Nova Religio* 11:97–120.

14 Anissimov, Myriam. 1999. *Primo Levi: Tragedy of an Optimist*. New York: Overlook Press, p. 257.

15 Levi, Primo, Marco Belpoliti and Robert Samuel Clive Gordon. 2001. *The Voice of Memory: Interviews, 1961–1987: Primo Levi*. New York: New Press: Distributed by W.W. Norton, p. 186.

16 Arendt, Hannah. 1948/1979. *The Origins of Totalitarianism*. Orlando: Harcourt Brace, p. 478.

17 Arendt, Hannah. 1958/1998. *The Human Condition*. Chicago: The University of Chicago Press, p. 50.

18 Jordan, June. 1997. *Kissing God Goodbye: Poems, 1991–1996*. New York: Anchor Books; "Poem for a Young Poet" by June Jordan from *Directed by Desire. The Collected Poems of June Jordan*. Reprinted with the permission of the June M. Jordan Literary Estate Trust, and Copper Canyon Press. www.Junejordan.com

19 Sampson, Anthony. 1999. *Mandela: The Authorized Biography*. New York: Knopf, p. 12.

20 Glendon, Mary Ann. 2001. *A World Made New: Eleanor Roosevelt and the Universal Declaration of Human Rights*: Random House Trade Paperbacks, p. 67.

21 Ibid., p. 142.

22 Arendt, *The Human Condition*, p. 57.

23 Ibid., p. 175.

24 Ibid., p. 209.

25 Ibid.

26 Lessing, Doris. 1987. *Prisons We Choose to Live Inside*. New York: Harper & Row.

27 Herman, *Trauma and Recovery*; Stacey, W. and A. Shupe. 1983. *The Family Secret: Domestic Violence in America*. Boston: Beacon Press.

28 Habermas, Jurgen. 1984. *The Theory of Communicative Action*, Vol. 1. Boston: Beacon Press.

29 Aberbach, David. 1995. "Charisma and Attachment Theory: A Crossdisciplinary Interpretation." *International Journal of Psycho-Analysis* 76:845–55, p. 846.

30 Weiss, R. 1991. "The Attachment Bond in Childhood and Adulthood," in *Attachment across the Life Cycle*, edited by C.M. Parkes, J. Stevenson-Hinde and P. Marris. London and New York: Tavistock/Routledge, pp. 66–76.

31 Lifton, Robert Jay. 1999. *Destroying the World to Save It: Aum Shinrikyo, Apocalyptic Violence, and the New Global Terrorism*. New York: Henry Holt, p. 13.

32 Borum, Randy. 2004. *Psychology of Terrorism*. Tampa: University of South Florida: DTIC Document.

33 Among others: Asch, *Social Psychology*; Zimbardo, Philip. 2007. *The Lucifer Effect: Understanding How Good People Turn Evil*. New York: Random House; Singer, M.T. and J. Lalich. 1995a. *Cults in Our Midst: The Hidden Menace in Our Everyday Lives*. San Francisco: Jossey Bass; Zimbardo, P. and S. Anderson. 1993. "Understanding Mind Control: Exotic and Mundane Mental Manipulations," in *Recovering from Cults*, edited by M. Langone. Norton: New York, pp. 104–125.

34 See, for example Twemlow, Stuart W., Peter Fonagy and Frank C. Sacco. 2005. "A Developmental Approach to Mentalizing Communities: I. A Model for Social Change." *Bulletin of the Menninger Clinic* 69(4):265–81.

35 Southern Poverty Law Center. 2015. *Teaching Tolerance*. Retrieved February 13, 2015 (http://www.tolerance.org).

36 Grimm, Sonja. 2010. *Germany's Post-1945 and Post-1989 Education*. Washington, DC: World Bank.

37 Lalich, *Bounded Choice: True Believers and Charismatic Cults*.

38 Egan, Nancy. 2001, *The Police Response to Spouse Abuse: An Annotated Bibliography*: John Jay College of Criminal Justice. Retrieved April 30, 2001 (http://www.lib.jjay.cuny.edu/research/spouse.html).

39 Evans, Martin. 2014. "New Domestic Violence Law Will Outlaw Coercive Control," in *Telegraph*. London, UK.

40 Levs, Joshua [Director] 2001. *Atlanta's House of Prayer*. National Public Radio. 3 April 2001.

41 Travis, Alan. 2015. "University Professors Decry Theresa May's Campus Anti-Terrorism Bill," in *Guardian*. London: Guardian.

42 Arendt, *The Origins of Totalitarianism*.

43 Lifton, Robert Jay. 1993. *The Protean Self: Human Resilience in an Age of Fragmentation*. New York: Basic Books.

44 Human Rights Council. 2014. *Report of the Detailed Findings of the Commission of Inquiry on Human Rights in the Democratic People's Republic of Korea*. UN Human Rights Council.

45 Lewin, Kurt and Martin Gold. 1999. *The Complete Social Scientist: A Kurt Lewin Reader*. Washington, DC: American Psychological Association.

46 Asch, *Social Psychology*. New York: Prentice-Hall; Asch, Solomon E. 1951. "Effects of Group Pressure Upon the Modification and Distortion of Judgements," in *Groups, Leadership, and Men*, edited by H. Gvetzkow. Pittsburgh: Carnegie Press, pp. 177–90.

47 Milgram, S. 1992. *The Individual in a Social World: Essays and Experiments*. New York: McGraw-Hill; Sherif, M., O. J. Harvey and B. J. White. 1961. *Intergroup Conflict and Cooperation: The Robbers Cave Experiment*. Norman: University of Oklahoma Book Exchange.

48 Lifton, *The Protean Self: Human Resilience in an Age of Fragmentation*.

49 Crenshaw, Martha. 2011. *Radicalization and Recruitment into Terrorism*. Paper presented at the Processes of Radicalization and De-Radicalization, April, Bielefeld, Germany.

50 Asch, *Social Psychology*, p. 257.

APPENDIX A

The Group Attachment Interview

This section will be of interest to attachment researchers.

The Group Attachment Interview (GAI) is designed to assess the presence and quality of an attachment bond formed between an individual and a group.

The GAI is based on the Adult Attachment Interview,[1] which is designed to assess "the individual's state of mind with respect to attachment."[2] The GAI is coded from an interview that lasts about an hour, during which the participant is asked various questions about their relationship to their group (in this study, their past relationship). The design of the interview is intended to "surprise the unconscious."[3] The interview transcript is coded to assign an attachment classification "which appears best to represent their overall state of mind with respect to attachment."[4] These classifications are: Secure, Preoccupied, Dismissing, Unresolved/disorganized (the full term for disorganized attachment) and the rarely occurring Cannot Classify.

The core task presented to the participant in the GAI (as with the AAI) is to reflect on past attachment experiences whilst at one and the same time maintaining a coherent and collaborative discourse with the interviewer. The ability to successfully negotiate this indicates a Secure, or Autonomous, state of mind regarding those attachment experiences (even in cases where those experiences may have had negative aspects). Various other types of incoherencies in response to the task map to the other types of attachment status (as detailed below).

The GAI focuses on a person's relationship to the group to which he or she belonged. The main change from the AAI interview is to substitute the section of the interview that asks the respondent to give (and later support) five adjectives to describe each caregiver, to instead give five adjectives to describe the relationship with the group:

> Now I'd like to ask you to choose five adjectives or words that reflect your relationship, as you remember it, with [group x], starting from when you first became involved? [if participant is an ex-member add: and up to when you ceased to be involved with the group . . .][5]

I also adapted coding standards for the GAI from the AAI protocol. The most important of these changes is in the definition of loss, trauma or abuse in relation to the group. In some regards, this differs considerably from the parallel definitions in the AAI. The GAI coding was driven by the concept of disorganized attachment, where fright without solution is the result of the conflict that occurs when the attachment figure is both the source of and the solution to threat. Thus I looked for situational markers of "probable experience" where fear arousal was described, or fear of loss of the group or attachment figures, as well as situations where assault/leniency processes occurred. The following is a list of those elements I coded as possible loss, abuse or trauma experiences for the purposes of the GAI:

- Reference to leaving or trying to leave the group
- Group sessions such as: "hot-seat," criticism or "therapy" sessions
- Interviewee describes feeling trapped
- Interviewee describes a situation in which they were fearful
- Interviewee appears to be objectively trapped, utterly dependent on the group for resources
- Verbal abuse causing interviewee to be fearful
- Discussion of experiences with weapons
- Discussion of physical abuse or violent incidents
- Discussion of loss of close persons (either on entry to, or exit from, the group)
- Discussion of entry process (where dynamics of assault/leniency were pertinent)

As with the AAI, disorganized attachment is termed Unresolved (disorganized/disoriented) – or "U/d." It is coded based upon discussion of abuse or loss that displays "lapses in the monitoring of reasoning or discourse, or reports of extreme behavioral reactions . . . during the discussion of these events."[6] These lapses "suggest momentary but qualitative changes in consciousness"[7] indicative of a "collapse of behavioral and attentional strategies"[8] in relation to the attachment figure. These lapses:

> often occur in a high-functioning individual and are normally not representative of the speaker's overall conversational style. For this reason, among others, transcripts assigned to the unresolved/disorganized . . . category are given a best-fitting alternate classification.[9]

These alternate classifications are: Ds (Dismissing), E (Preoccupied), F (Secure/autonomous) or CC (Cannot Classify). However, these alternate categories may be muddied or more difficult to ascertain where the current state of mind regarding attachment is Unresolved/disorganized. Further, each alternate assignment of Ds, E, or F is given a subcategory assignment (numeric) *and* a subtype (a or b).[i] Additionally,

---

i The subtypes are not part of this analysis and will not be discussed here, but they were coded for, and are documented in Table A.1 for possible future analysis.

Cannot Classify cases are noted by designating CC and then, the next best fit, followed by other possibly fitting categories, as, for example "CC/E3/Ds3a."

The Ds Dismissing and E Preoccupied statuses are considered to represent insecure or anxious attachment, as opposed to the secure F status. These three statuses are all, however, considered organized and systematic approaches to attachment (though not equally optimal). The Unresolved/disorganized and Cannot Classify statuses are not organized and represent segregated systems, or multiple and contradictory internal working models or attachment representations.

The major categories of states of mind in respect to attachment are:

> **Ds – Dismissing of attachment**: "Actively dismissing of the likelihood that [group] attachment experiences have affected personal development."[10] Often these transcripts are short, with idealized descriptions of [the group] that are not well supported by specific memories, or they are dismissing of "potential negative effects" of group involvement, "often while laying claim to personal strength."[11]
>
> **F – Secure/ "Free" – Autonomous**: "[V]alues attachment relationship and experiences and regards them as influential, but appears objective in evaluating any particular relationship and its influence. Interview is coherent. Generalized descriptions of [relationship with group] are supported by specific memories; fluent; non-contradictory; at ease with the topic."[12]
>
> **E – Preoccupied with attachment figures and experiences**: "The influence of [the group] or attachment-related experiences can neither be dismissed nor coherently described, and seems to preoccupy attention. [Individuals] may oscillate between good/bad evaluations of past or [group]."[13] These transcripts are often long, with long, entangled and angry passages, or many markers of "passivity of thought" indicating the inability to fully grasp or complete a thought process.
>
> **U/d – Unresolved (disorganized/disoriented)**: "[Individual] has experienced attachment-related traumas which cannot yet be clearly reconciled with present-day life."[14] Specific markers of disorganization and disorientation in reasoning, discourse and behavioral reactions to abuse or loss are delineated below.
>
> **CC – Cannot Classify**: "The patterning of interview responses makes it impossible to assign either Ds, F, E or Ud category placement."[15] There is a global incoherence in the interview, and often contradictory Ds and E discourse markers coexist.

Group Attachment Interview results

The overall results of the analyses are presented in Table A.1.

As anticipated, nearly all Newman Tendency former members had markers of Unresolved/disorganized/disoriented states of mind with respect to attachment to the group. That is, they continue to show signs of dissociation and disorientation in

TABLE A.1 Group Attachment Interview Results

Group	Age at interview	Year left group	Total years in group	Unresolved/ Disorganized?	Classification descriptor	Major classification or best-fitting alternative to U/d
Newman Tendency	35	2002	2	Yes	U/d Preoccupied	E3a
	36	1992	4	Yes	U/d Preoccupied	E3a
	40	1991	8	Yes	U/d Preoccupied	E2
	41	1993	8	Yes	U/d Cannot Classify	CC/E3/Ds3a[16]
	41	1992	8	Yes	U/d Dismissing	Ds3/a or b
	46	1992	7	Yes	U/d Cannot Classify	CC/E2/Ds2
	46	1990	5	Yes	U/d Secure[17]	F5
	49	2000	10	Yes	U/d Preoccupied	E3
	52	1992	16	Yes	U/d Preoccupied	E3
	52	1983	7	Yes	U/d Secure	F_-[18]
	57	2002	5	Yes	U/d Secure	F1a
	63	1974	4	No (Borderline)	Secure	F4b
Green Party	34	1999	3	No	Secure	F3a or b
	40	2002	1	No	Secure	F1
	41	2003	4	No	Secure	F3a
	43	1989	2	No	Secure	F4b
	44	2002	7	No	Dismissing	Ds3
	50	1991	3	No	Secure	F4b
	50	2000	3	No	Secure	F4b
	51	2004	13	No	Secure	F2
	52	2004	4	No	Secure	F3
	54	2004	5	No	Secure	F1a
	64	2003	4	No	Dismissing	Ds2

their thought processes regarding their experiences with the Newman Tendency. Further, many showed elements of preoccupied attachment to the group in the secondary, alternative classifications.

None of the Green Party former members (GPers) were classified as Unresolved/disorganized. First, there were few events that fit the categories of trauma or abuse as identified above, and thus there were few opportunities to code for U/d discourse in relation to such events. (However, the GPers did leave the Green Party, and so could be scored for U/d responses to loss.) Second, where those events did occur, the participants showed only mild, or no signs of disorganization or disorientation in regard to them.

The nine GPers' F transcripts were often hard to subclassify. This may be due to the fact that these relationships did not, in fact, rise to the level of attachment relationships, and so much of the discourse, while coherent and collaborative in a general sense, did not neatly fit the Secure subclassifications. It is possible, therefore, that these transcripts represent the GPers' general discourse style, rather than being reflective of any attachment bond to the Green Party (given that such a bond had not been established).

Notes

1 George, C., N. Kaplan and M. Main. 1996. *Adult Attachment Interview Protocol.* Berkeley: University of California.
2 Ibid., p. 1.
3 Ibid.
4 Main, M. and R. Goldwyn. 1998. *Adult Attachment Scoring and Classification Systems.* Berkeley: University of California, p. 1.
5 Stein, Alexandra. 2004. *Group Attachment Interview.* Minneapolis: University of Minnesota.
6 George, Kaplan and Main. 1996. *Adult Attachment Interview Protocol.* Berkeley: University of California, p. 178.
7 Hesse, Erik. 1999. "The Adult Attachment Interview, Historical and Current Perspectives," in *Handbook of Attachment: Theory, Research and Clinical Applications,* edited by P. Shaver. New York: Guilford Press, p. 405.
8 Lyons-Ruth, K. and D. Jacobvitz. 1999. "Attachment Disorganization: Unresolved Loss, Relational Violence, and Lapses in Behavioral and Attentional Strategies," in *Handbook of Attachment: Theory, Research and Clinical Applications,* edited by P. Shaver. New York: Guilford Press, p. 549.
9 Hesse, Erik. 1999. "The Adult Attachment Interview, Historical and Current Perspectives," in *Handbook of Attachment: Theory, Research and Clinical Applications,* edited by P. Shaver. New York: Guilford Press, p. 405.
10 Main and Goldwyn. 1998. *Adult Attachment Scoring and Classification Systems.* Berkeley: University of California, p. 4.
11 Ibid., p. 151.
12 Ibid., p. 4.
13 Ibid.
14 Ibid.
15 Ibid.
16 Cannot Classify assignments are, like U/d assignments, followed by alternate classifications.
17 Note that when assigning Unresolved/Disorganized, a major classification or best-fitting alternative is also assigned.
18 Unable to assign sub-category to this transcript.

APPENDIX B

Eye-level versus abusive, authoritarian relationships

"Eye-level," egalitarian relationships	Abusive, authoritarian relationships
Two-way communication	One-way communication: top-down. Bottom-up communication is only for purposes of monitoring the follower
Each person is seen as basically OK and worthy of support	Abuser assumes the follower must change to meet the abuser's criteria
Not necessarily equal (e.g., parent/child, student/teacher), but basic trust exists and a sense that each person has something to offer the other	The abuser has the right to all the power and has all the answers
Questions are allowed, encouraged and responded to directly	Questions are discouraged, sidestepped, avoided, or turned around back onto the follower.
Negotiation and compromise are practiced	Abuser demands obedience with no negotiation: loyalty is based on "all or nothing" commitment
Respect for both parties' wants and needs	Only the abuser's need are important or valid
Other relationships are allowed and encouraged	The abuser isolates the follower
Intimidation and fear are not used to gain compliance and control of the other	Abuser uses physical or psychological intimidation

INDEX

Page numbers for figures are in italics.

zone and 160–1; isolation and loneliness of 113–14; lifestyles of 123; names for 89–90; as psychopathic 2–4, 12, 108, 112–13, 160–1; as safe havens 26; single truth and 19; as skilled 80; social structures and 14; structures created by 108–26
learned helplessness 75
left brain 35, 40, 75–81, 139, 154–5
left-wing political activities 52, 115
Lessing, D. 166n
Let's Develop: A Guide to Continuous Personal Growth (Newman) 55–6
Levi, P. 161, 197–8; *The Drowned and The Saved* 167
Lewin, K. 210
LGATs (large group awareness training programs) 52–3. *see also* personal growth groups
lieutenants 17, 116–20, 161, 164–5
life blips 59–60
lifers 17, 96, 120, 153, 175
Lifton, R. 12, 47, 102–3, 136, 139, 147–50, 155, 162–9, 193, 204; *The Nazi Doctors* 165–6
limbic area 75–6, 83
Lindsey, J. 21
linear thinking 76
lines experiment 57, 142
Little Red Book, The 3
Little Red Guards 88
loaded language 147–51, 186–8
Lofland, J. 121, 176; *Doomsday Cult* 129n
logic 140
London transport bombing 85, 156
loneliness 113–14, 208
loose ties 209
Lord's Resistance Army 7, 22, 46, 175, 209
Lorenz, K. 29
losing track 190
loss 20, 181, 215
lost boys 92
love 40, 88–9, 152, 211; disorganized attachment and 35; fear and 19, 114; leaders and 108–11, 133–4; in North Korea 174; threat and 16–17, 109, 115–16
low-risk populations 30
loyalist poetry 136
loyalty 19, 23, 97–100, 108–10, 151
LSD 69
Lying for the Lord 62n35

M15 22, 43n
magical thinking 13
Main, M. 32–3, 36, 74, 181n; "Adult Attachment Scoring and Classification Systems" 109n, 186n, 192n
majority effect 57, 142–4
Making of a Moonie: Choice or Brainwashing? (Barker) 129n
malnourishment 71, 123
Malvo, L. 14nii
Mam, K.: *An Oral History of Family Life under the Khmer Rouge* 147n
Manchurian Candidate (film) 13
Manchurian Candidate, The (Condon) 82nv
Mandela, N. 110–11, 200
Manifesto on Method, A (Newman) 153–4
manipulation 14, 60, 85, 110, 113–14, 166, 207
Mannheim, K.: *Ideology and Utopia: An Introduction to the Sociology of Knowledge* 14niii
Maoist China 12–13, 102, 136–7
Mao Zedong 26, 88, 114, 119
marriage 55, 81, 92–5, 135, 141
Martin, J.: *Power, Authority, and the Constraint of Belief Systems* 132n
Marxist Leninist organizing 11
Marxist phraseology 154
Marxist therapy 4
Masoud: Memoirs of an Iranian Rebel (Banisadr) 197
mass killings 80–1
mass loyalty 110
mass suicide 66
material dependency 184
material reward 113
material support 102
Mawdudi, A. 53–4
meaning 75, 154, 169
mediation models 210
Medicaid 11
MEK 27–8, 36–9, 119, 133–5, 140. *see also* Iranian Mojahedin
memory 75–6, 154, 180, 184–90, 193, 204
mental health problems 92
mentalizing 112–13
mental manipulation 60, 110, 207
metabolic shutdown 74–5
metabolized memories 185
Middle East 204
Milgram, S. 57
militant atheism 13
militaristic cults 175

terrorism 7, 21, 43n; recruitment into
  45, 206, 211; suicide 2–6, 21–2,
  85; typical 60
testimonials 57
Theory of Everything 132
therapy 4, 37–8, 55, 93n; individual and
  group 45, 50, 57–8; mandated 44;
  Marxist 4
therapy/encounter-group collectives 15
thought: clarity of 38–40, 80, 139;
  critical 53–7, 79, 128, 139, 142–5, 206;
  disruption of 64, 136; feeling and 127–8,
  139–42; inability of 156; reform 12–13,
  19, 165; route 151–5
thought-terminating clichés 139, 147, 151
threat 20, 31, 34, 37–9, 63, 69–72, 78, 139,
  184; attachment behavior and 29–33, 36,
  74–5; leaders and 15–16, 109–11; love
  and 16–17, 109, 115–16
3H0 (Healthy, Happy, Holy Organization)
  138–9
time: monopolizing of 52, 57, 64–8, 98,
  123; sense of 185–8
Timerman, J. 166
Titanic, The (film) 174
Tobias, M.: *Take Back Your Life: Recovering
  from Cults and Abusive Relationships* 112n,
  176n
Tokyo 3, 69
Torah 122
torture 83, 123, 166
total conversion 19
total ideologies 7, 14niii, 15, 89,
  128–9, 146–7
totalist groups: attachment theory and
  28–40, 162–6; brainwashing and 19–22;
  direction and quality of interactions in
  124; disorganized attachment and 36–40,
  43; dissociation and 35, 38–9; exiting
  160–79; family, friends, and 88–107; fear
  and 27; first contacts 47–50; historic
  context of 116; ideology and language in
  18–19, 28, 53–4, 127–59; indoctrination
  and 63–87; inner circles of 17, 50,
  115–23; lieutenants of 17, 116–20,
  161, 164–5; outcomes of 21–4, 28,
  123–4; propaganda by 43–4, 53–7, 148;
  recruitment into 43–62; religion and
  13–15; stated programs of 44; structure
  of 14–18, 28, 108–26, 132
totalist self 193–4
totalist systems 7, 12–13, 23–4
totalitarian movements and states 1–3,
  6–7, 12, 44, 47, 91, 94, 97, 108, 115, 175,
  202–6

Tourish, D. 156
training camps 65, 91
traitors 91
transformation, total 137–8
transmission process 17–18, 54, 111–12
trauma 3, 14, 100, 154–5, 204; arousal
  continuum and 75; bonds 2, 34, 38,
  120; chronic 37, 77, 84; disorganized
  attachment and 75–9, 168–9, 180–95;
  dissociation and 35, 38–9; forced
  review of 70; memory and 180,
  184–90; reexperiencing of 77niv;
  relational-induced 75; sharing of 37–8;
  theory 15
Trauma and Recovery (Herman) 71
Trenton, G. 45
Trotskyist cults 1
truth, single 19, 68, 132–7, 142, 202
Tsouli, Y. 49
Tutu, D. 200
Twelve Tribes group 122, 138

ubuntu 200
UFO cults 89
Uganda 22, 46
ultra Orthodox Jewish sects 1, 122–3, 175
"Umuntu ngumuntu ngabantu" (proverb) 200
unanimous majorities 142–4
unbelievers 91, 134
UN Declaration of Human Rights
  200, 209
Understanding Terror Networks (Sageman)
  131n
undifferentiated others 104–5, 120
undue influence 57–8
Ung, L. 91
Unification Church (UC) 49, 52, 56–7,
  62n35, 121, 129–30, 144, 171. *see also*
  Moonies
union organizing drives 45
United Kingdom 7, 60, 100, 207
United Nations 123
United States 7, 13, 141
unpaid labor 22, 56
unpredictability 92n
UN refugee camps 46, 65
unreliability 31–2
unresolved/disorganized attachment. *see*
  disorganized attachment
Us and Them 53–4, 134

value-free assertions 146n
values, shared 203
verbal abuse 215
victims, blaming of 141, 161